The Good Old Days
in Hampton and
Newport News

For Alene
hoping to revive memories
Greetings
Parke Rouse

Courtesy Fort Monroe Casemate Museum

A bay steamer docks at Old Point's pier in the era of the first Chamberlin Hotel.

THE GOOD OLD DAYS
in Hampton and Newport News

by
Parke Rouse Jr.

THE DIETZ PRESS
Richmond, Virginia

Copyright © 1986 by Parke Rouse, Jr.

Printed in the United States of America

Second Printing, 1987

ISBN 0-87517-056-0

Design by Richard Stinely

TITLE PAGE: Union observer in Civil War scans Hampton Roads from balloon above Fort Wool and Fort Monroe.

For Lewis Archer McMurran Jr.

CONTENTS

Preface ... ix

I. The Era of Farmer and Fisherman

Chapter

1. When Pirates Roamed the Bay ... 3
2. Sally Cary and George Washington ... 6
3. When Hampton was Invaded ... 9
4. The Civil War and George Ben West ... 13
5. Lincoln Visits Fort Monroe ... 29

II. From Forests into Towns

6. Collis Huntington's Magic Touch ... 34
7. Mysterious Arabella Huntington ... 38
8. The Railroad Comes to Town ... 49
9. The 65ers Who Built Hampton ... 55
10. The Rise of a German Baker ... 59
11. Armstrong's School for Blacks ... 63
12. The Hotel That Made Old Point Famous ... 87
13. When Newport News Began ... 73
14. Celebrating Jamestown's Birthday ... 77
15. An Early High School Graduation ... 81
16. The Great White Fleet Returns ... 85

III. Years of the First World War

17. The Brewery: Victorian Curiosity ... 91
18. Daredevils of Curtiss Field ... 95
19. Death on the Lusitania ... 99
20. A Year That Changed the World ... 103
21. Memories of the First World War ... 107
22. Songs of Lonesome Soldiers ... 111
23. Thomas Wolfe at Langley Field ... 115
24. Washington Avenue in Wartime ... 118
25. Saloons and Bordellos ... 122
26. Stars of the Academy of Music ... 126

IV. A Calm Between Two Storms

27. Hurrah for Jackson School! ... 133
28. The Gold Coast of the James ... 136

29.	Life Along the Waterways	141	42.	'Live Up to Your Potential'	189
30.	A Bridge to Southside	145	43.	Sundays and Blue Laws	193
31.	Marching Through Daniel School	149	44.	Movies of the 1930's	197
32.	Model Ts and Sunday Drives	152	45.	Newspapering on 25th Street	200
33.	Building Boats on Hampton Roads	156	46.	Hampton's Biggest Trial	203
34.	Hampton's Oystermen and Crabbers	159	47.	Judge Spratley and the New Deal	206
35.	Courtly Judges, Tipsy Lawyers	163	48.	Hampton's Crabs and Terrapins	209

VI. Looking Forward and Aft

36.	Langley Rises from the Swamp	167	49.	Big Ships for a Big War	212
37.	The Crabber-Typhoon Rivalry	171	50.	German Sailors in Hampton	215
38.	"Happy Am I" Elder Michaux	174	51.	When Newport News Was Fifty	220
39.	Stores on Washington Avenue	177	52.	Homer Ferguson: Local Hero	223
			53.	The Muses Smile	226
			54.	Facing a New Century	231
				Index	235

V. The Beginning of the Suburbs

40.	The Flight to the Suburbs	183
41.	Pearl Bailey and Ella Fitzgerald	186

PREFACE

How We Got from There to Here

DESPITE their age and importance, Hampton and Newport News have rarely been the subject of books. This is an effort to correct that. Most of it is taken from Sunday newspaper accounts I have contributed to The Daily Press from 1980 to the present, with occasional magazine articles I have written for the *Virginia Magazine of History and Biography* and other journals.

I do not offer this as a formal history (I wrote one of Newport News in 1969, published as *Endless Harbor*) but as glimpses of events and people in the life of the lower Peninsula. Of the two cities, Hampton is much the older, having grown from a two-man settlement by Virginia's Jamestown colonists in 1610 at Old Point Comfort. It can claim to be the oldest continuously settled English-speaking community in the New World. Newport News came much later: it was undeveloped farmland until Union forces seized it after Virginia seceded in 1861. Its industrialization began in 1880, when Collis Potter Huntington chose it as the eastern terminus of the Chesapeake and Ohio Railway. Huntington's shipyard was begun in 1886, and the city was incorporated in 1896.

The merger of the two cities into one seems to me desirable and inevitable.

The focus of most of these essays is on people who gave life or color to the two cities: shippers, investors, soldiers, scholars, and others. But my emphasis is chiefly between the year 1918, when my parents moved to Newport News from Smithfield, until the 1940s, when I left the city to pursue my fortunes elsewhere. However, I have occasionally looked back in these pages to our colonial and 19th century beginnings.

Among the personalities from Hampton and Elizabeth City who figure in the early years are the seafaring Barrons and the land-owning Carys of Ceely's plantation on the Hampton Roads shore. Colonel John Baytop Cary, who conducted Hampton's pre-Civil War Hampton Academy and became Richmond's first superintendent of schools after 1870, was a member, as was James Barron Hope, who became a Norfolk orator as founder-editor of the *Norfolk Pilot*, now a part of *The Virginian-Pilot*.

Hampton's greatest surge came at the end of the Civil War. Many Union veterans who had seen the area's potential in the war contributed to its new growth. Chief among them was Samuel Armstrong, a Freedmen's Bureau official who created Hampton Institute. Another was James Sands Darling, a New Yorker who built a boat works, an oystering company, and the Peninsula's street railway system. His son Frank and his daughter-in-law Mollie became civic leaders. Similarly, Francis Anton Schmelz, a Civil War baker from Germany, established a thriving business. His sons George and Henry Schmelz created banks in Hampton and Newport News, joined Darling in the trolley system, and owned a daily paper which merged into today's Peninsula newspapers.

Other post-Civil War leaders included Harrison Phoebus, who operated the Hygeia Hotel at Old Point; James McMenamin, who created a large crab-packing house; Harry Houston, printer and publisher of the onetime Hampton newspaper, the Hampton *Monitor;* Harry Holt, clerk of Elizabeth City County; and such other families as the Cummings, Hopes, Sinclairs, Phillips, Healys, Spratleys, Woodwards, Howes, Armstrongs, Bookers, and Bentleys.

Two figures best illustrate the start of Newport News. One was George Benjamin West, whose family owned the 400-acre farm called Newport News Point when the Civil War came. West survived the war to reclaim part of his family's land, become rich, and to start a bank, hospital, and a boys' preparatory school in Newport News. The other major figure is Collis Huntington, the wealthy California and New York railroad man who brought the Chesapeake and Ohio Railway to Newport News in 1880-81 and started the shipyard in 1886. The rest is history.

I hope these vignettes will interest others in the many unexplored events and people of early Hampton and Newport News. What I have written is just a beginning.

Parke Rouse, Jr.
Williamsburg, Virginia

ACKNOWLEDGEMENTS

THE AUTHOR wishes to express thanks for many people who have helped with this book. He is especially grateful to Mrs. Dorothy Bottom Duffy, editor of the Daily Press, who engaged him in 1980 to become a contributing editor to the paper and to write twice-weekly local columns. These form the bulk of the text, with the addition of other material originally published in the Commonwealth Magazine and in the Virginia Magazine of History and Biography.

I would like to thank my old friend Lewis McMurran Jr. for his kindness in providing information for some chapters herein. Other help has come from Sinclair Phillips and Alexander Crosby Brown of Newport News; Mrs. Harriet Houston Donaldson and Dr. Chester Bradley of Hampton; and Cary and Carolyn McMurran of Williamsburg.

I am also indebted to several members of my family who have helped me recall events and people mentioned here. My mother, Pauline Dashiell Rouse, has been a constant help as has my aunt, Segar Cofer Dashiell, of Smithfield.

For assistance in locating illustrations I am indebted to the research library and photographic department of the Daily Press; and especially to librarian Terry Hammond, to Judy Mowrey, and to Kevin Dowling; to Alex Brown and his splendid collection of pictures originally printed in *Endless Harbor: The Story of Newport News,* in 1969; to Col. Leo Johns and John Quarstein of the Newport

News Historical Committee; to Ardie Kelly, librarian of the Mariners Museum; to John Michael Cobb, curator of the Syms-Eaton Museum of Hampton; to Phyllis Stephenson of Newport News Shipbuilding; to the Casemate Museum at Fort Monroe; to the Virginia State Library in Richmond; and to the publications office at Langley Field, all of whom kindly lent me photographs from their collections.

I hope that the governments of Newport News and Hampton will give attention to the need for more orderly photographic records of their cities. No single complete and unified picture source is now available in either city. I hope eventually it will be.

BIBLIOGRAPHY

Bentley, John B: *Gravestone Inscriptions of St. John's Episcopal Church, Hampton, Va.:* Published for St. John's Church by the Hugh S. Watson Jr. Genealogical Society of Tidewater, Va., 1975

Brown, Alexander Crosby, editor: *Newport News' 325 Years: A Collection of Historical Articles.* Newport News: Golden Anniversary Corporation, 1946.

———: *The Good Ships of Newport News.* Cambridge, Md.: Tidewater Publishers, 1976.

Engs, Robert Francis: *Freedom's First Generation: Black Hampton, Va., 1861-1890.* Phila.: University of Pennsylvania Press, 1979.

Jester, Annie Lash: *Newport News, Virginia—1607-1960.* Richmond: Whittet and Shepperson, 1961.

Lavender, David: *The Great Persuader.* Garden City, N.Y.: Doubleday, 1970

Rouse, Parke S. Jr.: *Endless Harbor: The Story of Newport News.* Newport News: Historical Committee, 1969.

———, editor: *When the Yankees Came: Civil War and Reconstruction on the Virginia Peninsula.* By George Benjamin West, Richmond: Dietz Press, 1977

Smith, Edward O. *History of the Newport News Shipbuilding and Dry Dock Company, from October 1880 to December 31, 1934.* Newport News, 1965.

Starkey, Marion Lena: *The First Plantation: a History of Hampton and Elizabeth City County, Va., 1607-1887.* Hampton: Houston Printing Co., 1936.

Taylor, Donald Ransone: *Out of the Past—the Future: a History of Hampton, Virginia.* Hampton: Prestige Press, 1960.

Tyler, Lyon Gardiner: *History of Hampton and Elizabeth City County, Virginia,* Hampton: The Board of Supervisors of Elizabeth City County, 1922

The Good Old Days in Hampton and Newport News

Casemate Museum

Hampton Roads was a busy sailing ship artery before the Civil War. On Old Point Comfort, in the foreground, stood Fort Monroe. On the Peninsula shoreline at right were Hampton and farms at Newport News Point. Across the water lay Norfolk, Virginia's largest town.

I.
The Era of Farmer and Fisherman
1607-1865

Syms-Eaton Museum

Blackbeard, notorious Atlantic Coast pirate, terrorized Virginia shippers until a Hampton-based British warship in 1717 killed him and captured his crew.

1. *When Pirates Roamed Hampton Roads*

IN colonial times, piracy flourished in Chesapeake Bay and along Atlantic sea-lanes which Tidewater tobacco ships traveled.

To combat the pirates, Great Britain dispatched a succession of patrol vessels to the colony. Most of the 17th-century ones operated out of Hampton, which was Virginia's major port from Jamestown's day until Norfolk grew important, just before the American Revolution.

A reminder of those days remains in the name of Blackbeard's Point on Hampton's waterfront, where the bloody and bearded head of the bay's most notorious pirate was hung up to public view in 1717.

Another relic of Hampton's efforts against piracy is a little-known tomb in the deserted graveyard of Hampton's early Pembroke church, close to Interstate 64 and to the Hampton Institute campus. It is the eroded and now-illegible tombstone of Peter Heyman, who was collector of customs for the lower James River district in the year 1700. Since the James River was then considered to encompass what later was named Hampton Roads, the lower James customs office was located at Hampton.

The eroded Pembroke Church tombstone contained this tantalizing inscription:

'In memory of Peter Heyman, Esq., grandson of Sir Peter Heyman of Summerfield in the county of Kent (England). He was Collector of Customs in the lower district of James River and went voluntarily on board the King's ship 'Shoreham' in pursuit of a pirate who greatly infested this coast. After he had behaved himself seven hours with undaunted courage, was killed with a small shot the 29th day of April, 1700. In the engagement he stood next the Governor, upon the quarterdeck, and was here honorably interred by his order.'

Back of that eroded tombstone is an heroic incident forgotten by all but a few history buffs.

It began with an outburst of piracy in the lower Chesapeake in the 1680s. Small, fast pirate ships operated by crews of renegades from the Caribbean islands hid out in the creeks and bays of the Eastern Shore, watch-

4 When Pirates Roamed the Bay

Mariners Museum

Small British merchantmen sailing to and from Chesapeake Bay were frequently attacked by pirates near the Virginia capes.

ing out for ships passing through the capes.

Whenever they saw an unescorted merchant vessel, the pirates would sail out and demand its surrender. If the merchant captain resisted, the pirates would open fire to dismast and disable the vessel, then board it and capture its cargo.

The brigands captured or sank so much Virginia tobacco and imported English goods that the British government in 1664 sent to Virginia H.M.S. Quaker, a ketch, to guard the Virginia Capes against pirates. However, the Quaker proved too slow and small for the job. For that reason, most merchant ships learned to confine their sailings to the twice-yearly tobacco fleets that gathered each fall and spring in the lower bay. On a given day they would sail for Great Britain under convoy of British warships.

Even so, piracy was still rampant in the year 1700. In that year the British Admiralty dispatched H.M.S. Shoreham, a larger ship, from Britain to Hampton. She was a frigate of 28 guns, manned by 120 officers and crewmen.

The "Shoreham" had just arrived for duty in April 1700 when the notorious Caribbean pirate, Louis Guittar, sailed into the capes. After plundering and destroying five small vessels, Guittar was surprised to see the Shoreham bearing down on him. He didn't know it, but Lieutenant Governor Francis Nicholson was aboard her, along with Peter Heyman, Hampton's collector of customs. As commander of Virginia's army and navy, Lieutenant Governor Nicholson was anxious to arrest Guittar.

In a day-long battle between the two ships, 39 pirates were killed by British guns. After her sails and lines had been shattered, Guittar's ship, La Paix, was run aground by the Shoreham and compelled to surrender. Of the 100 pirates captured, three were hanged and the rest sent to prison in England.

Peter Heyman was the only man aboard the "Shoreham" we know to have been killed.

Redoubling his efforts against piracy, Governor Nicholson that spring ordered the militia of Elizabeth City, Princess Anne, Norfolk, Northampton, and Accomack counties to station lookouts along their coast. They stayed on duty until that fall, when 300 Virginia and Maryland tobacco ships had safely gathered in the bay in those months and sailed in convoy to England.

After Britain went to war with France in 1702, Virginia shippers faced the added threat of French warships and privateers. The House of Burgesses in Williamsburg petitioned England to send more naval ships, but because of the British Isles' wartime needs, the mother country could spare only a few vessels for the Chesapeake.

Alarm spread through the colony again in 1709 when a French privateer fleet was rumored to be entering the bay to capture black slaves and other "good booty." The Virginia militia was again called up, cannons were placed around the lower bay shoreline to fire warnings, and lookouts were again posted at strategic points.

So dangerous were the sea-lanes from Virginia to England in those days that many Virginians forswore trips to the homeland. Virginia ships which traveled in convoy had to fly the English ensign at all times and fire a gun in case of danger, to alert the other vessels. The naval officer commanding the lead convoy was designated as admiral, with another designated as rear admiral behind the convoy. That's how rear admiral originated.

Of all Chesapeake pirates, the most celebrated was Edward Teach or Tech, known as Blackbeard. His scraggly beard hung down to his waist, and he preyed on Virginia commerce for years. Going into battle, Blackbeard "wore a sling over his shoulders, with three brace of pistols hanging in holsters like bandoliers, and stuck lighted matches under his hat, which, appearing on each side of his face, his eyes naturally looking fierce and wild, made him altogether such a figure that imagination cannot form an idea of a Fury from Hell to look more frightful."

In 1717 Blackbeard and his pirates stationed their ships at the entrance to the Chesapeake and compelled ships to pay them tribute to pass. When British naval sloops drove him off, Blackbeard sailed south to Ocracoke Inlet on the North Carolina coast and looted that area.

North Carolinians called on Virginia's Governor Alexander Spotswood to send navy ships from Hampton, and Spotswood dispatched two British sloops.

The resulting battle of Ocracoke became the most famous pirate battle in American history. H.M.S. Pearl, one of the two British ships, finally overtook Blackbeard's ship, and Lieutenant Robert Maynard, RN, and his crew fought with the pirates hand-to-hand. Twelve of the Pearl's crew were killed, and 22 were injured.

The British warship Pearl returned from combat bearing Blackbeard's head, which was displayed at Blackbeard's Point on Hampton River.

Blackbeard was killed after sustaining 25 wounds. The British then seized his ship and crew. The pirate's head was cut off as a trophy and nailed to the Pearl's bowspirit. When the sloop Pearl returned to Hampton, Blackbeard's head was hung up on what is now Blackbeard's Point on Hampton River.

Fifteen of Blackbeard's surviving pirates were placed in Williamsburg's Public Gaol, and 13 were hanged. Piracy in the Chesapeake declined after that.

Today, exhibits by the National Park Service at Ocracoke Inlet record Lieutenant Maynard's victory over Blackbeard. I hope Hampton will someday dig up and record the earlier story of Peter Heyman, who lies buried in Pembroke's ancient cemetery.

2. Sally Cary and George Washington

ONE of the belles of early Virginia was born in Elizabeth City County, the collateral ancestor of many prominent Americans. What's more, she was so admired by George Washington that his biographers have criticized him for impropriety.

She was the beautiful Sarah Cary, known as Sally Cary, who was born in 1730 at Ceely's plantation on Hampton Roads near Salter's Creek, in what was once Elizabeth City County and is now Newport News. Her surviving likeness in an old portrait shows us a lovely woman. When she married wealthy George William Fairfax of Alexandria in 1748, many prominent suitors were disappointed.

George Washington, who was only 16 in 1748—two years younger than Sally—met her through his brother Lawrence, a Fairfax employee, and he was smitten by Sally from the first. But she was already married, and George went to work for her husband. All he could do was worship Sally from afar.

A year before he died in 1799, the 66-year-old Washington wrote from Mount Vernon to Bath, England, to tell Sally that nothing in his life had "been able to eradicate from my mind the recollection of those happy moments, the happiest in my life, which I have enjoyed in your company."

That was strong stuff, I must admit.

Biographer Douglas Freeman took offense at that "happiest in my life" remark when he wrote of Washington. He said he realized that G.W. was just being gallant, but he felt he had said too much and was disloyal to George's wife, Martha, who had followed her husband and kept Mount Vernon going all those years while George was off fighting those British.

Dr. Freeman tried to explain Washington's effusion to Sally as the compliment of an aging belle, who was safely separated by the wide Atlantic. Indeed, Sally in 1798 was a childless, 68-year-old widow who had been away from Virginia more than 25 years. Fortunately, she apparently never told anyone what Washington had written her. It was discovered in her papers after she died in 1811.

The Carys were the most prominent family on the lower Peninsula before the Revolution. Various Carys had plantations in Warwick and James City counties—Peartree Hall, Richneck and Carisbrooke among them. Progenitor Miles Cary of Warwick had several sons, who acquired extensive Peninsula lands. His descendants Henry Cary Sr. and Jr. were highly

The beauteous Sally Cary of Ceely's plantation near Hampton wed George William Fairfax and was admired by George Washington.

successful architects and Tidewater contractors. They built most of early Williamsburg.

The plantation called Ceely's, where Sally Cary was born, had passed through several 17th century families before Miles Cary of Richneck plantation in Warwick married Mary Wilson Roscow, the daughter of Colonel William Wilson of Hampton. William Wilson had built a plantation house there in 1706 on a tract of 2,000 acres "on both sides of Saltford's (Salter's) Creek" he had bought from Thomas Ceely.

William Wilson's home on Hampton Roads was a two-story brick house with wings. It was on or near the site of the 20th century Elizabeth Buxton Hospital, later Mary Immaculate Hospital.

Sally Cary was the daughter of Miles and Mary Wilson Roscow Cary, born in 1730. She was the eldest of the Cary children, all of whom married well. Her brother, Wilson Miles Cary I, married Sarah Blair, daughter of President John Blair I of the council in Williamsburg.

Sally's sisters did almost as well as she. Mary married Edward Ambler of Jamestown and had a daughter who married John Marshall. Anne married Robert Carter Nicholas of Williamsburg, treasurer of Virginia. Elizabeth Cary, the youngest, married Bryan Fairfax, a kinsman of Sally's husband who became the eighth Baron Fairfax.

Apparently Sally Cary met George William Fairfax in Williamsburg in the 1740s, when he was attending the assembly. He was one of the wealthiest Virginians of his day, inheriting part of the Fairfax proprietary in Northern Virginia. He built a plantation, Belvoir, near Alexandria, which burned after the Revolution.

Evidently Sally and George Fairfax were a happy couple. He wrote to a friend from Williamsburg before the marriage: "Attending here on the General Assembly, I have had several opportunities of visiting Miss Cary, a daughter of Colonel Wilson Cary, and finding her amiable person to answer all the favorable reports made, I addressed myself [proposed to her], and having obtained the young lady's and her parents' consent, we are to be married. . . ."

They were married December 12, 1748, probably at Ceely's plantation. They lived until 1773 at their plantation, Belvoir, after which they moved to England.

George Washington saw a lot of Sally after he was hired by Fairfax to survey his inheritance. When the 23-year-old George left Mount Vernon in 1755 to lead his militiamen with General Braddock against the French, he

John Baytop Cary ran Hampton Academy before Civil War. After the war he was first superintendent of Richmond public schools.

Syms-Eaton Museum

wrote Sally frequently. His first letter began:

"Dear Madam: In order to engage your Corrispondence, I think it expedient just to deserve it: which I shall endeavour to do by embracing the earliest and every opportunity of writing to you. . . ."

George continued to write Sally even after he became engaged to the widow Martha Dandridge Custis. In September 1758, for example he asked Sally "when [do] you set out for Hampton and when [do] you expect to return to Belvoir again?"

Four months after that question, George married Martha Custis and brought her to Mount Vernon. After that, George stopped writing to Sally until he penned his indiscreet letter in 1798. They never met after the Fairfaxes went to England in 1773.

In his last letter to Sally, 66-year-old ex-president Washington began:

"My dear Madam, Five and twenty years, nearly, have passed away since I have considered myelf as the permanent resident of this place (Mount Vernon), or have been in a situation to endulge myself in a familiar intercourse with my friends. . . . During this period, so many important events have occurred and such changes in men and things have taken place, as the compass of a letter would give you but an inadequate idea of."

"None of which events, however, nor all of them together, have been able to eradicate from my mind, the recollection of those happy moments, the happiest of my life, which I have enjoyed in your company. . . ."

Fortunately, Martha Washington had died before that letter came to light.

As for Sally Cary's Peninsula birthplace, few traces remain today. In 1813, British soldiers in the War of 1812 came ashore at Ceely's and burned Hampton. By the end of the Civil War, Ceely's was abandoned. A younger Wilson Miles Cary of Baltimore, presumably a great-great nephew of Sally's, rode to the Peninsula on horseback in 1868 and reported that the "fine old brick mansion" had been burned by squatters, who were living after Emancipation on the site.

That Cary descendant learned that his family's Richneck house, three miles from Warwick Courthouse, had also been destroyed. It is now marked by an historical marker.

One of the last Carys on the Peninsula was John Baytop Cary, who conducted Hampton Military Academy from 1851 until the Civil War broke out. After serving in the Civil War, he became Richmond's first public school superintendent in the 1870s. Public schools in Richmond and Hampton bear his name.

Like the O'Haras of Tara, the Carys and their mansions have gone with the wind. However, beautiful Sally has left a legend behind her.

Angered by the British invasion of Hampton in 1813, the United States began to build Fort Monroe at Old Point in 1819. Casemates lie behind the lighthouse.

3. *When Hampton was Invaded*

THOUGH Hampton is America's oldest continuous English-speaking settlement, it has virtually no buildings besides St. John's Church that go back beyond the 19th century. That's because the town was burned twice: once by the British in the War of 1812 and again by Confederates in the Civil War. The Confederates were trying to keep it from falling into the hands of the invading Yankees.

Few people have written of Hampton's invasion by the British. The best source I know is Benson J. Lossing's *Field Book of the War of 1812,* which that 19th century historian compiled after visiting Virginia scenes of combat in our second war with the British. The war began in 1812 and dragged on until Andrew Jackson won the Battle of New Orleans in 1815.

It was a fruitless war. My encyclopedia says it "brought few decisive military gains for either side," either British or American. In fact, few mementos of it remain in Tidewater despite Hampton's nightmare and an attempted British invasion of Craney Island, both in the spring of 1813. The next year British ships returned to the Chesapeake, went up the Potomac and burned Washington. President and Mrs. James Madison had to flee the White House.

The British invaders first sailed into Hampton Roads on June 19, 1813. In Richmond, Governor James Barbour sent all available Virginia militiamen to defend Norfolk, Portsmouth and the Peninsula. General Robert Barraud Taylor, a peacetime Norfolk lawyer, commanded Virginia forces.

The Virginia militia and U.S. Navy ships quickly fortified Craney Island at the entrance to the Elizabeth River, hoping to avert attacks

9

When Hampton was Invaded

Daily Press

Saint John's Church survived Hampton's invasion by the British in 1813. Still in use on Queen Street, it is one of the nation's oldest churches.

on Norfolk and Portsmouth. At Craney Island the British struck on the morning of June 21, 1813, landing 2,500 British troops on the beach from frigates and troop ships.

U.S. Navy ships and General Taylor's Virginia troops shelled the British invaders at Craney Island so successfully that they finally turned back. It was a joyous victory, though Taylor's army feared another invasion attempt at some other place. "The enemy has been completely foiled," crowed the Norfolk Gazette and Public Ledger, somewhat prematurely.

Three days later the British struck again. "Accounts just received (are) that the enemy landed last night at New-Port-Neuse, at the entrance of James River," announced the Norfolk Gazette on June 25. "An attack upon Hampton is probably meditated."

By sunup on June 26, 1813, British marines were going ashore from warships at Ceely's plantation, which stood on the Newport News boulevard, near the later site of the old Mary Immaculate Hospital. From there they marched by Kecoughtan Road to Hampton, then a town of 1,000 people.

Before Hampton learned of this threat, however, its defenders were misled by 40 British landing craft, which appeared to threaten Blackbeard's Point. As a Hampton defense force under Major Stapleton Crutchfield rushed to halt them, the invaders from Ceely's plantation marched into Hampton. Crutchfield's force of 435 Virginians killed and wounded about 200 of the Britishers, but the 2,500 invaders overwhelmed them and took over Hampton.

A few soldiers with the British then ran

Casemate Museum

Simon Bernard, trained in engineering by the French army, was the principal designer and builder of Fort Monroe.

wild. Led by 18 French soldiers who had been captured by the British in Spain and promised their release if they would fight for Britain, the angry British took revenge for their defeat at Craney Island. They pillaged and burned buildings, raped women and plundered stores. As Major Crutchfield reported to Governor Barbour:

"The unfortunate females of Hampton who could not leave the town were suffered to be abused in the most shameful manner, not only by the venal, savage foe but by unfortunate and infuriated blacks, who were encouraged in their success. They pillaged and encouraged every act of rapine and murder, killing a poor man by the name of Kirby, who had been lying on his bed at the point of death for more than six months, shooting his wife in the hip at the same time and killing his faithful dog lying at his feet."

The British navy's second-in-command, Rear Admiral John Cockburn, moved to the handsome residence of Mr. and Mrs. John Westwood, no longer standing, to direct the occupation. The British seized Old Point Comfort lighthouse and commandeered large quantities of supplies from nearby plantations.

The leader of the invading troops was Lieutenant Colonel Charles James Napier, later to become a British general and scholar. He objected to some of his troops' behavior but was overruled. He wrote in his diary, "Every horror was perpetrated with impunity—rape, murder, pillage—and not a man was punished."

Several of Hampton's houses then had windmills to grind wheat and corn, and these were stripped of their sails. The ancient communion silver of St. John's Church also was seized.

Writing to the Richmond Enquirer a few days later, Colonel Richard E. Parker of the Westmoreland Militia said "Hampton exhibits a dreary and desolate appearance which no American can witness unmoved. . . . Men of Virginia! Will you permit all this? Fathers and brothers and husbands, will you fold your arms in apathy and only curse your despoilers? No!"

General Taylor protested to the British com-

The first Hygeia Hotel was built at Old Point in 1820 but torn down for better visibility in the Civil War. It was replaced by a larger hotel, later burned accidentally.

When Hampton was Invaded

Field Book of the War of 1812
Wharves for coastal schooners lined Hampton Creek in 1852. Benson Lossing made this sketch at the foot of King Street, when Hampton had fewer than 2,000 residents.

mander, but he was told the British were retaliating for American "cruelty" at Craney Island. Taylor appointed four of his offices to investigate the charge, but they found no American cruelty.

Accounts of Hampton's conquest published in the Northern press identified the town as "Little Hampton," to distinguish it from the Hamptons on Long Island in New York.

Except for Captain Napier's diary, which did not come to light till later, the British never acknowledged misconduct at Hampton except by their 18 French mercenaries, called "Chasseurs Britanniques." The British general, Sir Sidney Beckwith, said he had ordered the French out of town and back to their ship as soon as he learned of their misconduct. He blamed it on cruelties the French had encountered while fighting for Napoleon in Spain. "They could not be restrained," Beckwith said, lamely.

But Hampton was merely a foretaste of the British burning of the White House and the Capitol by Admiral Cockburn the next year. Cockburn's invaders were finally defeated at Fort McHenry at Baltimore in September 1814. That was when Francis Scott Key wrote, "The Star-Spangled Banner." It was another triumph for America's citizen soldiers.

The Hampton invasion infuriated Virginia and created widespread anti-British sentiment. Jefferson, Madison and Monroe were strongly critical of His Majesty's government. "Remember Hampton!" remained a rallying cry. There were demands for more American soldiers and stronger coastal defenses. "Our force was altogether insufficient at Hampton," wrote Sergeant James Jarvis of Portsmouth. "Had our people been equal or two-thirds the number of the enemy, the Hamptonians would not have been compelled to retreat. They fought like heroes."

That's why James Monroe, who succeeded President Madison, proposed that a series of 12 coastal forts be built along the Atlantic and Gulf of Mexico. One of the largest, Fort Monroe, was started in 1819. On the Rip Raps offshore the Army built Fort Calhoun, which became Fort Wool. President Monroe discouraged other would-be invaders with his Monroe Doctrine.

Several actors in the Hampton drama became famous. Cockburn was chosen by the British to convoy Napoleon to St. Helena in 1815 and made Admiral of the Fleet. Sir Charles James Napier became a general and one of Britain's warrior statesmen. But Americans—especially Hamptonians—never forgave them.

Harper's Weekly magazine ran this sketch of Federal troops landing at Newport News in May of 1861, a few weeks after Virginia voted to secede from the union.

4. The Civil War and George Ben West

WHEN Virginia voted on April 17, 1861 to secede from the union, it doomed itself to become the battleground of the war between North and South. It had not long to wait. On May 27, farmers living at Newport News Point, at the juncture of Hampton Roads and the James River, saw troop-laden vessels approaching their shore. The Yankees had come: The feared invasion of the Peninsula was at hand: The first assault on the Confederate capital at Richmond was about to take shape.

One of Newport News' few residents that Monday morning in May was a pudgy lad of 22 whose family owned a large farm and a dock at Newport News Point. He was George Benjamin West, whose carefree youth ended forever that day. Thinking back later of the placid Sunday before the Yankees came, George Ben West wrote, "This was the last happy day spent in our pleasant home, and how happy we were in the enjoyment of the present...." Ahead lay his family's hasty flight from Newport News, four years of hectic refugee life in Richmond and Lynchburg, and finally the Wests' return to Newport News in 1865 to a desolated farm and a changed world.

West's memoirs, which he wrote between 1906 and 1917, are a graphic account of Southern suffering—a minuscule *Gone with the Wind* of bravery and suffering, buoyed up by hope. In George West's own case, there was a happy ending. Newport News grew into a city in 1881 when it became the terminus of the Chesapeake and Ohio Railway, and George Ben West opened a bank and lived comfortably until his death in 1917 at the age of 78. He was a man of importance in the shipbuilding city.

West's memoirs paint a picture of a prosperous slave-owning family reduced overnight to fear and flight. Though all of the family except his mother and brother survived, they found on their return to Newport News in 1865 that their house and farm buildings had been destroyed and most of their lands sold for delinquent taxes. Dismayed by family deaths and losses, West's aged father, Parker West, died soon afterward.

West's memoirs describe how the Federal troop ships approached the West wharf near the present 18th Street in Newport News on that fateful day in May:

> On Monday Morning, May 27, soon after breakfast, several boats were seen loaded with troops going up the river, and being so near the land, it was apparent they intended to land at the wharrves . . . I was the only male at the house, father being out in the field attending to his hands. Mr. Marrow [George Ben West's brother-in-law], whose wife and children were there, had gone to the Casey farm, and brother was at his own place. One can imagine the great excitement produced by the sight of the troops. War seemed to have come in the midst of perfect peace.
>
> I went at once in search of father, who was so large and fat and so troubled by rheumatism that he could not walk but had to attend to his farming riding in a "Carry-All." I met Jeff Crandol, who was still on duty but had left his post on the beach for reasons I never knew and was returning to it. I informed him of the landing of the troops and told him to report [it]. . . . I could not find father, so I returned home. Soon brother came up on horseback. Being a member of the [Confederate] cavalry company, he had to report. . . .
>
> Very soon after, a squad of Marines came to the house and advised father to go and ask protection of the commanding officer, who turned out to be General [Wolcott] Phelps. They said many of the soldiers were the roughs and jailbirds of Boston and would steal and destroy everything unless it was guarded. We took their advice, and father and I went over and found the General laying off the entrenchments, afterwards built.

United Virginia Bank

George Benjamin West was a boy living at Newport News farm in 1861 when Federal troops landed and fortified the point. He returned after Appomattox.

> This battery extended in a semicircle [along the James River], and at this point was built quite a strong earthwork on which were mounted afterwards some heavy guns. General Phelps was the colonel of the 1st Vermont [Regiment] but on account of his West Point training had been made brigadier general, though the Massachusetts colonel was his senior in point of service. There were three regiments landed. The 7th New York, all Germans, were stationed next to our house, all on our land; the 1st Vermont in the center: and the Massachusetts next. . . .
>
> We found the General in the centre of the camp, and as soon as the request was made and the house pointed out he turned to a corporal and said "Take three men and go with Mr. West and guard his property and do

as he tells you." They returned with us. . . . Our yard enclosed all the outhouses, barns, stables, etc. . . .

The negroes in the fields had on the landing gone to their quarters and left the horses and mules in the fields. The quarters were near the [Newport News Creek]. . . . Our cook, Aunt Lucy, and her family lived in the kitchen in the yard, but her two boys, who were in the field, went to the [slave] quarters and we did not see them again. . . . We after awhile caught all the horses and put them in the stables. In the excitement of the morning the family, fearing to have the rifle and uniform of Mr. Marrow in the house, had gotten Aunt Lucy to put them under our smokehouse, which was on low pillars and the rear exposed to anyone who should look under. When we began to realize this and that Aunt Lucy or her daughters might tell some soldiers, it became a question how to get them out unobserved by anyone on guard, for we were sure that if found they would accuse Mr. Marrow as the owner. . . .

We had dinner cooked for the guard, and as all the other soldiers had gone to camp to dinner, we invited them to go to the front porch to eat. We also got all the negroes out of sight, and then I took the bundle and rifle and carried them to the barn and hid them in a large pile of oats. In the afternoon we feared that the oats might be taken to feed any horses that they might have, and . . . we concluded it were better to have the rifle and uniform in the house. We had no difficulty in getting the guard to their supper on the porch, and I brought the uniform and rifle back to the house. . . .

Father did not go over to the camp on business again, but when we wished any information or favors, I would write a letter in father's name and take one of the guard as a protection and have the interview with the general. I am glad to record that I was always received by him as well as his adjutant with

Daily Press

Federal troops in 1861 took over Warwick Courthouse north of Newport News. This sketch was made in 1862 by a sergeant and shows tiny courthouse at right.

16 The Civil War and George Ben West

the utmost courtesy and consideration, and the requests were always granted in a kind and cordial manner. . . . I could hardly believe.

Phelps had instructed the pickets to arrest all without passes or having any kind of stolen goods. There were a hundred or more around headquarters having every kind of household goods, and some with carts loaded with plunder. I did not know then that the neighbors had left their homes and that most of the plunder was from deserted homes; but thought they had been taken from the people and imagined all sorts of cruel treatment to our friends. . . . I learned afterwards that the thieves, finding out that they would be arrested, had left most of the plunder in the thickets outside of the pickets, all of which was afterwards brought into camp in the night. . . .

How could he sleep, fearing as well as hoping that a battle would take place in the camp? So again we did not undress but watched at the windows all night and at the least noise, those who were sleeping would be aroused. . . . How said it must have been to father to see so much destruction of what it had required him so many years to accumulate. . . .

After six days of fear and sleeplessness the Wests decided to move with their servants to Williamsburg or some other place outside the Federals' Peninsula beachhead. When George Ben West made the request of General Phelps, West later recalled, "he readily agreed to let us leave and said he would furnish us a guard which should be instructed to go with us as far as we siehd, and that we could take not only the negroes who were willing to go but that he would give us the guard to carry those who did not wish to go . . ."

The Wests decided to take only their house servants, who were anxious to go with them. For several days they loaded farm carts with food, clothes, and a few household goods. Many valued articles were left behind in hopes they could reclaim them later. George Ben West and his brother William supervised the loading, George Ben wrote:

We were all very busy till late, packing up the things we thought we would be able to take,

The Union mounted coastal guns called columbiads along waterfront of Parker West plantation site at Newport News beginning in 1861. They tried to halt Confederate shipping.

Hampton Institute Library

The Civil War and George Ben West   17

Daily Press

Union troops at Newport News raided nearby farms for provisions. This sketch by a New York Illustrated News combat artist is titled 'A Foraging Party.'

and we left behind a great many things packed that we could not carry. . . . One cart was loaded with bacon, the others with trunks, bedding, and bed clothes, some crockery, no book or single piece of furniture except a skeleton loung for father to sleep on. . . .

Father drove one of the carts. The others were driven by my sisters and the negroes. We had only one single carriage. Sister Mary drove this and in it were Mammy Watson and mother, with Bettie and Hannah's baby. The corporal and his guard came over early to accompany us, and father was very impatient to lead and was at the head of the procession. . . . He must have thought that he would never again have the comforts that he was leaving, yet by nature he was sanguine, hopeful, and of a happy disposition, full of energy and pluck and was able to bear his loss in a wonderful manner.

Early on the morning of June 2 the Parker West family got in its farm wagons and headed westward along a dirt road which led westward through scattered farms and pine forests of Warwick County, now the city of Newport News. They were headed for the Confederate line of General John Bankhead Magruder, dubbed "Prince John" for his imperious ways. Before they reached that line, however, a Federal force halted them and demanded they return, but George Ben West produced their pass from General Phelps and they went on. After a night's halt with a Warwick County farmer, they set out again and met Magruder, who was engaged in building Confederate defense lines across the Peninsula. West's account continues:

After breakfast we started and met General Magruder near the picket, with some cavalry, reconnoitering. He stopped and inquired as to the number and position of the Yankees, whether they had thrown up entrenchments, and intimating he would attack them. He seemed to feel very sorry for father and told him to go to Yorktown and he would furnish us quarters and would supply all our wants as long as he had anything to eat himself. We have always felt very kindly to him for his kindness and offer, and in fact he was kind to all the refugees. . . .

"What a week this had been! I was completely broken down, and all of us were half sick. My sickness and the reports about Magruder going to attack Newport News caused me to give up all idea of going back for the furniture and negroes. . . ." Accordingly, the West caravan moved on to Williamsburg, where they rented a house and lived austerely, sleeping on the floor and hoping for news that the Confederates had driven Federal forces out of Newport News.

"After the battle of Bethel June 10 we did not feel so safe in Williamsburg, and brother and father thought it best for us to move to Richmond."

Accordingly, the West women and children boarded a James River steamer at Chickahominy landing, ten miles west of Williamsburg, while Parker West and his sons drove their wagons westward through James City, New Kent, and Henrico Counties to arrive a day before the womenfolk.

One afternoon the latter part of June '61 we reached Richmond and attracted as much attention and curiosity as any army corps did a year or two after. We were not an attractive sight driving through the city, and I had to often reply to inquiries as to where we were from and why we were moving. I suppose some of them got an idea of what war was . . .

Parker West rented a house on Richmond's Church Hill, near old St. John's Church, with a detached kitchen, smokehouse, and stable. For it they paid $12,50 a month, at first in gold and later in Confederate currency. "We did not form many intimacies with the Richmond people," George Ben West recorded. "We refugees were poor and kept very much to ourselves. I do not think father had $100 when we left home, and most of this was gone. He could do nothing, and we all decided we would almost starve before we would sell any of the slaves, and none of them could bring much hire."

After reaching Richmond, William, the elder West son, entered full-time Confederate service, but the family urged George Ben West to remain as long as possible with his ailing parents and young sisters. Through the influence of General Virginius Groner, a family friend, he found a civilian job in the Confederate Quartermaster Corps. He earned $50 monthly, which was pooled with receipts of his father's sale of his horses, mules, and carts to provide furniture, food, and clothes for his family.

I was employed to have charge of some warehouses on the [James River] basin where were stored the baggage of the soldiers from the South who had each left home with trunks and valises and mess chests, etc., and as transportation could not be secured beyond Richmond, the [Confederate] government rented these warehouses and stored the baggage. . . . I remember the 12th Georgia Regiment's baggage was oftenest called for and am quite sure that the Regiment had more baggage stored than the whole Army of Northern Virginia had with them in 1864.

Even though Mrs. Parker West and her five daughters earned a few dollars weekly by sewing soldiers' uniforms, the family sank into debt. At last, General Groner obtained the discharge of young William West from the Confederate cavalry and had him assigned to the Adjutant-General's office in Richmond. To provide further funds, the Wests' eldest daughter, Mary Emily Marrow, made her way through federal lines to Hampton and brought to Richmond furniture and other goods she had left behind. Wrote Parker West of the 1861-62 winter:

That fall and winter we had quite a good

The Civil War and George Ben West 19

Casemate Museum

Union forces made use of observation and signal balloons on the Peninsula during the Civil War. This sketch was made in a Union camp near the James River on Peninsula.

time, being all together except Mr. Marrow, and it was seldom that we did not have stopping with us some of the Peninsula soldiers. Our [Confederate] armies had been for the most part victorious in every engagement, and our friends had for the most part not done much fighting, and so none were killed or wounded, and we were sure the war would soon be over and therefore gave ourselves up to all the enjoyment possible under the circumstances.

While working in the Quartermaster Corps office one afternoon, George Ben West got his first view of Robert E. Lee, who was then headquartered in Richmond:

A gentleman came in to see if there was a boat going down the river that afternoon as he wished to go down to Shirley [the Carter family plantation, where Lee's mother, Ann Carter, had been reared]. He was dressed in a sort of fatigue suit with no mark of rank, and did not give his name. When he went out, all the clerks wondered who he could be. All of us were sure from his manner and appearance that he was some distinguished man. It was the universal verdict of all that he was the handsomest and courtliest man we ever saw, so we wished to know who he was, and we found out it was General R. E. Lee. At this time he did not wear a beard, only a moustache, which was only slightly iron gray.

I saw him often that spring and summer, and he then wore only the mustache....After the fights around Richmond [the Seven Days' Battles] his office was in the Custom House, and I often saw him and President Davis on their horses, going out to the camps. Davis rode a dark bay Arabian and Lee his gray. Though Lee was considered a fine horseman and was so distinguished looking, yet to my mind the President was the best rider. He is the only man I ever saw who looked like he and horse were one.

The Wests' hopes for an early Confederate victory were dashed in the bloody Seven Days' battles between McClellan's invaders and Lee's defending army in June and July, 1862. Young West wrote:

This spring and summer we began to realize war in all its horrors. The evacuation of the Peninsula, the fight at Williamsburg [May 4-5, 1862], and fights around Richmond were participated in by our friends and acquaintances, and daily we were hearing of the death or wounding of some of these. How anxious were we to hear and yet dreaded to hear who the killed and wounded were. This was the most disastrous year to the troops from the Peninsula of any during the war.

When Magruder fell back from Yorktown and the Army of Northern Virginia had to come from the Rapidan to defend Richmond, there was great excitement and grave fear that the city would fall into the hands of the enemy. There was a rumor that General Joseph E. Johnston advised the evacuation of the city to draw the Yankees farther away from their base of supplies. At any rate the government made provisions to move in case it became a necessity. Brother even had his ticket to Columbia, S.C., to superintend the removal of the records of the Adjutant General's office to this place. Our department was to be removed to Richmond.

Alarmed for their safety, the older Wests in the spring of 1862 decided Richmond was no longer safe for them or their daughters. Accordingly, the ailing Mr. and Mrs. Parker West gathered their daughters and house servants and went up the James River canal to Lynchburg, some 150 miles west of Richmond in the Piedmont area. It was a timely flight, for the thunder of cannon could be heard in nearby Richmond during the crucial seven days. George Ben West was briefly pressed into military service in this crisis:

A Union soldiers' hospital near Old Point continued to treat the injured. It was the forerunner of the Veterans Administration Hospital at Hampton.

Virginia State Library

When Confederates realized Hampton would be overrun by Union troops from Fort Monroe, Colonel John Magruder ordered the city burned. Some burned their own homes.

The Yankees had crossed the Chickahominy Swamp, and there was great excitement in Richmond as well as along the lines of the entrenchments that protected the city. The inner line had not been mounted with any artillery, and I had to send out lumber to the batteries to temporarily mount some heavy guns and was out in all the rain . . . Oh what a sad time it was! The whole city filled with the sick and wounded, every available place a hospital, and a great many private houses with some loved one or acquaintance. The hearses were busy all the day and did not take only one body but as many as could be put in. The dead could not be buried as fast as they were hauled out and had to lie in the cemeteries sometimes 24 hours before the graves could be dug.

I saw a man brought back from Oakwood [Cemetery] sitting up in his coffin who had been carried out as dead but had come to while lying on the ground. No doubt some were buried alive, and many died for want of proper attention and care. The people of Richmond did everything in their power to help, especially the ladies, who nursed in the hospital and furnished all the delicacies they could get. On my way to the office I passed the Seabrook Tobacco warehouse that was used for a hospital, and through the windows could see the hundreds lying on the cots, where the tobacco hogsheads had been accustomed to be store - nothing but a series of sheds enclosed by a brick wall.

Returning from a trip to visit his parents at Lynchburg, George Ben West spent his first night on a canal boat. The shy young man was surprised by the conviviality of the passengers:

I could not understand how we would sleep till they swung in the centre of the boat berths in three tiers [high]. I fortunately got in one of the side ones, for to me it looked very danger-

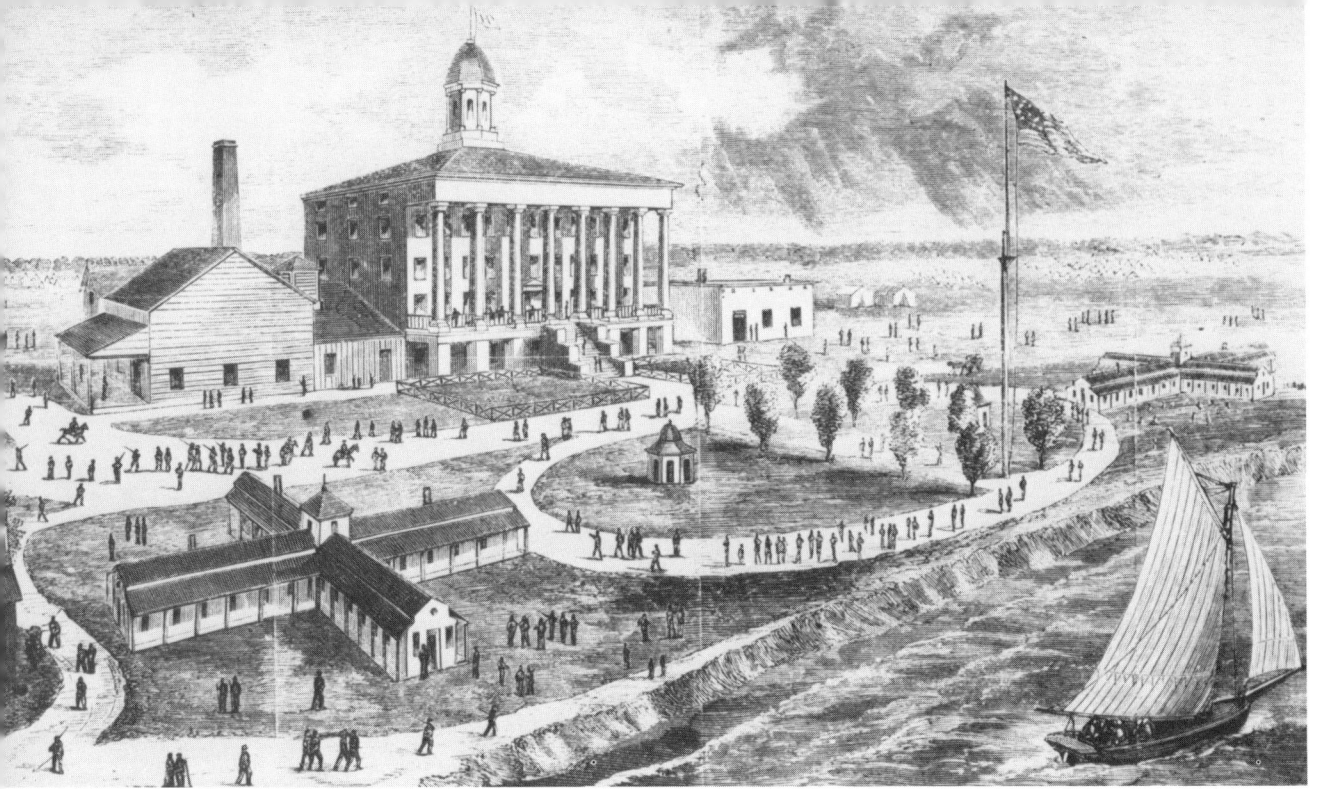

Federal forces erected their Chesapeake Hospital on Hampton Roads shore between Strawberry Banks and present Hampton University. It grew into Veterans Administration Hospital.

ous, seeing the men swing out one above the other. I never saw such familiarity among strangers; everybody tried to have a good time and make others enjoy themselves. Many had snacks with them, or fruit, and it would always be handed to all the passengers so that, though very slow and tedious travel, there was so much of sociability and informality, it was delightful.

The two West brothers continued to share a rented house on Richmond's Church Hill until William died of typhoid fever during an epidemic. Surrounded by the dead and dying, his younger brother wrote, "His death did not seem to affect me, for I suppose I had seen and heard so much of death that it had lost its terrors and I was so sick that for once in my life I do not think I would have cared whether I lived or died."

With McClellan's threat to Richmond successfully repelled, Mr. and Mrs. Parker West and their daughters returned to their rented refugee quarters. The war was rapidly worsening for the Confederacy, and food was scarce and expensive. The Wests bought their last sugar in 1863 for $20 a pound. For lack of coffee or tea, they drank concoctions made of toasted corn, burned peanuts, meal bran, or sweet potatoes. "Money depreciated so rapidly that our salaries amounted to hardly anything," George Ben West recalled.

Early in 1865, the last year of the war, George Ben West's mother died of a long illness. The Confederacy's own end was near. About noon on Sunday, April 2, just after church time, George Ben West wrote that "we heard quite a stir in street and found out it was parties from the St. Paul's Church in earnest conversation and deep excitement, and by inquiry found out the message sent by General Lee [in Petersburg] to President Davis about evacuating the city." As soon as he could, young West got leave from his office and rushed home to tell his father and sisters. He was determined to join Lee's army south of

The Civil War and George Ben West 23

the James River, and he told his family good-bye. He wrote:

> Of course the parting with my loved ones was exceedingly sad, tho' not a one tried to persuade me to remain. I did not know what I would do or where go, but intended to follow the army and stay as long as there was any chance of success. I had no idea the cause was in such a critical state. Tho' I had been so situated that it would have been almost criminal to have left the family and gone into active service, and tho' I believed I was doing more good and a greater work than I could do in the field . . . yet I had not been very well satisfied with myself when I remembered that my friends and acquaintances were bearing the burdens and risks of a soldier, and I in a bomb proof in Richmond.

Young West went to his office to quit his job, "and all along the streets we could see

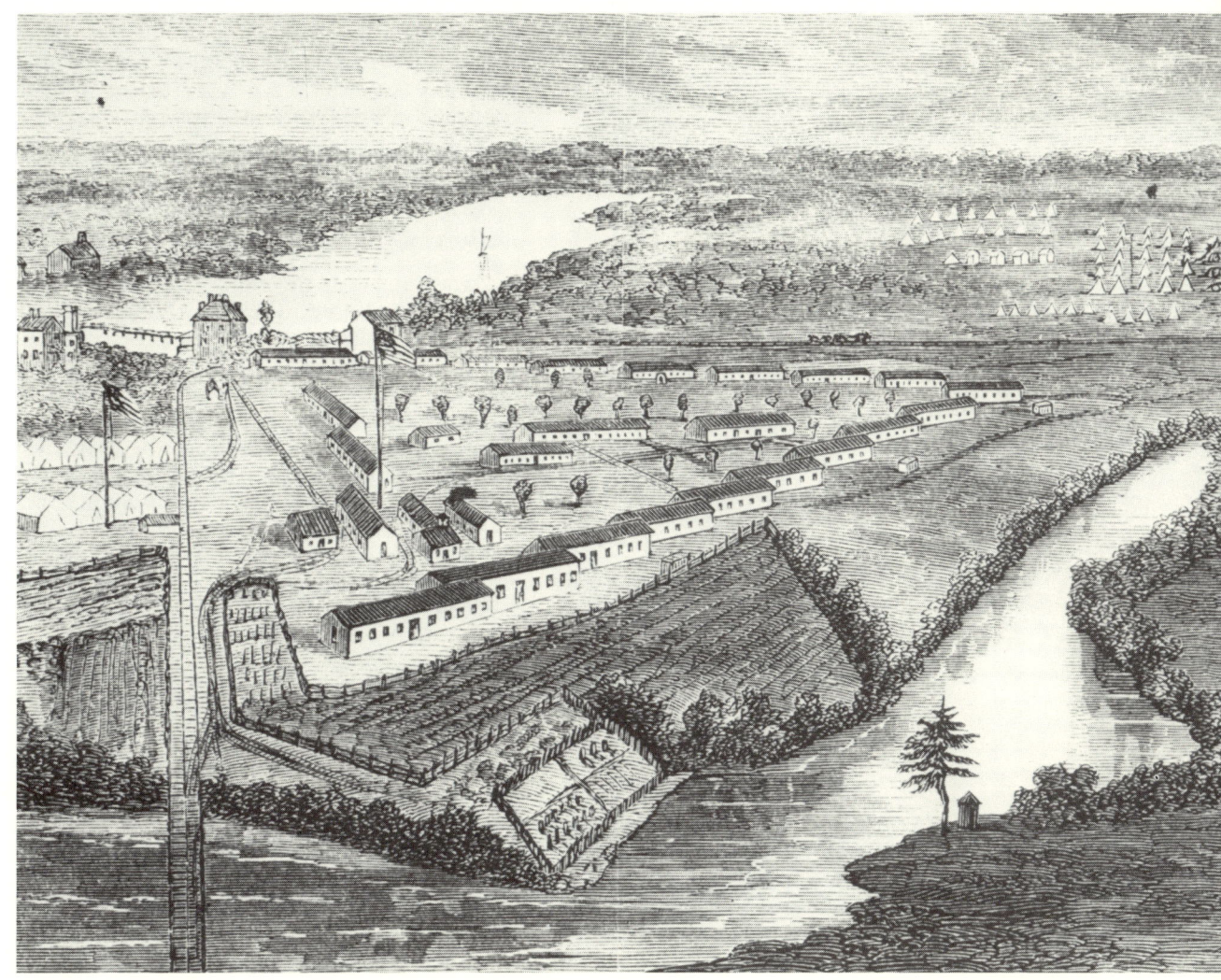

Casemate Museum

As Civil War casualties grew, the Federal hospital near Hampton had to be expanded. This 1864 Harper's Magazine woodcut shows barracks at military Hospital.

men hurrying and families watching and bidding farewell to loved ones; but everything was solemn and subdued - no noise of wailing and crying - only silent tears and deep sighs." Returning through the streets, he saw Confederate supplies being given away and destroyed to prevent their falling into the enemy's hands when Richmond fell. He wrote:

> On our return we saw many drunken, and some lying in the gutters with the liquor flowing around them. We passed Major Ferguson's in the wagons just before midnight, and the warehouse had been opened or broken in and the people were carrying away their plunder. Had not the stores been robbed they would have been burned in a fiew hours, and it is unfortunate that the government could not have been to all who remained in the city the stores that they could not carry away. . . .
>
> I left Richmond on a baggage wagon from our stables. Our train got mixed up with the artillery, and our progress was very slow. We could only have gone a few miles when the day broke. We got away from the army trains and traveled all day, but I do not remember anything of the country; it was all new to me. I did not know where we were going, did not inquire, nor did I care. My thoughts were on those I left behind . . .

West's wagon train was attacked in southern Virginia by a Federal cavalry unit:

> "In a short time the whole camp was panic-stricken . . . Some took short cuts down the hill and swam across the stream. The road and bridge were jammed. It was the only time I ever saw a stampede, and had I not been in it, could not have imagined the mad rush, unreasonable fear, and selfish desire for their own safety . . . In all of our trip we had fallen in with many soldiers who in one way and another had been separated from their commands and would follow along with us, sometimes a considerable distance. Some of these went back and in a short time word was sent us that the Yankees had been driven off.

West's wagon train reached Danville and started out again, this time headed for Greensboro, North Carolina. Here he learned that Lee had surrendered several days earlier. "Mr. Davis and his Government were here [in Greensboro] and were uncertain what to do. After hearing from General [Joseph E.] Johnston and learning he would have to surrender, it was decided that the Government should be transferred across the Mississippi."

West decided to follow Jefferson Davis, but his commanding officer, Major John C. May-

Daily Press

Long after the Civil War, Confederate casualties in Newport News were re-interred at Greenlawn Cemetery under this cenotaph.

nard, urged him to return to Virginia. He was issued a discharge from service in Greensboro by Major John Withers, Assistant Adjutant General of the Confederacy. With a dozen other discharged Virginians, George Ben West set out by horseback to return through rural North Carolina and Virginia to Richmond, where they arrived late in April, 1865. Hurriedly he rushed to his family's house on Church Hill, only to find that they had started back down the Peninsula to Newport News. Soon he followed them by boat down the James, docking at Old Point Comfort. He wrote:

What a change on the Peninsula: The space between Mill Creek and Hampton, instead of cultivated farms, was covered with temporary houses and tents, used for [Federal] hospitals and quarters. Hampton had been burnt by Magruder, as it has become a refuge for Negroes and Yankees in '61. The Peninsula troops were of the burning party, and many a young man set fire to his own father's house; and this was the case with my brother. He fired our [Hampton] house in the parlor. There were very few brick houses, so the whole town was leveled - only the chimneys standing as sentinels, and they too were soon pulled down to make flues for the little shanties and tents which soon began to appear on the site. The Old St. John's Church walls remained standing . . . Sad, sad such times, yet youth is sanguine.

Recalling all this as he penned his memoirs in the year 1906 to 1917, George Ben West expressed amazement that Virginia had revived so strongly from the war and Reconstruction. He himself was a good example of the New Virginia which was rising from the ashes of the old. After regaining possession of a small part of his father's lands at Newport News, he shared in the prosperity which accompanied the construction of the Chesapeake and Ohio Railway terminus there in 1880-81 and the creation of the shipyard in 1886-90.

George Ben West himself founded the city's second bank, the Citizens and Marine, and he helped build the town's earliest Baptist church and its first private academy for young men. [Newport News Academy soon closed, but the Citizens Marine-Jefferson Bank became part of United Virginia.] He became a trustee and benefactor of the University of Richmond, and he created a trust which eventually provided a million dollars for Riverside Hospital's outpatient clinic.

Though West lived on in a changed industrial age, he retained the principles and the pride of the rural Virginia which had produced him. He deified Lee, Stonewall Jackson, and other leaders of the South's Lost Cause. Always a bachelor, he remained a kindly, courteous, and rotund figure, beloved by his family. All his life he loved to tell of the day the Yankees landed at Newport News, for he believed he had seen the worst of times and lived to tell the tale. Like Robert E. Lee, he believed that "Misfortune, nobly borne, is good fortune." He is an important figure in Peninsula history.

A paddle-wheeled transport ship discharges Federal troops at Camp Butler in Newport News in 1861. The area is now covered by docks and coal piers.

II.
From Forests into Towns
1861-1909

President Lincoln came to Fort Monroe twice in the Civil War. He was there in 1862, when the Peninsula campaign began, and in 1864 seeking to negotiate a truce with the Confederacy.

5. Lincoln Visits Fort Monroe

PRESIDENT Lincoln paid an important visit to Fort Monroe in the winter of 1864-65. There he met secretly with three major Confederate officials in an effort to end the war. The house Lincoln used is still an important site at that base.

It's a shame that effort failed, for Lincoln was willing to recommend to Congress that Southern slave-owners be paid for their slaves by the United States if the South would return to the Union. It didn't work. As we know, Lee fought on to defeat on April 9, 1865, just two months after the peace conference. The South thereby lost it hopes for independence and its slaves, too.

The Monroe Conference took place February 3, 1865, in the cabin of the River Queen, a ship which was docked at Fort Monroe. Accompanying the president down the river from Washington was Secretary of State William H. Seward. They met with three Confederates from Richmond: Confederate Vice-President Alexander H. Stephens of Georgia, Judge John A. Campbell of Alabama and R.M.T. Hunter, of Virginia.

It was an awkward reunion for Lincoln and Stephens, for they had been friends and fellow Congressmen before the war.

Stephens was a small, wiry little man weighing less than 90 pounds. Like Robert E. Lee and many other Southerners, he had opposed secession, but when the war came, he accepted the vice-presidency of the Confederacy. He arrived on the River Queen in a huge overcoat, muffler and several shawls. Lincoln broke the tension with humor, as he often did. "Never have I seen so small a nubbin come out of so much husk," he said to the tiny Stephens.

Nothing came of the meeting except Lincoln's release from a Northern military prison of Stephens' nephew, who had been taken in battle. The war ground bloodily on. Grant's siege of the Confederate capital at Richmond that spring soon forced Lee to evacuate Richmond and Petersburg. A few weeks later came the surrender at Appomattox.

Lincoln had a big hand in his army's conduct of the war, and he often sailed down the Potomac to Virginia in the four years of fighting. He came to Monroe and to Berkeley on the James twice, and he visited Norfolk and City Point—now Hopewell—on other occasions. After the Confederacy evacuated Richmond, Lincoln came to the ex-Confederate capital to see the city for himself. Harper's

30 *Lincoln Visits Fort Monroe*

Casemate Museum

Wounded Union soldiers were discharged at Hampton for treatment at a military hospital. Union naval forces controlled Hampton Roads in the war.

Weekly printed a lithograph showing the president in the State Capitol, surrounded by admirers.

Lincoln's earlier Fort Monroe visit came in May 1862, a year after the war started. He was impatient at General George B. McClellan's delay in pushing up the Peninsula to Richmond. The president and Secretary of War, Stanton, came by ship to Fort Monroe about May 5, the same day McClellan captured Williamsburg. The president stayed at the commanding officer's quarters at Monroe while federal forces on Fort Wool—the Rip-Raps—shelled Confederates on Sewell's Point. By May 11, the Union army entered Norfolk, which had surrendered. Lincoln watched some of the action from Fort Wool.

The house which sheltered Lincoln at Monroe, known as Quarters 1, is still in use there. It is built in the neat Southern form of other officers' quarters, including the house wherein Lieutenant and Mrs. Robert E. Lee had lived with their family in the 1830s. Both are built in a style which suggests 19th century Mississippi cotton mansions, appropriately framed by old live oaks, which give the casemate area of Monroe such an old-time Southern flavor.

Lincoln came by ship to Berkeley plantation in Charles City County twice in the summer of 1862, just three or four months after his May visit to Monroe. By that time McClellan had been stopped by Robert E. Lee in the Seven Days' Battles around Richmond, and he was resting his army of 125,000 men at what was then called Harrison's Landing, now Berkeley.

By then Lincoln was fed up with McClellan. On his second visit to confer with "Little

Mac" that August, McClellan presumed to advise Lincoln on national policy, and Lincoln decided to fire him as commander of the chief Union Army. He did so in November, replacing him with General Burnside. Grant came several generals later.

Lincoln visited Grant's center of operations near Petersburg nearly three years later, in April 1865, staying at Appomattox Manor, the Epes plantation on the James. The house is now owned by the Park Service, and memorabilia of Lincoln's visit are exhibited there.

It's interesting to speculate what might have happened if that Fort Monroe peace conference in February 1865 had brought peace. Would Lincoln have been able to get from Congress the $400 million he proposed to reimburse Southern slave-holders for their freed blacks? And would such a peace have been acceptable in North and South?

I suspect not. By 1865, bitterness between the two sides had reached such intensity that it compelled a fight to the finish. For that, the nation is still paying a price.

Two other visitors to the Peninsula in the Civil War and soon after have left a graceful record of their visits.

One was an unknown Union soldier who died at Newport News Point in 1861 or 1862,

Casemate Museum

An 1861 illustration in the New York Illustrated News showed Commandant's Quarters at Fort Monroe, where Lincoln stayed in May 1862, at the beginning of the Peninsula Campaign.

In March 1862 the Confederate ironclad Merrimack fought the Union dreadnought Monitor in Hampton Roads, midway between Hampton and Newport News. Sidney King painted this mural.

The Commandant's Quarters at Fort Monroe, shown in 1890, has housed several presidents and many military leaders. The fort is one of the nation's oldest in service.

after the Union army had seized it and built Camp Butler there, named for Union general Benjamin Butler. The soldier was eulogized after the war by Henry Wadsworth Longfellow, who presumably read of the unknown warrior's death after General George B. McClellan had led his Peninsula Campaign from Old Point to Richmond in an unsuccessful attempt to capture the Confederate capitol.

Longfellow's sonnet reads:

"A Soldier of the Union Mustered Out"
Is the inscription on an unknown grave
At Newport News, beside the salt-sea wave.
Nameless and dateless, sentinel or scout
Shot down in skirmish, or disastrous rout
Of battle, when the loud artillery drave
Its iron wedges through the banks of brave
And doomed battalions, storming the redoubt.

Thou unknown hero sleeping by the sea
In thy forgotten grave! With secret shame
I feel my pulses beat, my forehead burn
When I remember thou hadst given for me
All that thou hadst, thy life, they very name,
And I can give thee nothing in return.

A very different poem was penned by the California poet Joaquin Miller in the 1880s when the Chesapeake Dry Dock Company—soon expanded into the Newport News Shipyard—opened with the drydocking of the United States Navy monitor, Puritan.

Collis Huntington, who headed the Chesapeake and Ohio Railway and the shipyard, brought Miller to town on his private railroad car. The two men, both Californians, were drawn together by their interest in outdoor life and gold-mining. For Joaquin Miller had been a miner, express rider, newspaper editor, and judge before turning to poetry.

Miller titled his poem "Newport News," and it portrays the rustic town as it began its life a century ago:

The huge sea monster, the Merrimac,
The mad sea monster, the Monitor,
You may sweep the sea, peer forward and back,
But never a sign or a sound of war:
A vulture or two in the heaven's blue,
A sweet town building, a boatman's call,
The far sea-song of a pleasure crew,
The sound of hammers. And that is all.

And where are the monsters that tore this main?
And where are the monsters that shook this shore?
The sea grew mad, and the shore shot flame!
The mad sea monsters they are no more.
The palm, and the pine, and the sea sands brown,
The far sea songs of the pleasure crews,
The air like balm in this building town,
And that is the picture of Newport News.

Casemate Museum

A Fort Monroe guard company musters inside the moat about 1890. Until the air age, the base was an important coastal defense for the Chesapeake area.

6. Collis Huntington's Magic Touch

THE industrial age entered Chesapeake Bay close on the heels of the Civil War. Coal-burning steamships gradually replaced the schooners which had hauled America's commerce, and railroads slashed their way through worn-out tobacco fields to create larger ports at Norfolk, Newport News, and Baltimore.

All this was symbolized in a hulking, six-foot-two-inch titan of finance who as early as 1837 recognized Cheaspeake Bay as a coming center of industry.

He was Collis Potter Huntington.

Little except farmland surrounded the Chesapeake when Huntington sailed into Newport News Point as a 16-year-old boy, peddling watches and hardware for New England manufacturers. Pine trees fringed the blue waters, and "buy boats" moved lazily from one wharf to another, loading wheat, corn, and tobacco. But the ambitious Connecticut youth recognized the area as "ideal for enterprise," he wrote later.

The vision of the Chesapeake stuck in Huntington's mind throughout the years of the California Gold Rush, when he went west and made a fortune selling mining gear in Sacramento. Then, becoming a great railroad builder after the Civil War, he turned his eyes again toward the riches which he had seen in the Chesapeake hinterland.

Huntington recognized the need for railroads linking the growing west to the ports of the Great Lakes and Chesapeake Bay. In the troubled years of reconstruction, he laid his plans. To the railway which his "Big Four"—Leland Stanford, Mark Hopkins, Charles Crocker, and he—had cut from the Pacific to Chicago, he would attach an eastern railroad extending to Chesapeake Bay and the Atlantic's shipping.

Because the Baltimore and Ohio Railway already served the upper bay area, Huntington decided to confine his search to Newport News and four other lower bay sites fronting on deep water: Norfolk, Yorktown, West Point, and the mouth of the Piankatank River. Secretly choosing Newport News at last, he had his agent quietly buy up acreage from farmers down the Virginia Peninsula to serve as right-of-way for his Chesapeake and Ohio Railway.

When he revealed his plan in 1872, Huntington expressed belief that the Peninsula, "so designed and adapted by nature" for man's use, would become a great metropolis.

Collis Potter Huntington was photographed shortly before his death in 1900. As usual when he worked, he wore a cap. At his rear was a large print of his newest project, the shipyard.

Applauding his choice, Scribner's Monthly for December 1872 declared that "Nowhere on the four continents is there a more magnificent expanse of landlocked water than this Hampton Roads in which the navies of the world might rise at their moorings . . ."

As the one-hundredth anniversary of Washington's victory at Yorktown approached in 1881, the C. & O.'s main line stretched westward from Newport News. In Williamsburg it ran down the middle of Duke of Gloucester Street. On the hundredth anniversary of Cornwallis' surrender, October 19, 1881, Collis Huntington played opulent host to a trainload of Senators and Congressmen who came to Yorktown to dedicate the Victory Monument, which crowns that town.

But Huntington in 1881 had only begun to industrialize the lower Chesapeake with his C. &. O Railway. Steamships were by that time rapidly replacing sails, and he saw the need for a shipyard on the Chesapeake to repair the steel ships which were flocking to the C. & O.'s Newport News coal piers. In the depression year of 1886 he decided to charter his Chesapeake Dry Dock and Construction Company, built along the lower James near his railway terminal. Its name soon changed to Newport News Shipbuilding and Dry Dock Company. Today it is simply Newport News Shipbuilding.

Though he lived in New York, Collis Huntington frequently rolled into Newport News on his private railroad car to check on the growth of his empire. When his shipyard opened in 1889 with the drydocking of the United States Navy's Puritan—one of the new ironclad monitors—Huntington brought with him the two wild-haired poets, Walt Whitman and Joaquin Miller, whose earthy verses he admired. Miller recorded his impressions in a poem titled "Newport News."

36   Collis Huntington's Magic Touch

Begun in 1886 as a ship repair facility, the Newport News yard in 1889 began to build ships. The Spanish-American War expanded it to a major builder.

The Huntington enterprises attracted thousands of men to Newport News from Virginia and North Carolina farms, seeking jobs. Many were victims of the panic and depression which had followed the postwar boom. Others were emancipated blacks, who had been encouraged by Federal policy to leave their former masters and seek refuge behind Union lines in the last years of the Civil War. It was a new age.

Collis Huntington's vast capital attracted other business to Newport News, just as the Norfolk and Western and the Virginian Railways were doing in Norfolk and Portsmouth across the water. The area drew an endless procession of farm families for the next hundred years from former "black belt" counties south of the James and in eastern North Carolina. The Newport News yard also attracted skilled shipbuilders from Clydebank, Glasgow, and Plymouth in the British Isles. In place of "The palm, and the pine, and the sea sands brown," Hampton Roads became a melting pot of races and nationalities.

Powerful as he was, Collis Huntington was bitterly fought by the financiers of New York and Boston, who saw New York and Boston threatened by the rise of the Chesapeake region. (Eventually he sold his railroad interests and concentrated on the shipyard.) He was assailed as a "robber baron" who used wealth to achieve seflish gains. While this was true, it was also true that he possessed great vision. He had brought the Industrial Age to the Chesapeake region and given jobs to thousands at a time of need.

To induce more ocean trade to come into Hampton Roads, Huntington signed agreements with European and British shipping lines. In the same years, coastwise steamboat services operated to connect Chesapeake Bay ports with the Atlantic and gulf coasts. Not until highways blossomed after World War I did the graceful white passenger boats disappear from the Chesapeake. Their rotting docks today testify to their passing.

By the time Collis Huntington died in 1900, the character of Chesapeake Bay was changing. His friend Joaquin Miller, who shared his bravado, hymned him as "first to lead the steel-shod cavalry of conquest through the Sierras to the Sea of Seas . . . who has done the Greater West and South more enduring good than another other living man . . ." The heyday of giants ended a year later, when Congress at President Theodore Roosevelt's behest introduced the first antitrust laws.

The modern outgrowth of Huntington's enterprises if familiar. Although he never spanned the continent with his rail system, he lived to see Hampton Roads grow into the port he had visualized in 1837. His shipyard a few years after his death had become the largest privately-owned yard in the world, building many of the greatest passenger and warships ever to fly the American flag.

The growth of the city which he built up from a village illustrates the change which industrialization brought in the hundred years after the Civil War to seaside towns which line the Chesapeake. Once they looked to the water for their cargoes, their travel, and their news. Today, the Chesapeake plays a less visible but still important part in the urban life which surrounds it.

So war-torn is the twentieth century that a ring of military bases has been built around the Chesapeake, further detracting from its native charm. But despite the hum of jets and the clatter of coal trains, the smell of saltwater still rises from the creeks and rivers which feed the bay.

Can these be kept unspoiled? Most people who live along the rural reaches of the bay are determined that they shall be. They cherish Joaquin Miller's vision of the old Newport News waterside:

> A vulture or two in the heaven's blue;
> A sweet town building, a boatman's call;
> The far sea-song of a pleasure crew;
> The sound of hammers. And that is all.

Collis Huntington has left his legacy, but Joaquin Miller's vision is worth remembering, too.

7. Mysterious Arabella Huntington

WHAT is it that poor get for free but the rich must pay for? The answer is privacy. To escape the gaze of the curious, America's rich have often gone to expensive ends. But no one in recent America hid herself more successfully than the mysterious Arabella Yarrington, who in the 1860s became the inamorata, and later the wife, of Collis Potter Huntington, the Californian who spanned the nation with railroads before he died in 1900.

Belle Huntington: that name in the Edwardian age had a golden ring to art dealers, to European hostesses, and to international society in France and Spain. Back in her native Virginia, however, few knew that rich Mrs. Huntington of New York and Paris was poor Arabella Yarrington, who had worked as a seamstress and barmaid in post-Civil War Richmond. Inquirers today can find few records of her career, even though Huntington archives are preserved at Syracuse University, at the Huntington Library in California, and at the Mariners Museum in Newport News. Arabella saw to her privacy before she died in 1924.

Lacking fact, the world has made many surmises about the strong-willed southern girl who in 1900 became "the world's richest woman." Some whispered she was a mulatto, though that was untrue. Others said she was ashamed that her father had been a machinist and her mother a boardinghouse keeper. Still others said she was attempting to conceal an illegitimate child by Collis Huntington during the lifetime of his wife. Only after the first Mrs. Huntington died in 1883 did Collis marry Arabella. It was a strangely quiet wedding, with none of Collis's family present and little word in the press.

What the world knows of Arabella dates chiefly from her later marriage. This was to Collis's favorite nephew, Henry E. Huntington, in 1913, after he had divorced his wife, Mary Alice Prentice, mother of his four children. Uniting two-thirds of Collis's $450,000,000 fortune (Arabella's son, Archer Huntington, got most of the rest), Henry and Belle turned a California ranch into the Mediterranean palace which became the Henry E. Huntington Library and Art Gallery, today a center of historical study.

It is at San Marino that Belle's memory is best kept—not in Richmond, where she grew up, nor in New York, where she chiefly lived. However, the memory is not of a southern beauty but of an imperious old lady, dressed in the black widow's weeds she wore from the time of Collis's death until her own in 1924. It is this Belle—a pillar of respectability—who largely survives. Though the English portraitist Sir Oswald Birley had wanted to portray her for posterity as a grande dame, she preferred to be remembered as a stern matriarch. A teacher, visiting the Huntington Library with her class, mistook her portrait for "Mrs. Siddons as the Tragic Muse."

In some ways, Arabella was a typical tycoon's wife of the Edith Wharton era. She spent her husband's millions to enjoy and transplant the riches of Europe back home to America. But Arabella was more complicated. To Collis she was a beautiful, romantic southern belle. To her adored son Archer she communicated surprisingly sophisticated tastes for travel, the arts, and literature. In her last husband, Henry Huntington, she inspired a taste for paintings, books, gardens, and architecture which became their gift to the nation. To both her Huntington husbands and her son she was a figure loved for her brains and charm, however arrogant she became with age.

In his book on the art dealer Lord Duveen, S. N. Behrman called her one of the most fascinating unsung heroines of her generation. Robert Wark, curator of the Huntington Art Gallery, writes: "Quite aside from her personal achievements, which were considerable, she was a key factor in the lives of the three most important members of the Huntington family. . . . The influence she exercised in one way or another through these men is awesome to contemplate."

The arrogance of her nature was reflected by an art dealer who trailed her around Europe eight months without selling her anything. "Mrs. Huntington allows herself manners which even the Empress of Germany cannot afford," wrote James Henry Duveen, Lord Duveen's brother. Her family and staff catered to her whims. When she tired of San Marino's heat, husband Henry knew they must depart. Once she had announced "We're leaving for New York immediately," her husband would sorrowfully tell his valet, "Pack my things—let's go."

Mariners Museum

Arabella Yarrington, born in Richmond, became Collis Huntington's second wife in 1883. She became one of America's richest women and a well-known art collector.

What is known of Arabella's birth and youth rests largely on research in Richmond and New York, chiefly by art historian James T. Maher for his *The Twilight of Splendor,* published in 1975. In that architectural account of Henry E. Huntington's San Marino estate, the author indicates the difficulty of reconciling Arabella's account of her parentage and first marriage with existing records. "Arabella Huntington is not so much forgotten as misremembered, when she is remembered at all," Maher writes. "She protected herself from the press so adroitly that, despite the fact that she had been married to two of the best-known men of the era, and had herself been one of the richest Americans of history, no accurate obituary of her could be written when she died."

Her only printed biography, an appreciation by the late Cerinda Evans, published by the Mariners Museum of Newport News in 1959, was prepared, Miss Evans admitted, "from statements by her relatives and associates." Her letters and other personal documents are not in the Huntington archives, and her son, Archer, who was then living, told little of his

Casemate Museum

New American fortunes in the 1880s spawned fancy resort hotels like the first Chamberlin at Old Point. Belle Huntington preferred the spas of Europe, often accompanied by her son Archer.

mother's life. Even the date and place of her birth are uncertain. The inscription on her tomb at San Marino reads "Born June 1, 1850, Union Springs, Alabama," but other sources indicate it occurred in Richmond before 1850.

Her parents were apparently Richard Milton Yarrington, a machinist, and his wife, Catherine, the former Mrs. Edward M. Maddox, who kept a Richmond boardinghouse in the 1850s on the south side of Main Street, in the commercial area along the James River, between Seventeenth and Eighteenth streets. It was at that time a declining area adjoining Richmond's Shockoe Bottom. Yarrington was perhaps connected with the Mrs. James Yarrington who earlier had kept a Richmond boardinghouse at Twelfth and Bank streets, fronting Capitol Square, in which Edgar Allan Poe had married his fourteen-year-old cousin, Virginia Clemm, in 1836.

A Richmonder of the 1880s recalled that Arabella was the daughter of a policeman. The *Richmond Directory* shows that a John Blair Yarrington was on the Richmond police force in 1850, and later. However, Arabella's father was more probably the Richard Milton Yarrington who was listed in Richmond directories of 1850, 1852, 1855, and 1856. He was at times a machinist, builder, millwright, and boardinghouse owner. Richard Yarrington died in May 1859; however his wife's boardinghouse continued through the Civil War and afterward.

Close by the Yarringtons' was Fourteenth Street, a once-prosperous thoroughfare where saloons and faro houses centered in the Civil War, when Richmond was capital of the Confederacy. According to one nineteenth-century Richmonder's recollections, the tall and beautiful Arabella grew up in this music hall atmosphere. By another Richmonder she was remembered as a seamstress who sewed for well-to-do ladies. In the household were also her sisters, Emma and Elizabeth Page, and her brothers, Richard Milton and John Duval Yarrington.

To Richmond in 1868 came the tall, Rabelaisian Collis Potter Huntington. He had just achieved the linking of the Mississippi Valley to the West Coast with his Southern Pacific Railroad, and he was looking for new worlds to conquer. A West Virginia promoter had aroused his interest in merging three short railroads in Virginia to tap Ohio Valley coalfields, and Collis had come south to investigate. From Lexington, Virginia, Robert E. Lee, on September 21, 1868, had endorsed the Chesapeake and Ohio as well situated to "become one of the most prominent of the eastern branches of the Pacific Railroad."

Soon Huntington was deeply involved. The Chesapeake and Ohio was reorganized in 1870 with him as president, and plans were made to extend it from the Atlantic Ocean to meet the Southern Pacific at New Orleans. According to Richmond legend, Huntington stayed during these 1868-1870 visits at Mrs. Yarrington's boardinghouse. And there, it was said, he met her daughter, the beautiful nineteen-year-old Arabella.

Huntington was 48. Though long married, he and his childless wife, Elizabeth, had grown apart during his long absences on business. A huge man of simple tastes, he was so absorbed in business that home meant little. A spicy raconteur and outdoorsman, he was more at ease in mining camps than in society. Known for toughness, independence, and shrewdness, he prided himself on spending less than $200 a year on his personal needs.

Married and middle-aged though he was, Collis Huntington in his bachelor quarters in Richmond fell in love with Arabella Yarrington. However, not until 1884, when his first wife had been dead ten months, did Collis and Belle abandon their attempted secrecy and unite in marriage.

The fifteen years between their Richmond

Daily Press

The four-story Warwick Hotel, center, was Newport News' biggest building when this picture was made in 1889. At left are C&O piers and in background the shipyard.

meeting and their New York marriage was difficult to reconstruct, so well did Arabella lay her screen. She claimed to have married "a Mr. Worsham of New York" in 1869, and after his death to have borne his son in New York on March 10, 1870. However, Collis habitually referred to Archer as his son, and Archer Huntington called Collis "Father," both in Collis's lifetime and in the account that Archer wrote in *Who's Who in America* after Collis's death. As David Lavendar wrote in his biography of Collis, *The Great Persuader:* "Efforts to discover information about her background lead to such blank walls as to leave one wondering whether she systematically has eliminated any traces of her youth."

The "Mr. Worsham of New York" who allegedly fathered Arabella's son was John Archer Worsham of Richmond. He could indeed have married Arabella, as she later claimed. However, serious doubt exists that Worsham was ever any more in her life than a friend who helped Arabella hide her secret. Contrary to the belief fostered by Arabella that Worsham "lived only a short time after the marriage," he continued to reside in Richmond through 1877, when he was operating "club rooms," or gambling facilities, at 1341 East Franklin Street.

Instead of being a New York financier, as Belle's biographer supposed, he was actually operator of a faro parlor where Civil War and Reconstruction Richmond drank and gambled in a gamy atmosphere in the 1860s and 1870s. Richmond City Council records for 1861 recount one police raid on Worsham's gaming house in which a faro table and other gambling apparatus were seized with $553.50. Arabella's alleged "husband" continued to be so engaged until 1877, despite testimony planted by Arabella in the *New York City Directory* that year which listed Arabella as "Worsham Bell D. wid. John, h 109 Lex av."

With the Confederacy's demise in 1865, Worsham's opportunities in Richmond momentarily ended. He therefore moved to New York and with a partner bought a house near the new Fifth Avenue Hotel, where he opened another faro parlor, styling himself as "banker." Arabella, her mother, and her brothers and sisters later followed their Richmond friend to New York. There on March 10, 1870, Arabella gave birth to a son she named "Archer Milton Worsham." Significantly, no marriage license for Arabella and John A. Worsham exists, nor any birth certificate for their son.

No reference to John Archer Worsham appears in the *New York Directory* after 1868, suggesting that he returned to Richmond, where he was living again with his wife Annette in 1870. However, the New York Census for 1870 lists a "John DeWersion," his wife "Bell DeWersion," and their three-month-old child John, as living that year with Mrs. Yarrington and her unmarried children at 5 Bond Street. Moreover, Worsham's deed of sale of his New York house in 1866 was by "John A. Worsham and Annette Worsham his wife." Apparently, John Archer Worsham never married Arabella Yarrington but remained married to his wife Annette until she died in Richmond on January 3, 1874. His own demise was reported in the *Richmond Daily Dispatch* for May 28, 1878:

J. A. Worsham, a leading member of the sporting fraternity of Richmond . . . died Sunday afternoon, May 26, at the residence of his nephew. . . . Mr. Worsham prided himself upon the reputation for fair dealing he had acquired in the long years of varying fortune during which he had been "in the business." . . . Many members of the Legislature who have eaten at his richly-laden boards will testify to his hospitality and geniality. During the war he was liberal to our soldiers. . . .

He died poor.

As for Arabella, her fortune rose rapidly after her son's birth. In 1871 she moved to an affluent area at 109 Lexington Avenue in New York with her mother and son. Four annual issues of the *New York Directory* list "Bell D. Worsham" at that address. Who paid for this luxury? The answer is suggested by the fact that her brother John went back to Richmond about 1871 to work for Collis Huntington's Chesapeake and Ohio Railway. Huntington himself continued to reside with his ailing wife in New York, not far from Arabella. Occasionally he went by private car to visit his railroads in Virginia and California, sometimes—it was said—accompanied by Arabella.

It was easy to understand. The Arabella of that period is revealed in a portrait of a beautiful young woman, with dark hair and eyes, a small mouth, and dress of the latest style. Beyond this, it is clear that Arabella Yarrington was a woman of superior intellect, with a taste for the advantages which education, travel, and money could provide. However modest her background, she was an apt student of language, history, and the arts, personally directing the education of young Archer as he and she traveled widely over Europe and the United States.

The years between the birth of Arabella's son in 1870 and her marriage to Huntington in 1884 were glossed over in accounts of her life until James Maher's book appeared. There he documented the association between the beautiful "widow" and the aging Huntington. In 1872 Collis Huntington bought the house at 109 Lexington Avenue where Arabella lived, paying $14,000 and assuming a $6,000 mortgage. In 1874 Catherine Yarrington, Arabella's mother, bought a still larger house at 68 East Fifty-fourth Street in New York, paying $30,000 cash and assuming a $13,000 mortgage; the same day she conveyed it to Arabella "for and in consideration of natural love and affection and of the sum of One Dollar lawful money."

Arabella moved again three years later, buying a larger house at 4 West Fifty-fourth Street, paying $150,000 cash, and assuming a $100,000 mortgage. She signed the conveyance "Belle D. Yarrington Worsham." Not content with her sizeable house and grounds, Arabella in 1878 acquired adjoining property for $33,000 and in 1880 added another lot for $27,500 cash and a $15,000 mortgage. She had paid altogether $331,000, the equivalent of $3,000,000 today. It was indeed a classy neighborhood, for she sold her house later to Mr. and Mrs. John D. Rockefeller, Sr. More recently, in 1938, it was torn down to make room for the garden of New York's Museum of Modern Art.

From her travels, Arabella developed a passion for elegance and high living. In the early 1880s she had her New York mansion at 4 West Fifty-fourth Street doubled in width and redone in Victorian style. It included also a Moorish sitting room, embossed *trompe l'oeil* wallpapers, and other features of the classical and Empire styles. By this time her association with Collis Huntington was becoming known, and she acquired more confidence. Visiting Texas in 1877, she was noticed in the society column of the *Austin Statesman:* "Mrs. B. D. Worsham, mother, and son . . . are in the city, stopping at the Raymond House. Mrs. Worsham is a niece of Collis P. Huntington, the railroad man."

The English art dealer James Henry Duveen wrote in *Secrets of an Art Dealer:* "One of the most extraordinary women I have ever known was Arabella Huntington: extraordinary because of her indomitable mind and an outrageous spirit which compelled her to outvie all competitors. Long before I met her, Arabella was the unofficial wife of Collis P. Huntington."

Occasionally, Belle, as she came to be known, traveled as "Mrs. Worsham" and accompanied Collis in his private car to visit his rail empire. At Newport News, where the Chesapeake and Ohio built its Atlantic terminus in 1881, the mysterious dark-haired lady on board the train was rumored to be a mulatto. Most of the time she preferred to be in New York or Europe, where she could be with Archer anonymously and indulge her taste for the luxuries she had missed in her youth.

After a long illness, Huntington's wife, Elizabeth, died of cancer at their New York residence on October 5, 1883. Ten months later Belle was quietly married to Collis at her home, in the presence of her mother, son, and a sister. Henry Ward Beecher performed the rites, and Collis rewarded him with four $1,000 bills. The *New York Tribune* assured readers that Arabella's "family and that of Mr. Huntington [are] on terms of the closest intimacy. She is wealthy in her own right. Her first husband died several years ago." Actually, John Archer Worsham had died in Richmond six years earlier.

The press saw in the marriage of Collis and Arabella a symbolic reunion of the divided North and South. Wrote Hubert Bancroft in *Chronicles of the Builders:*

In this union were brought together two types of development that distinguish two widely different sections of the United States, each of which is marked by an intellectual and physical character that is superior in originality, independence, and strength; he being an exponent in his personality of the possibilities of New England stock, the eulogy of which is in the history of the United States; she of rare beauty, imperial in form and carriage, and full of charity and tenderness, idealizing an aristocratic and scholarly ancestry peculiar to the best blood of the South, though differing in the details of sentiment, opinion and manner.

The last forty years of Belle Huntington's life were years of unprecedented American luxury. The beautiful girl grew into a fierce grande dame, courted by awed art dealers but loved by Collis, Archer, and—fourteen years after Collis's death—by his nephew and heir, Henry Edwards Huntington. Freed of the fear of public opinion, Arabella lived more openly and traveled more royally. She was one of that generation of American wives which Henry James thought found fulfillment in artistic stimulation while their husbands laid up great fortunes.

Arabella began her career as Mrs. Huntington by moving into Collis's house at 65 Park Avenue upon their marriage in 1884. The New York real estate broker Charles MacRae, in the course of selling Arabella's Fifty-fourth Street house, wrote to John D. Rockefeller that year that Arabella "has laid out to live in Mr. Huntington's house . . . at Park Av & 38th Street . . . which she is having entirely altered to suit her." Huntington deeded his deceased wife's house to Arabella on June 17, 1884—a month before they were married. Collis and Arabella also bought a 113-acre estate at Throgg's Neck, overlooking Long Island Sound, making it their legal residence. Additions and redecorations ordered by Arabella doubled the $250,000 cost, but Collis rarely begrudged his wife anything.

Belle's taste for palaces had begun to blossom. Fashionable New York was moving uptown, and she wanted to be in the vanguard. She and Collis soon bought property at Fifth Avenue and Eighty-first Street but then decided to buy and alter a house on Fifty-first Street. Finally, they traded Arabella's house at 4 West Fifty-fourth Street for the Rockefellers' house at Fifth Avenue and Seventy-second Street. James Maher estimates that Arabella's real estate had by this time cost Huntington $1,131,500.

But Huntington could absorb such costs. Arabella wanted to build a Fifth Avenue mansion, and no other site thus far had satisfied her. In 1889, when Huntington was opening his Chesapeake Dry Dock Company at Newport News, he bought lots in New York at Fifth Avenue and Fifty-seventh Street to satisfy his wife. There, two blocks from Central Park, the Huntingtons' townhouse finally took shape in 1892-1893, amid the huge *fin de siècle* mansions built by Cornelius Vanderbilt, William C. Whitney, and the great-aunt of Edith Wharton, Mary Mason (Mrs. Isaac) Jones. Arabella Huntington had arrived.

Collis in 1892 went on to buy Arabella a mansion on San Francisco's Nob Hill and a summer retreat, Pine Knot Lodge, in upstate New York. He was the classic aging husband intent on pleasing an ambitious new wife. The Yankee colossus and his Confederate bride were ideally happy.

Through his Southern Pacific, his C&O, his Newport News shipyard, and his other interests, Collis Huntington in the 1880s has become one of America's richest men. To consolidate his interests he now created the Newport News and Mississippi Valley holding company, with himself as president, his brother-in-law Isaac Gates as first vice-president, and Arabella's brother John as second vice-president.

The union of Arabella and Collis was strengthened by his generosity to her relatives. Collis spared no expense to educate and befriend Archer, who early dropped the Worsham name and became a Huntington. Enamored of Hispanic culture, Archer lived abroad and married Collis's niece, Helen Huntington. They became familiar with many Europeans and expatriate Americans of the early twentieth century. When Helen divorced Archer and married English playwright Harley Granville-Barker, Archer in turn married sculptress Anna Hyatt.

For her part, Arabella befriended Clara

Prentice Huntington, whom Collis and his first wife had adopted. Clara was in her mid-twenties when Belle married Collis, and stepmother and stepdaughter became friends. Belle persuaded Collis to let Clara travel with a chaperone in 1888 to Europe, where she soon was engaged to an impoverished German prince. Collis was incensed, and he and Arabella hastened to Paris, where Arabella calmly persuaded him to approve the marriage and to provide a $1,000,000 dowry.

Huntington's favorite nephew was Henry Edwards Huntington, who was close to Arabella's age, and she also became fond of this good-natured in-law. Collis had first hired him in 1871 to extend the Chesapeake and Ohio westward from Virginia to Kentucky, and Henry had married a sister of Collis's adopted daughter. Next to her son, Henry E. Huntington was the most trusted member of Collis and Belle's family.

Both Archer and Henry Huntington were men of bookish tastes, unlike Collis. Each was influenced by Arabella to specialize, Archer in Spanish art and literature, and Henry in English books and paintings, plus the history of the American West. Collis in old age designated Henry as his trustee to manage Belle and Archer's holdings after his death. The influence of Arabella on her son was described by Arthur Pope in his biography of Archer, *Last of the Titans,* in 1956:

Archer Huntington's mother was a remarkable woman. She made the education of young Archer, for which she was exceptionally qualified, her main business. She spoke French like a native, was proficient in French history, and a real connoisseur of many of the arts of France. She had read to and with her boy the English classics before he was nine, and she inspired him with high intellectual and artistic ambitions.

Archer's second wife, Anna Hyatt Huntington, added:

Archer told me many times how grateful he was to his mother for introducing him early in life to the best English literature. She also took him abroad when very young to see all the museums of Europe and their historical interests; so that his young mind was thoroughly attuned to the rich satisfactions the arts afforded.

Under Arabella's prodding, Collis in his seventies slackened his labors and began collecting art with her. Together they accumulated a remarkable collection of eighteenth- and nineteenth-century paintings which Archer after their deaths gave to the Metropolitan Museum of Art in New York. Collis also became interested in New York art auctions and authorized one galley to bid for him under the code name "Carlos," though he never developed the specialized interests of his wife, son, or nephew. In the opinion of one San Francisco architect, "Mr. Huntington's views on architecture would shame a Digger Indian." Stories circulated of the old man's aversion to the French furniture which collapsed when he plopped his huge frame into it in his New York house. The lodge in the Adirondacks was more his style, and there Collis Huntington died on August 13, 1900, at the age of 79.

Arabella's inheritance, estimated at $150,000,000, set off an orgy of collecting which was the talk of the art world. After her San Francisco house on Nob Hill was destroyed in the 1906 earthquake, she continued to load her New York quarters with masterpieces. In 1907 she spent several millions to buy the Rudolph Kann collection, offered in Paris by the Duveen brothers. According to Curator Robert Wark of the Huntington Art Gallery, she "embarked on an incredible spending spree that lasted for the better part of a decade and turned her, within a few years, into one of the most important art collectors of her generation."

Mysterious Arabella Huntington   47

Mariners Museum

Beautiful as a girl, Belle Huntington grew to be an imperious dowager. She traveled widely, owning houses in New York, San Francisco, and Paris.

In the course of the spree she bought another palace in 1908, this time in Paris. It was the Hotel de Hirsch at No. 2 Rue de l'Elysée, and its construction in modern terms had cost $25,000,000—lavish even in Arabella's language.

The pictures she bought in these years included two Rembrandts, a Franz Hals, a Vermeer, a Cuyp, a Lawrence, a Reynolds, and nearly 200 others. Other acquisitions by Arabella included Rembrandt's "Aristotle Contemplating the Bust of Homer," which Archer later sold to yield funds to build the American Academy of Arts and Letters in New York, and Velasquez's "Duke of Olivares," which Arabella gave in 1910 to Archer's creation, the Hispanic Society of America. Most of Arabella's Italian and Flemish Renaissance paintings and her tapestries, "The Four Seasons," are now at the Henry E. Huntington Library and Art Gallery at San Marino; the others are at the Metropolitan.

The contagion of collecting slowly drew Henry E. Huntington to Arabella. Though slightly older than Henry, she remained handsome, for she was only 50 when Collis died. Aunt and nephew were divided at first by a continent, for Collis had sent Henry in 1892 to California to protect Huntington interests. The settlement of Collis's estate often drew Arabella thereafter to California or Henry to New York. Understandably they traveled on private trains, Arabella's boasting a parlor car, sleeping car, diner, kitchen, and library.

In 1906 Henry Huntington suddenly divorced his wife. It had not been a happy marriage, and Henry's interests influenced him to seek the company of Arabella and her knowledgeable son. The original motive seems to have been his growing zeal for collecting, though love was to follow. "The enthusiasm and drive for collecting surely came primarily from Arabella," wrote Robert Wark:

There is little evidence of Henry being stricken with this disease until he came under her influence, and there are many indications that she guided and even prodded him in making several of his important early purchases. But it is also clear that Arabella had no particular predilection for British art. Her own tastes were much more catholic, running to Italian Renaissance and Dutch seventeenth-century paintings and French eighteenth-century materials.... And so it was Arabella who provided the initial drive for the formation of the Huntington Art Collection, and if it was Lord Duveen who found and sifted much of the material, it was Henry himself who determined the basic character of the collection and the direction in which it grew.

No one was surprised when Henry and Arabella were married in 1913, seven years after his divorce, when both were 63. It was far different from Arabella's marriage to Collis. She continued to wear widow's weeds for "Mr. Huntington," as she always referred to Collis, even after she married "Ed," as she called his nephew. The attraction now was their mutual interests, for both sought means of preserving their treasured collections for the future. The quest led within a year to San Marino, where they made their main residence in 1914. From then on, it was the focus of their collecting and planning. Thus the careers of two powerful and strong-minded people coalesced.

Though Henry retired in 1908, he continued to buy real estate, rare books, and art. The industrious habits of a lifetime drove him to work on, usually eighteen hours a day. He remained chairman of the Newport News shipyard, and he uncomplainingly accepted his losses when the United States scrapped ships there after the Washington Disarmament Conference of 1921. When a Newport News ship was spared by the lobbying of yard president Homer Ferguson, Huntington split the "profit" with the yard. Through Lord Duveen, he bought Gainsborough's "Blue Boy" for $620,000 and gave a comparable sum to Ferguson for shipyard executive bonuses.

Henry Huntington in the 1920s continued as a patron of Lord Duveen, buying works of such British masters as Gainsborough, Reynolds, Lawrence, and Constable. In 1920 he moved his library of British books and manuscripts from New York to San Marino, though many bibliophiles felt it should remain in the East where American scholarship then centered. Like Leland Stanford, however, Huntington foresaw the rise of the West Coast as a cultural center and sought to hasten it.

Arabella died three years before Henry, in 1924, after having chosen the site of their mausoleum at San Marino. After her death he built the Memorial Collection to Arabella at San Marino, housing Archer's gift of Renaissance paintings and his own of French and Italian porcelain, furniture, and sculpture. Wrote Curator Wark: "They were purchased at the end of his life as a grand, final gesture of thanks and affection to the woman whose interest and energy were responsible for the art side of the institution he founded."

From her son Archer, Arabella's death evoked poems of deepest grief. Tributes to "Aunt Belle" were unanimous among the younger Huntingtons. Yet Arabella's background remained as much a mystery to them as it was to her friends and contemporaries. Obedient to the end, Archer destroyed any papers his adored mother had left behind—she who did not want the world to know the secrets of her youth or of her early relationship with Collis Huntington.

For nearly a century Arabella's story has intrigued those who heard the whispered rumors. Understandably, she used every means to protect the reputation of herself, her husband, and her son. Slowly the facts of Arabella's life have emerged, however. Despite pieces still missing, her life can be seen as the triumph of a tough and imperious spirit. Though she lived a century before the modern women's rights movement, she achieved her ambitions in a man's world. When all the facts are known—if ever—Arabella may prove to be the most remarkable of all the Huntington's—Collis, Henry, and Archer included.

8. *The Railroad Comes to Town*

NEXT to the landing at Jamestown in 1607 and the invasion by General McClellan's Union army in 1862, the most important event in Peninsula history was the coming of the Chesapeake and Ohio Railroad in 1881.

That was the start of industry in eastern Virginia. Soon afterward came the Newport News shipyard, the Norfolk and Western Railway to southside, and trolley lines, gas works, and street lighting.

Today the C&O is only one of the many industries in our midst. But its coal and freight lines to and from Newport News make jobs and money for our communities. Those rail lines keep the Peninsula in competition with Norfolk and Baltimore for shipping dollars. We've been losing out since the C&O merged with Baltimore's Baltimore and Ohio, but we'll come back.

To me, the revival of the Peninsula in the Reconstruction era is a Cinderella story. Most of it was due to one big, bearded industrial giant—Collis Huntington of New York and California. After he died in 1900, his nephew, Henry E. Huntington, took over. The two men made the Chesapeake and Ohio a top railroad. In the process, they helped Newport News become the nation's biggest shipbuilder.

Part of the sprawling CSX network, today's C&O stretches from the Boat Harbor in Newport News to Toledo, Ohio, growing from a tiny Louisa Railroad of pre-Civil War days. It was started in the 1850s to carry farm produce from Louisa County eastward to the Richmond, Fredericksburg & Potomac line at Doswell, in Hanover County. By the outbreak of the Civil War in 1861 it had become the Virginia Central Railroad and ran from Richmond west to Jackson's River, now Clifton Forge.

The Civil War wrecked Virginia, but Yankee capital soon flowed south to help rebuild it. In 1867 the legislature of Virginia and West Virginia approved the building of a rail line from "the waters of the Chesapeake to the Ohio River." They called it "The Chesapeake & Ohio Railroad."

There wasn't much money in bankrupt Virginia, but Collis Huntington brought some. He'd already built a railroad out west, and he wanted to build another in the east to tie to it and provide cross-country service.

Collis was a shaggy 6-foot, 2-inches. He'd made a fortune in the 1849 Gold Rush, and he thought big. He came to Richmond soon after Appomattox and in 1869 joined forces with stockholders of the Virginia Central. He knew

49

50   *The Railroad Comes to Town*

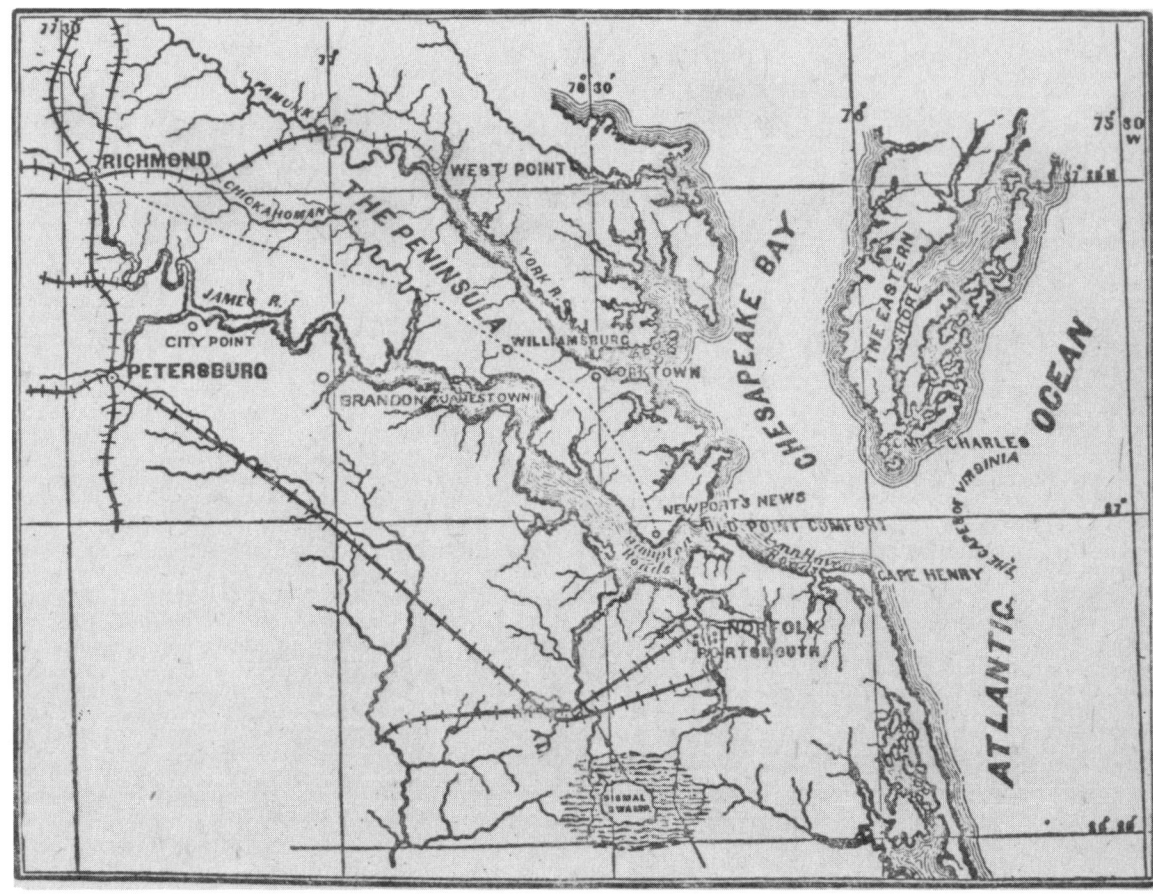

Daily Press

A map in Scribner's Monthly in 1872 showed the projected route of Collis Huntington's C&O Railway, down the Peninsula. The competing Norfolk and Western was shown on the Southside.

the U.S. had entered the age of coal and steel. He saw the money to be made in hauling coal from West Virginia and Kentucky to ships calling at Hampton Roads.

In Richmond, Collis met a tall, handsome young woman who worked in a gambling saloon near Capitol Square. She was Arabella Yarrington. They had an affair, and she bore a child. He kept her in luxury in New York and married her after his first wife died of cancer. Then he "adopted" Belle's young son as Archer Huntington, who later founded the Mariner's Museum. The Collis and Belle romance was a secret until Archer died in the 1950s.

When Collis bought into the C&O in 1869, he expanded it rapidly. In 1873 he ran it west to Huntington, W. VA., on the Ohio River, naming the town for his family. He also began looking around on the Peninsula to find the best route to Hampton Roads. After considering Norfolk, West Point, Yorktown, and a site on the Piankatank River, he chose Newport's News Point.

It's a little-known fact that Huntington had visited Newport's News in 1837, when he was a 16-year-old peddler of watches and hardware. He remembered it all those years as an ideal deepwater site for industry.

Moving rapidly, Huntington had his Penin-

The Railroad Comes to Town 51

sula line surveyed in 1873. Then a Wall Street panic hit the nation's postwar revival. The rail extension was halted seven years till the Virginia Assembly in 1880 gave it the go-ahead. Col. Carter Braxton, CSA, engineered the last mileage of the right-of-way (Lee Hall to Newport News) that year. Construction began in February 1881.

To keep the C&O's lower Peninsula tracks all in one county, Elizabeth City ceded a little land along the route to Warwick.

Except for tiny Williamsburg and Hampton, the Peninsula in 1880 was forests and small farms. Warwick County had only 2,258 people. Hampton was a town of 2,000 rebuilding from its Civil War burning. Newport News Point was a fishing village of two or three docks, scarred by Federal fortification left from the war.

A Warwick County deed of January 1881 names two Northern men as agents of the C&O to buy up right-of-way land and build the C&O. They were given authority to acquire "the necessary land and waterfront and riparian rights and to erect thereon such wharves, shops, round-houses, warehouses, elevators, coal tipples, timber yards, cotton and tobacco presses" as necessary.

The Hampton Monitor reported that year that "2,200 hands are at work on the C&O Railroad between Richmond and Yorktown laying the track." One work force moved east from Richmond while another worked west from Old Point. A Norfolk paper reported on Aug. 23, 1881, that the workers had gone on strike for higher pay, fewer hours, and more frequent paydays.

For awhile it looked as though Huntington

Casemate Museum

The C&O in 1883 ran a spur from Newport News to Phoebus, thus serving ship traffic at Old Point. This dockside view shows the postoffice and Adams Express office there.

52 The Railroad Comes to Town

Casemate Museum

An 1862 photo of Kimberly Brothers' Army and Navy Stores at Fort Monroe shows sides of meat on display. Most Peninsulans raised most of their produce on small farms or backyard gardens.

wouldn't fulfill his promise to finish his railroad in time to bring congressmen by train from Washington to Yorktown on Oct. 19, 1881, to celebrate the centennial of Cornwallis's surrender. Two hundred striking workers had seized the locomotive in Newport News used for construction.

But the strike soon ended and the track was completed from Richmond to Newport News, with a temporary spur from Lee Hall to Yorktown. On Sunday, Oct. 16, Major J. J. Gordon, head of the C&O builders, drove a silver spike completing the track near Williamsburg.

To bring VIPs and other passengers to Yorktown, six C&O passenger trains rolled through Williamsburg from Washington and Richmond on Tuesday, Oct. 18, on their way to Yorktown. To finish the line on time, Williamsburg permitted a temporary track down Duke of Gloucester Street. However, it was soon replaced by the present right-of-way along Lafayette Street, behind the Governor's Palace.

From its start at Newport News in 1882, the C&O shipped coal around the world. Pier 9, photographed about 1890, could move 6,600 tons of coal per hour.

Newport News Historical Committee

From its 1890s depot at 23d Street and the James River, the C&O moved many passengers. Trains arriving from the Great Lakes met a passenger ferry to Norfolk there.

Two ceremonial trains on Wednesday, Oct. 19, signaled the Richmond-Newport News track opening. One came down the tracks from Richmond with James T. Bailey as conductor. And a two-car "Centennial Special" went from Newport News to Lee Hall and thence to Yorktown. George Ben West, a Newport News pioneer who later founded Citizens Marine Bank (now part of United Virginia Bank) and Riverside Hospital, wrote an account of the trip which survives.

After the Yorktown Centennial ended on October 20, 1881, C&O workmen early one morning tore up the temporary track from Lee Hall to the Yorktown U.S. Military Cemetery. That infuriated Yorktown citizens, who had wanted the spur to stay. Huntington usually had his way.

To connect with trains at Newport News, the C&O contracted for a steamer to take passengers to and from Norfolk. In 1884, however, the railroad started its own passenger ferry to Norfolk, known as "Smoky Joe." C&O steamer Virginia was succeeded by bus service in 1950. In 1971 Amtrak took over C&O passenger service down the Peninsula.

Huntington and his companies spent a lot of money on Newport News. His agents bought up all the land they could get, holding most of it in the name of the Old Dominion Land Company. He built the Warwick Hotel for travelers, started a gas company and a reservoir (later bought by Newport News), and provided a Union Chapel for early worship in his "company town."

A spur track from Newport News to Fort Monroe was opened in 1890. Later, service facilities for cleaning passenger cars were built at Phoebus.

But the coal mines of West Virginia and Kentucky proved the C&O's best long-term customers. After passengers and general cargo dwindled in the 1930s, coal shipments kept the C&O prospering on the Peninsula. I think of that often as I hear those big "blacksnake" coal trains rumbling through Williamsburg in the night, shaking nearby houses.

Yes, the coming of Huntington's trains in 1881 began a new age on this Peninsula. We must keep alive and growing.

Syms-Eaton Museum

The Frank Darlings' Cedar Hall was the center of Hampton's social and artistic life until torn down after the Frank Darlings' deaths. Several houses now occupy the site, overlooking Hampton River.

9. *The 65ers Who Built Hampton*

VIRGINIANS often make a distinction between "Come-Heres" and "Stay-Puts"—those who move to town and those who've been around since Adam. That's especially true in an old town like Hampton, which has been in business ever since the first English settlers in 1609 dropped a couple of settlers at Old Point to keep out Spanish invaders.

Burned to the ground in 1813 and again in the Civil War, Hampton has rebuilt each time. In its revival after 1865, it attracted as residents a lot of Yankees who had been Union soldiers or Freedmen's Bureau officials in the Late Unpleasantness. They liked Virginia and chose to stay.

Old Hamptonians called them "carpetbaggers" and "65ers," but they included some of the best citizens Hampton ever had. One I admire was Samuel Chapman Armstrong, who founded Hampton Institute. Another was James Sands Darling, who brought his wife and year-old son here in 1866 on a schooner loaded with lumber to rebuild Hampton's houses, burned in the Civil War.

"Old J.S.," as he's called, died back in 1900, at the age of 68, but he's still talked about. So too are his son, Frank W. Darling, who died in 1941, and his grandson, "Young J.S.," who died at 52 in 1951.

What impresses me about the Darlings is their Yankee enterprise and generosity—especially their generosity. There are countless stories of their help to Hampton Institute, to St. John's Church, and to aspiring students. Their civic spirit was wonderful to behold. They were loved by black and white.

Old J.S. was born in New York City in 1832, the son of an English-born ship joiner. He grew up in the present midtown New York, now covered wtih skyscrapers. When he was 11 his mother died, and he was hired out to an aunt to work on her Long Island farm. From there he went to his brother's Long Island shipway to learn a trade and became a partner.

The Darling brothers did pretty well till the Civil War came along. Discouraged in New York, 33-year-old James Darling, after Appomattox, sailed to Virginia to find a new career. He chose the burned-over village of Hampton. He installed his family in a house on King Street, close to his mill, now the site of Wyatt Brothers' Men's Wear, and brought a shipload of lumber down to build houses. Soon he bought a sawmill and grist mill on King Street,

James S. "Jock" Darling

The first James S. Darling sailed to Hampton after the Civil War. He became a leading businessman and philanthropist.

near his house. After Hampton grew west in the 1880s, J.S. built a new house on the present Victoria Boulevard, near Armistead Avenue.

Darling liked Southerners and had sympathized with them in the Civil War. He paid a "Hessian" to fight for him.

As Darling prospered in Hampton, he extended his reach. In 1879 he formed a partnership with William Smithers and built a fish oil factory on the Eastern Shore. Unfortunately, a hurricane soon destroyed it, and the partners lost their shirts.

Undiscouraged, 50-year-old Darling turned to tonging oysters in Hampton Roads. And there, as his grandson Frank Cumming tells the story, he was spotted by his old friend William Ballard, a prosperous Norfolk oyster-buyer. Ballard lent him money to rebuild. The revived fish-oil factory was long operated on Back River, near Grand View.

Darling went broke again when his lumber mill failed. However, his chief employee, Bill Sparks, a black millhand, refused to be turned off. "Boss, you can just feed me," he told Darling. The mill was restarted and it prospered. Darling paid his faithful helper, and in his will left him a farm on the Eastern Shore.

Darling and his son formed J.S. Darling and Sons, an oystering firm, in 1881. It closed in 1979.

In 1882, when Hampton bar was opened by the state for oyster-planting, J.S. rented acreage and began oystering. Hampton oysters proved highly salable, and J.S. had to hire hundreds of oyster shuckers. The mountains of oyster shells at his plant on Hampton Creek were a landmark long after his death. There were other measures of his succcess. I remember them in the 1930s.

In 1888, J.S. took another flyer and built a street railway with the Schmelz brothers to connect Hampton and Old Point. It flourished, and three years later they extended it down the new Victoria Avenue to Newport News. The trolley provided quick and cheap transport between the two cities. It also did much to build up Collis Huntington's shipyard, which he had opened at Newport News in 1886.

Many yard employees found Newport News expensive and built homes in Hampton.

Wrote the Phoebus Sentinel of Darling's railway in 1900: "Its effect on the growth and prosperity of Hampton was marked from the day the first car passed over it. Hundreds of people came to live in the West End of Hampton near the line. The cars quickly became crowded, and the electric railway recognized as a successful venture."

Many Peninsulans took Sunday outings to

Old Point over the trolleys. Mrs. Frederick Hartel of Williamsburg, whose father was then an Army officer at Fort Monroe, recalls stylish ladies and gentlemen stopping off the street car near the Old Chamberlin Hotel to enjoy Sunday band concerts. That was the age of Victor Herbert, Sousa, and "The Blue Danube."

After he built the trolley line, J.S. teamed up with his son Frank to create what the Phoebus Sentinel described as "a magnificent hotel" at Buckroe Beach, plus a dance and picnic pavilion. To his wife, who was visiting relatives in the North, young Frank Darling in the early 1900s wrote proudly of the first day's "good profit" of "several dollars." Unfortunately, though, the Buckroe trolley that same day struck a cow.

J.S. and the Schmelzes sold the trolley line two years before he died, bringing him a profit of $16,000, more than he expected. He gave a party for his trolley employees on Christmas Day in 1898 and divided the sum among them in checks ranging from $50 to $1,000. The old man wept as he thanked his men, and they wept in gratitude for the gift.

"No one was overlooked," reported the 'Sentinel,' "from the man who greased the tracks on up. It was a splendid Christmas gift."

The J.S. Darlings had three children, two of whom lived to maturity. Daughter Grace married James Cumming and had seven children. Three of them are living, all in Hampton: Frank, Daniel and William Cumming. The Darlings' son Frank married Mary "Mollie" Gorton, who taught Indian students at Hampton Institute. Their only child, J.S. Darling II,

Mariners Museum

Vendors sell outside the Chapel of the Centurion at Fort Monroe in 1885. J. S. Darling made Hampton a major oyster port and built a successful Peninsula streetcar system.

grew up at Cedar Hall, which the Darlings had built on Hampton Creek early in the 1900s. It was razed years ago and is now a waterside residential area.

Frank Darling's wife, Mollie, outlived both her husband and her son, dying in 1957 at Cedar Hall. She loved music, books, theatricals—anything creative. "Cedar Hall when the Darlings lived there was full of laughter," says a Hamptonian. Mollie organized the Cedar Hall Reading Club, several theatrical groups and taught Sunday school at St. John's for 40 years. The family gave St. John's its bell, stained glass windows, and other gifts. "The Darlings were forever doing things for people," a friend recalls.

J.S. Darling II inherited his parents' business and civic interests. He created and was chairman until his death of the Hampton Roads Sanitation Commission. His three children are Mrs. James Tormey, the former Ann Darling, of Hampton; Sally Darling, actress and off-Broadway producer, of New York; and J.S. "Jock" Darling III, conductor and harpsichordist of Williamsburg.

Yankees or not, the Darlings became part of the Peninsula mainstream at the end of the Civil War and have remained so ever since. Old J.S. may have been a "carpetbagger," but he soon became a rare and valuable citizen—one of the key figures in Hampton's revival. Many legacies of the Darlings and the Cummings live on in Hampton today, including Darling Memorial Field, which they built.

The moral of all this seems to be that newcomers have brought to the Peninsula many blessings. Yankees they were, but I say thank God for the Armstrongs, the Huntingtons, the Darlings, and the rest of the "Come-Heres." The Peninsula wouldn't be the same without them.

The Darlings' boatyard on Hampton Creek built and repaired vessels from the 1880s until the mid 1900s. Here an oyster boat prepares to slide down the ways in a 1926 photo by Cheyne.

Syms-Eaton Museum

10. *The Rise of a German Baker*

THE rise of the Peninsula from the ruins of the Civil War is an epic, taken too much for granted today. Seldom in history has a defeated people been so desolated as we Virginians were after Appomattox.

Yet the Peninsula made a comeback. From the cinders of Hampton and the ruined farms of Newport News, a great community developed. It began with the arrival of the C&O, followed by the shipyard and military bases. It owes similar credit to other men who created a trolley system, waterworks, banks, stores, and businesses galore.

The rise was slow during Reconstruction. It speeded up with the coming of the railroad in 1881 and the shipyard in 1886.

It was a revolution for a section of the world that had stuck largely to farming and fishing since Jamestown's time. Many people hated the change. Ellen Glasgow, who wrote novels in Richmond, said she missed the courtly manners of the plantation age. She didn't like industry.

But geography dictated that the Peninsula after 1865 would be a center of railways, shipping, and defense. And it has become one.

One man who anticipated that was Francis Anton Schmelz, a German who had emigrated to the United States before the Civil War. After serving in the Confederacy, he mustered out at Hampton in 1865 and started a bakery and confectionary on Queen Street. He did so well he sent his two sons to college.

Stories still circulate about the Schmelzs' enterprise. One is that they sent a load of pastries by trolley each workday from Hampton to the Newport News shipyard, to be sold outside the gates for snacks and lunch. Another is that Francis Schmelz got his start crabbing with a handline on the Hampton waterfront. With a piece of meat as bait, he was said to have caught enough crabs to get a start.

Virginia had few banks in the Schmelzs' days. Until then, merchants performed services now handled by banks. The first Peninsula banks I'm aware of were the First National and the Citizens and Marine, both started on Washington Avenue in Newport News in 1889.

The Schmelz brothers were George and Henry, those sons of Francis Schmelz, the emigre. They had prospered in their father's

The Rise of a German Baker

Syms-Eaton Museum

Henry Lane Schmelz, his wife, and daughters pose for a Cheyne photograph in his Hampton studio in 1907. Schmelz and his brother George were bankers and industrialists.

bakery and decided to open a small privately owned bank in the rear of Henry's King Street bakery.

The 1880s were a time of Peninsula growth. Bank credit was needed to buy real estate, build stores and houses, and open businesses. The Schmelz brothers provided it.

The Schmelzs' "back room bank" flourished. A 1911 newspaper says it "was so successful and the natural ability of the two brothers was so apparent that they decided to enter the banking business in all its branches." They opened their first full bank at King and Queen Street. It succeeded, and in 1902 it bought out the rival Bank of Hampton and consolidated under that name.

In 1890 the brothers started another bank, this time at Twenty-fifth and Washington Avenue in Newport News. It was originally a private bank, whose stock was held by the two brothers alone. It went public in 1912. By that time it had become the largest private bank in the South.

In 1931, long after the two brothers' death, Schmelz Brothers' Bank sold its assets to the First National of Newport News. The Schmelz Brothers had not been able to reopen its doors after the Roosevelt bank moratorium of 1931, but its assets were found fully adequate to pay off depositors. Nobody lost a cent.

The Schmelz boys also started other enterprises. With Frank W. Darling of Hampton they built the Newport News and Old Point Railway and Electric Company. Its purpose was to provide fast and cheap transport for workers at the shipyard. The company later became the Citizens Rapid Transit, which has recently become the Federally-owned Pen Tran.

Syms-Eaton Museum

This 1890s trolley operated from Hampton to Old Point and the Old Soldiers' Home. Service was later added to Newport News.

George Schmelz was also the chief stockholder in an infant Newport News paper which later merged to become today's dailies. He was chief mover in the Hampton, Phoebus, and Fort Monroe Gas Corporation and an officer of McMenamin Crab Picking House, then a big plant on Hampton Creek. It helped Hampton to become Crab Town.

In that age of local banks, George Schmelz served on the boards of two in Richmond and Hampton and one in Newport News. His office, where he jovially met all comers, was a corner of the Schmelz bank in Newport News. He came to work by trolley, like most people in that early day.

The brothers always lived in Hampton, George and his wife rearing five daughters and Henry and his wife two. The brothers married sisters, Mattie and Georgie Hickman. Their own sisters married Howard Collier and Robert Hudgins, both of Hampton.

Like many men then, George Schmelz taught a Sunday school class before morning service at Hampton's Memorial Baptist Church. His wife had given funds to build the church. Inspired by her example, Schmelz organized its men's class, which "is said to be the largest in Virginia, if not in the South," according to an early Daily Press.

Hampton was shocked in 1909 when Mrs. George Schmelz died at 50, leaving her five young daughters. It was equally stricken in 1911 when George himself died at Johns Hopkins at 57. Tributes poured in. "He was easily the most promising figure in the Peninsula business world," wrote an editorialist.

A newspaper account of Schmelz's funeral gives insight into Peninsula life in 1911. When the casket reached Richmond from Baltimore on its way to Hampton, it was met by an honor guard of friends, who accompanied it on the train the rest of the way. Delegations of mourners waited at C&O depots in Newport News and in Hampton.

At Hampton "Henry Lane Schmelz, almost crushed by his brother's death, received the condolences of his intimate friends as he made his way to his carriage." At the service, President Frederic W. Boatwright of Richmond College led a long procession of pallbearers. They included Frank W. Darling, Henry C. Blackiston, Nelson Groome, Hunter Booker, Albert Howe, and Jacob Heffelfinger of Hampton; Douglas Smith and Robert P. Holt of Newport News; Simon R. Curtis of Lee Hall; and John M. Miller, Richmond banker.

Three years after George died, his brother Henry followed at 61. He had been ill in bed for eight months. Wrote the Daily Press,

HAMPTON
Electric Light & Power Co.

RATES PER LIGHT FOR 16 CANDLE-POWER INCANDESCENT LIGHTS.

All-night lights (dark to day light).......... $1.50 per month.
One-half night (dark to 12 o'clock) ... . $1.00 per month.
Stores, up to ten o'clock, 80c.
Hotels,—billiard-rooms, parlors, halls, offices dining room, kitchen, &c. $1.00 per month.
Hotels,—bed rooms....50c. "
Private houses.... . ...60c. "

ARC LIGHTS.

All-night lights, ... $100.00 yearly.
Dark to 12 o'clock,.. ..75 00 "
Dark to 10 o'clock, ... 65.00 "

CHURCH LIGHTING.

Wiring and fixtures, $2.50 each light Rates for light, 5cents each light each night.
If church cannot afford to pay out in one sum the cost of wiring and fixtures, the company will charge 10 cents each ght each night. Contracts taken only or a year.

Syms-Eaton Museum

Hampton's pioneer utility company supplied power to run trolleys and to light homes and offices.

"There is little question but what Mr. Schmelz was the best all around banking man in Eastern Virginia." He was a director of banks in Hampton, Newport News, Phoebus, Norfolk, and Richmond.

I'm not aware of descendants bearing the name Schmelz on the Peninsula, but the family survives under other names. One member is William R. Van Buren Jr., president and treasurer of the Daily Press, grandson of George Schmelz. Other descendants bear the names Collier, Hudgins, Phillips, Robinson, Coenen, and Lasches, though not all are in this area.

The Peninsula's first three Schmelzes—emigrant Francis and sons Henry and George—played a notable part in the rise of this community. They rubbed elbows with other empire-builders: Harrison Phoebus of Old Point, Frank Darling of Hampton, and Collis Huntington of Newport News. Thanks to such men, Hampton and Newport News are an important industrial hub. As Huntington foresaw, it can grow even greater if we work at it.

Hamptonians gathered at Old Point in 1893 to watch warships rendezvous for voyage commemorating 400th anniversary of Columbus' discovery. A similar rendezvous marked the 1907 Jamestown Expositon.

Mariners Museum

11. Armstrong's School for Blacks

IN a tour of my World War II stomping ground, Hawaii, in the 1970s I came across the footprints of a Peninsula figure I always admired. He was Samuel Chapman Armstrong, a Hawaii-bred teacher who rose to be a general in the Civil War and spent the rest of his life teaching blacks to become citizens. He founded Hampton Institute, now a university.

In an historic house of an 1820 Congregationalist missionary at Hilo, I uncovered the story of the Rev. Richard Armstrong. He had come to Hawaii in a great American missionary outpouring of the early 1800s. Like many fellow Congregationalists from New England's colleges, he spent his life Christianizing the amiable Polynesians of the Sandwich Islands, today known as the Hawaiian chain.

The face of Richard Armstrong was gentle yet strong. Looking at his picture in the Lyman House Museum, I could understand how he was chosen to be commissioner of education for the islands. Though Hawaiians before Congregationalism had lived a good life of dancing and laughter, they lacked an alphabet and nearly everything else which Western ingenuity had devised since the Middle Ages. Along with Christianity, Armstrong and his Congregationalists brought to Hawaii reading, writing, arithmetic and medicine.

Armstrong's sixth child was Samuel, born on Maui in 1839 and sent back to Williams College in 1958 to be educated under the great Mark Hopkins. Besides his father's good looks he inherited a missionary impulse. He grew up wanting to help people, to spread the new England mixture of puritanism and materialism which has made those psalm-singing Yankees so rich and influential.

Sam Armstrong set out to be a teacher, but the Civil War broke out while he was in college. He was captured by Confederates at Harper's Ferry in 1862, but after an exchange of prisoners returned to duty and fought until the war's end.

After Appomattox he was sent to Old Point by the Freedman's Bureau to help the thousands of blacks who had been emancipated and were encamped around Fort Monroe, without homes or jobs. Armstrong began teaching them to read and write when suddenly he heard a call he thought came from God. It was to start a school for blacks like the Hilo Training School for Native Hawaiians which his father had created in Hawaii.

Young Sam, by this time a brigadier, begged

63

Armstrong's School for Blacks

Blacks flocked in the Civil War to claim freedom at Fort Monroe. Freedmen's Bureau educator Samuel Armstrong began class to train them which grew into Hampton University.

money from the American Missionary Society to buy Little Scotland, a farm on Hampton Creek, and this became his campus. The society first asked an older man to run the school. When he declined, they returned to Sam.

The Institute that began in 1868 had about 25 students, taught by whites. In many ways it resembled Howard, a school for blacks founded in the District of Columbia a year earlier by another Freedmen's Bureau general, O.O. Howard. Each has grown into a national institution, with students from many states and lands. They were pioneers.

The Institute was not popular with Virginians for a long time. The war was too recent and Yankees were regarded dubiously. The campus was a little world to itself. The Armstrongs and other white teachers were snubbed by locals, but the school grew. By 1874 it had $37,000, much of it raised by the student choir in concerts through the North, singing spirituals and gospel songs.

"I have been in the traveling show business the last two years," Armstrong wrote a friend. "Have given over 300 concerts with the Hampton students (ex-slaves). . .This is a

Armstrong's School for Blacks 65

rough and terrible fight with difficulties, but I think I'm on top."

The educator was considered by many whites to be a troublemaker. Liberal blacks called him a white racist. Still, Armstrong had faith and carried on. He believed that black people could only assume responsibility as citizens if they were educated and able to support themselves.

"I tell you," he wrote in the 1880s, "the present is the grandest time the world every saw. The African race is before the world and all mankind is looking to see whether the African will show himself equal to the opportunity. And what is this opportunity? It is to demonstrate that he is a man—that he has the highest elements of manhood, courage, perseverance and honor. That he is not only worthy of freedom but able to win it."

One of the Institute's early students was Booker Washington, who went there from Rocky Mount farm and later was principal of Tuskegee Institute in Alabama. Teachers were trained, as well as nurses, artisans and homemakers. Many became preachers, for Southern blacks were and remained church-oriented.

When his wife died and left him with two children, the general waited a decade before marrying again. On a trip north in 1892 he was

Daily Press

Well-dressed Hampton Institute students in 1900 studied mechanism of the cheese press. Photographer Frances Benjamin Johnston took this for her "Hampton Album," shown at 1902 Paris World's Fair.

paralyzed, but his friend Collis Huntington sent his private rail car to bring Armstrong back to Hampton. The two had become friends when Huntington came to Newport News in 1880 to create a port for his C&O railway and they worked together on schooling and jobs for blacks.

Armstrong died in 1893. Only a few months before he had walked out on the Institute shoreline to watch the Great White Fleet of American naval vessels return from its global voyage from Hampton Roads to celebrate the 400th anniversary of Columbus' arrival in the New World. He was buried on the campus with a stone from Hawaii at his head.

His widow, who went north with her children after his death, lived until 1958. Armstrong's son-in-law, Arthur Howe, was president of Hampton from 1930 to 1940. When the school reached its 80th anniversary in 1948 it chose its first black president.

The Armstrong name remained in Hampton as long as his nephew, Richard Armstrong, and his brothers, Kalani and Matt, lived on Armstrong Point, not far from the Institute. Since their deaths the area has retaken its earlier name, Ivy Home Farms.

But Samuel Armstrong will never be forgotten. The school he founded, now known as Hampton University, is today a prestigious and well-endowed liberal arts college which is known around the world. Like his missionary father in Hawaii, Armstrong left his world better than he had found it.

Daily Press

Hampton's historic Little Scotland plantation became campus of Hampton Institute. Early plantation house on the river has housed Samuel Armstrong and succeeding presidents.

12. *The Hotel That Made Old Point Famous*

IF you live on the Lower Peninsula you can't escape the influence of a man named Harrison Phoebus, who died in 1886. The name is familiar through the community of Phoebus, which is now part of the city of Hampton. When you talk to old-time Hamptonians, his name invariably crops up. He ran a hotel at Old Point that was famous. He helped bring the C&O Railway from Newport News to Fort Monroe in 1882.

Harrison Phoebus was one of the post-Civil War giants who made the Peninsula important, along with Collis Huntington, the Schmelz brothers, James S. Darling, and George Ben West. They started an industrial growth which accelerated with the Spanish-American War and the two world wars. They replaced Tidewater farming with shipping lines, railroads and factories.

It's significant that Phoebus, like most of our Reconstruction tycoons, came to the Peninsula from the North, Post-Civil War commerce in Virginia was largely the creation of Yankee capitalists.

Like Scarlett O'Hara in "Gone With the Wind," Peninsulans after the Civil War accepted a new commercial era as inevitable. Our industrialization has continued ever since, hastened by hot and cold wars.

Phoebus was a Marylander, born in 1840, who had fought for the Union in the Civil War. When he was mustered out of service in 1865, he went to work for the Adams Express Company of Baltimore. They liked his willingness to tackle any work, "from sweeping a floor to writing a letter," as he put it. So the company in 1866 sent him to Old Point as its agent, handling shipments which arrived by the bay steamers that docked there.

Phoebus became a one-man industry. He was Old Point's postmaster, notary public, U.S. commissioner, insurance agent, and representative of shipping companies. Like most people in those hard-up days, he took any work he could find.

Phoebus' big chance came in 1874, when he had a chance to control the old Hygeia Hotel at Old Point, with the backing of Samuel Shoemaker, a wealthy Baltimore friend. The resort hotel had been rebuilt after the war for families visiting Fort Monroe or seeking a rest on the wind-swept shore of Hampton Roads.

Two Hygeia and two Chamberlin hotels have successively attracted vacationers to Old Point from 1820 until today. The first tiny Hygeia, erected in 1820 to house constructors of Fort Monroe, was demolished by the Army after the outbreak of the Civil War, then replaced by a larger Hygeia after Appomattox. Its success attracted the rival Chamberlin Hotel in 1896. It

Casemate Museum

The first Hygeia at Old Point was opened in 1820 and visited by such figures as Chief Black Hawk, Edgar Allan Poe, Mark Twain, and Henry Clay. It was torn down in 1862.

Daily Press

General George McClellan's Union Army marches past original Hygeia in September 1862 in this Civil War engraving from Harper's Weekly of September 20, 1862.

Daily Press

In 1868 a second Hygeia hostelry began to grow at Old Point, starting with this restaurant and hotel on Old Point's Government Dock. It grew into a large, world-famous spa.

burned in 1920, as the Hygeia had earlier. In 1928 a second Chamberlin was built, fronting Hampton Roads where the first Chamberlin had reigned. The Government Pier which had served ships at Old Point for over a century was torn down after World War 2.

Casemate Museum'
This expanded four-story brick Hygeia was run by Harrison Phoebus from 1874 until he died in 1886. It offered European baths and famous cuisine plus the newly popular beach bathing.

Casemate Museum
John Chamberlin in 1896 built five-story brick hotel which bore his name. It captured some of the fame of Phoebus's Hygeia until it burned in 1920. It was busiest during Jamestown Exposition of 1907.

Daily Press
The fourth major resort hotel at Old Point is the second Chamberlin, built in 1928 and still in operation. Government Pier once fronting it was pulled down after World War 2.

It stood where the generals' houses at Monroe now stand, facing the shore and dock across a plaza with a central bandstand.

The tip of Old Point in that area has harbored three hotels before the present Chamberlin, which was built only in 1928. When Fort Monroe was laid out after the War of 1812, William Armistead built the first inn there in 1820 to house visiting engineers and officers. It was operated by Marshall Parks of Norfolk. The elaborate stone construction of Monroe required out-of-town artisans, who were brought from Norfolk, Washington, and Baltimore. Some ended up permanently on the Peninsula.

Parks named his hotel the Hygeia for the Greek-goddess of health. It was a simple frame building with porches, which served until demolished by the U.S. Army in 1862 to give Fort Monroe's guns full play on Hampton Roads shipping lanes in the Civil War. An ad for the hotel in the Norfolk Herald of 1822 declared:

"Here lov'd Hygeia holds her blissful seat
And smiles on all who seek her blessed retreat."

The Hygeia drew Americans plus British and French naval officers, whose sailing ships often rendezvoused in Hampton Roads before the Civil War. Old Point's historian, Dr. Chester Bradley, writes that it "became to the planters and statemen of the South what the Saratoga Hotel was to the North." Edgar Allan Poe recited poetry on its veranda on Sept. 9, 1849—only a month before he died in Baltimore.

After the hotel was torn down, a Hygeia restaurant was built on Old Point's dock in 1863 for travelers. After 1868, it grew into the second Hygeia Hotel. This was the large red palatial four-story Victorian structure which Harrison Phoebus took over in 1874. It stood

Daily Press

Harrison Phoebus was renowned as operator of Hygeia Hotel at Old Point from 1874 to 1886.

close to the water and had a dance pavilion, bath house, and pleasure dock.

Phoebus installed many gadgets and luxuries to compete with popular resorts like Niagara Falls, the Pocono Mountains, and the Virginia springs. He put in hydraulic elevators, gaslights, electric bells in bedrooms, and bathrooms on each floor. To compete with the medicinal waters of the Virginia springs, he put in baths—Turkish, Russian, thermo-electric, magnetic, mercurial, sulphur, vapor, and hot seawater.

You couldn't help but like Harrison Phoebus. He was an attractive man, never too busy to show an employee how to do his job. He traveled to Europe to see how its hotels were run. "Let every man follow his bent," he used to say. "Do not try to make a stone mason out of a carpenter or a mathematician out of a poet. If a man can write poetry, let him write it. If he can drive an express wagon, let him drive it. They are both good things."

When the C&O extended its tracks from Richmond to Newport News in 1881, Harrison Phoebus saw opportunity to attract inland patrons. He persuaded Collis Huntington to extend the C&O line from Newport News to Old Point the next year. The village on Mill Creek adjoining Old Point at that time was called Chesapeake City, but the C&O renamed it for Harrison Phoebus. The place was incorporated as Phoebus in 1900. In recent times it has become part of Hampton.

So successful was the Hygeia that it attracted another hotel to Old Point, the Chamberlin. Behind it was John Chamberlin, a Washington saloon and restaurant owner, who was intimate with politicians of the Cleveland and McKinley administrations. The slick John Chamberlin lobbied a bill through Congress in 1886 to permit him to build a hotel on Army land at Old Point, right next door to the Hygeia.

Congress probably wouldn't have passed the bill if Harrison Phoebus had lived. However, he died suddenly of a heart ailment in 1886 at 45. He was buried at St. John's churchyard in Hampton after a funeral procession of 65 carriages from Old Point. Harper's Weekly carried his obituary, describing his prowess as a hotel man and civic leader.

As you might guess, the Hygeia without Phoebus soon lost out to the new Chamberlin, after that five-story palace opened in April 1896. Many of Chamberlin's friends came to it—Cabinet members, senators, and tycoons. The Norfolk Herald called the hotel "magnificent" and "among the largest and most attractive of American watering place hostelries."

Like Harrison Phoebus, Chamberlin did not long enjoy his success. He died in August 1896, four months after the Chamberlin opened. The hotel's new owners soon bought up and razed the Hygeia. For 24 years after that the Chamberlin enjoyed some of the luster that Harrison Phoebus had brought to Old Point. It throve especially in the Jamestown Exposition of 1907, when guests included Mark Twain and William Howard Taft. Its guests made up a Who's Who of Edwardian America.

When war broke out in Europe in 1914, the Chamberlin went after the patronage of Americans who had once gone to European spas. It advertised "The gouty and rheumatic population need feel no alarm at the closing of the celebrated resorts of Karlsbad and Baden Baden. At the Chamberlin, every treatment given at Aix, Vichy, Karlsbad, Nauheim, or Harrogate is duplicated." Pretty fancy, eh?

Eight years after the Chamberlin burned to the ground in 1920, it was succeeded by the present Chamberlin. However, it never thrived as its predecessors had. Deprived of gambling, it has had to depend on vacationers and conventioners. The competition was growing.

In Virginia's long history as a host, its most famous hotel man remains Harrison Phoebus, the penniless Marylander who came to Old Point in 1866 as a clerk. He showed that one determined soul can create a world-famous resort. No wonder a town adopted his name. He made Old Point and Phoebus famous.

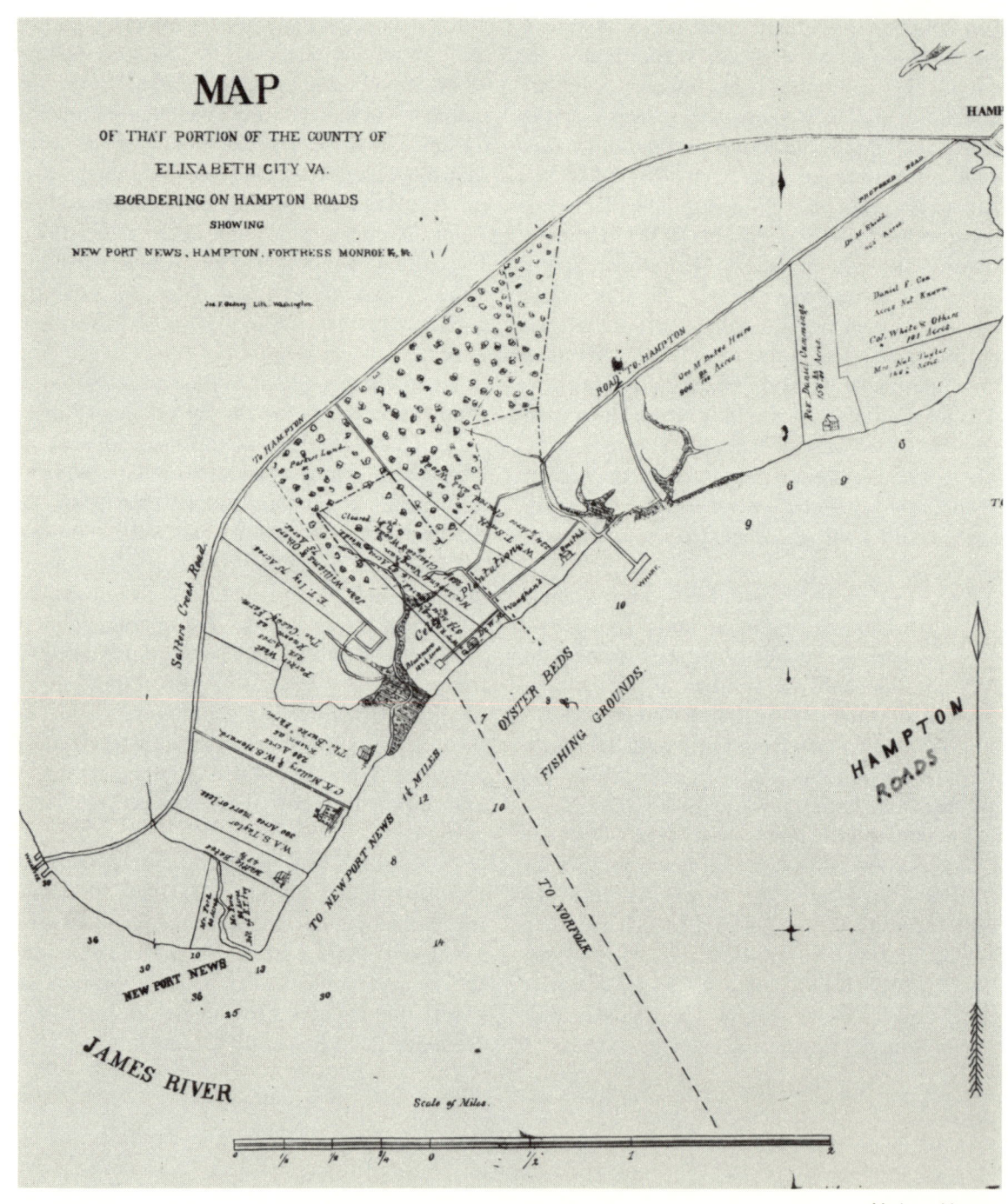

Mariners Museum

The Hampton Roads shoreline when Newport News became a town in 1881 was dotted by few farmhouses. A narrow road led from Parker West's farm on the James River to Hampton. Kecoughtan road went from Ceely's plantation to Hampton.

13. *When Newport News Began*

I'VE just come across a fascinating account of a newcomer to the Peninsula in 1883, when this area was still torn up by the Civil War. Hampton was rebuilding after its burning in 1861, and Newport News was no more than a railroad stop. It had become the terminus of the C&O two years before, but it had few buildings or streets.

The visitor was John Swinerton, a Northerner who came south to be manager of Lafayette House at Twenty-Seventh Street and Lafayette (later Huntington) Avenue. It was agreed that when Collis Huntington had finished his new hotel, the Warwick, Swinerton would take that over and run both. Swinerton wrote his account for the Newport News Pioneers in 1914.

Swinerton was an energetic hotelkeeper, with the gift for gab of his breed. He enjoyed hosting celebrities at the Warwick like Admiral George Dewey, General Phil Sheridan, General Winfield Hancock, and stage stars who came to town after 1900 to perform at the Academy of Music. He was a friend of Harrison Phoebus, who'd run the Hygeia Hotel at Old Point, and Phoebus' competitor, John Chamberlin, who built the first Chamberlin Hotel there.

Young John left New York on January 1, 1883, and arrived via a Bay Line steamer at Old Point. There he learned that the C&O's daily train to Newport News had departed, so he joined two other travelers to go to Newport News by horse and wagon for $1.50 apiece. It was a bad beginning.

"The roads were muddy and filled with ice," he wrote, "so we were nearly three hours in making the journey. I often think of this trip when I hear people complain about paying 15 cents in a warm, comfortable, and handsome trolley car, running every 15 minutes."

Lafayette House charged travelers $3 a night, and its rooms were in heavy demand. Its occupants were engineers and builders who had come to build piers and a grain elevator for the C&O and to construct the Warwick Hotel and other buildings for the Old Dominion Land Company's promised city.

Swinerton found most of the town's 1,000 residents living in the area of Eighteenth Street and River Road, later called "Hell's Half Acre," where the present railyards and docks are. Only nine buildings, he wrote, had been erected on the high ground west of the Warwick Hotel site at Twenty-Fourth Street.

(The Eighteenth Street area became run down as polite families moved to the West Avenue area.)

One early building was the interdenominational Union Chapel on West Avenue near Twenty-Sixth. Others were the Old Dominion's office, two saloons, a few small stores, and the old Hawkins farmhouse on the James River at Thirty-Fifth. It was then the home of engineer Walter Post, whom Collis Huntington had sent to town in 1880 to build C&O piers and—after 1889, the shipyard. In 1907 Post became president of the yard.

Huntington by 1883 had succeeded in buying most of Newport News Point up to about Thirty-Fifth Street. However, the Melson family, who owned the land needed to build Washington Avenue, refused to sell to him. When Swinerton asked why the new hotel was not built on the principal avenue, he was told: "That land is too valuable."

Swinerton didn't say so, but the Hawkins-Melson-Finch estate developed its Washington Avenue property independent of the Old Dominion. Most of the property is now owned by William E. Allaun Jr., who inherited it through his mother a Hawkins-Melson-Finch descendant.

The railway town in 1883 had no minister, no lawyer, and only two doctors. "Dr. Joseph Charles was kept busy," Swinerton told the Pioneers, "cutting off legs of Negroes who were injured working on the piers or railroad."

Walter Post, the C&O construction chief, was justice of the peace, and was called "Judge Post" by black and white. Most legal transactions had to be taken to Warwick Courthouse at Denbigh, or to Hampton.

"There were no white schools," Swinerton recalled. "There were very few white children. A colored school was kept at an old

Mariners Museum

Collis Huntington's Old Dominion Land Company opened its four-story Hotel Warwick at 25th Street in Newport News in 1883. It sought to attract midwest vacationers to come south over the new C&O.

Hotel Warwick's 1883 brochure showed grand stairway in its lobby and its water sports on the adjacent Casino grounds. Collis Huntington occasionally stayed there, as did visiting Academy of Music stars.

house across the C&O track near Twenty-Eighth Street."

The Warwick Hotel opened on April 11, 1883, about three months after Swinerton came to town. It was planned by Collis Huntington as a luxury hostelry to attract vacationers as well as businessmen, and it charged $4 a night. Advertisements showed its Victorian elegance, including a luxurious dining room and ballroom.

(The original wooden hotel served Newport News nearly a half century, till it was torn down as a fire hazard. A later brick Warwick still operates.)

At Old Point, competitor John Chamberlin was so impressed, he told the editor of the New York Home Journal that "The Warwick is the best hotel south of Washington." Swinerton adopted that as his motto.

"The hotel was opened with a banquet to the prominent men and their wives of the Peninsula," the hotel man recalled in 1914. "The C&O ran a special train from Old Point and Hampton, bringing the guests directly to the hotel over a spur track from Twenty-Eighth Street."

Swinerton promoted whist games at night in his hotel lobby for lack of entertainment. A participant was Theodore Livezey, first head of the Old Dominion Land Company. His son Walter, a teen-ager in 1883, penned Swinerton's daily dining room bill-of-fare. By 1914 he had succeeded his father as president of the Old Dominion Land Company.

Frequent visitors in the 1880s aboard private C&O railway cars were Collis Huntington, the California "robber baron" who built and owned most of the town, and Williams Wickham, president of the C&O. Wickham, a native of Hanover County and a Confederate general in the Civil War, had a city street named for him. So did Huntington later, along with Post and Orcutt.

The Warwick's grounds included a park which extended from Twenty-Fourth Street westward up West Avenue to Thirtieth Street. A wooden entertainment hall, called the Casino, was built in the park, close to the river, and gave its name to the area. In its early days the Casino was a recreational center for hotel guests and it had a pleasure pier, now gone, and beach bathhouses. Dances were held in the building, and speakers came to town for Chautauqua lectures. Evangelist Billy Sunday held revival services on the Casino grounds in the 1930s.

"After the Warwick opened, it was the center for everything," Swinerton recalled. "On the ground floor was the only drugstore and the only barber shop in the place. The Court House, Customs House, Post Office, and the first bank (the First National, later to become First and Merchants) were for awhile located under the hotel."

Joining Walter Post in 1889 in the Huntington hierarchy was Calvin Orcutt of New Jersey, who came to head Newport News Light and Water Company, an offshoot of the Old Dominion Land Company, and the new shipyard.

Orcutt had worked for Huntington in New York before making the Peninsula his main base. Swinerton and the Warwick whist-players liked him. "We were always glad to see Mr. Orcutt," the hotel manager said. "He was jolly and chuck full of optimism, ready for a game of pool after supper, and never ready to quit." Orcutt often sat in the Warwick lobby regaling visitors with visions of the city's future.

Like the Chamberlin and Hygeia, the Warwick attracted Northern vacationers each winter. "The hotel enjoyed the patronage of the best class of tourists from the North. It was kept up to a high standard, the rates being $4 per day and $21 to $25 per week," Swinerton wrote. "It had as good a chef as could be found, and the best that the New York markets could supply was none too good for the Warwick."

Though downtown streets had been laid out in 1883, little else greeted Swinerton when he first arrived.

"There was a boardwalk up Twenty-Seventh Street to Washington Avenue," for pedestrians, he wrote, "another went to the Twenty-Eighth Street C&O crossing. Street lights were unknown here at that time. I recall one dark rainy night a drummer from Boston arrived. After supper he asked where the business streets were. I told him 'Washington and West Avenues and River Road.' When daylight came and he could see nothing but open fields, he enjoyed the joke."

Well, that was Newport News 98 years ago. By the time John Swinerton died in 1934, aged 93, it had become a city of 30,000 people. Since its merger with Warwick County in 1958, it has expanded to 150,000.

It's still not the huge city it someday will be, but our generation has a chance to realize John Swinerton's expectations. The Peninsula has good years ahead.

14. *Celebrating Jamestown's Birthday*

One of the memorable events of Virginia's history was the Jamestown Exposition of 1907, which introduced modern tourism to the reviving post-Civil War Virginia Peninsula. It celebrated the 300th anniversary of the start of English settlement at Jamestown.

The summer-long celebration centered at grounds of the site of the present Norfolk Naval Base, but it radiated across Hampton Roads to Hampton, Newport News, Williamsburg and Jamestown. Many Exposition visitors came by the C&O to the Peninsula. And excursion boats brought others to Jamestown's long steamship dock, now razed.

Many ads and printed programs for the Exposition survive. Typical is an advertising folder published by the Old Dominion Steamship Line in 1907, with an aerial view of Hampton Roads full of ships.

The scene was of the International Naval Review, visited by President Theodore Roosevelt aboard the presidential yacht, Mayflower. It recalled an earlier Hampton Roads naval extravanza, in 1893, when "the Great White Fleet" of United States naval vessels sailed from Hampton Roads on a round-the-world goodwill tour.

My interest in the 1907 Old Dominion ad was attracted by its daily passenger ship voyages from New York to Norfolk. In those steamboat days, you could sail from Gotham to visit the Jamestown Exposition from April to November of 1907 and then go back for only $10 round trip, including stateroom berth. Meals were only $1 or so additional.

The ships left Pier 26 in New York's North River every weekday at 3 p.m., reaching Norfolk at 10 next morning. There, if you wanted to, you could catch another passenger steamer and go up the James to Richmond.

The ad indicates the variety of passenger ships which by 1907 were opening up Hampton Roads to other Atlantic ports. This area's railroad and passenger ship service after the Civil War showed the rapid growth of local population. Coastal Virginia was building an industrial economy based on railroads, shipyards, military bases, cigarette-making and resorts like Old Point, Buckroe Beach, Ocean View, and Virginia Beach.

Even Newport News in 1907 went after tourists. Collis Huntington had built his big wooden Hotel Warwick in the 1880s, and the Old Dominion Land Company had created a waterside park on West Avenue as its front yard, with a casino building. The original hotel has been razed, but a later brick one is being restored today.

"In the early days, Newport News was considered not only an industrial center, but also a pleasure resort," wrote Harold Sniffen, of the Mariners' Museum, 40 years ago in the book, *Newport News' 325 Years*. "The Hotel Warwick attracted vacationists and advertised a casino, refreshment pavilion, bowling alley, as many as sixty bath houses, and a 'Pleasure pier.'"

Among ship lines serving Hampton Roads the Old Dominion was in 1907 foremost. The company operated seagoing ships connecting with Atlantic ports plus a network of Chesapeake inlet "feeder" lines. The feeders brought freight and passengers to the two Hampton Roads transshipment points, Old Point and Norfolk. Old Point's pier was a busy hub.

According to Sniffen, "These feeders ran south from Norfolk through the Albemarle-Chesapeake Canal into North Carolina; across the mouth of Chesapeake Bay to Cherrystone (north of Cape Charles); up the Chesapeake to Mobjack Bay; to Old Point and Hampton; up the James River to Richmond; to Newport News and thence across the James to Smithfield; and up the Nansemond to Suffolk."

He lists among Old Dominion steamboats serving early Newport News such long-gone vessels as the Hampton, Pamlico, Northampton, Luray, Accomack, Isle of Wight, Enola, Hampton Roads, Ocracoke, Mobjack, Berkley, Brandon, and Pocahontas.

Mementoes of many of these ships are in the Mariners' Museum.

The 1907 shipping advertisement shows that Old Dominion's New York-to-Norfolk line was served by five vessels: the S.S. Monroe,

Virginia State Library

A Hotel Warwick brochure shows Casino Park with dressing rooms for swimmers. The park was long used for sports and political gatherings. Most of it is now used for buildings.

Celebrating Jamestown's Birthday 79

Mariners Museum

Two spectacular early Navy fleet gatherings brought sightseers to the Peninsula. In 1893 a two-month Naval Rendezvous honored Columbus's voyage. This travel poster shows Norfolk in foreground and Peninsula beyond.

President Theodore Roosevelt in 1907 dispatched a naval fleet from Hampton Roads to impress Japan on round-the-world tour with America's might. He returned in 1909 to receive the ships in an Old Point review.

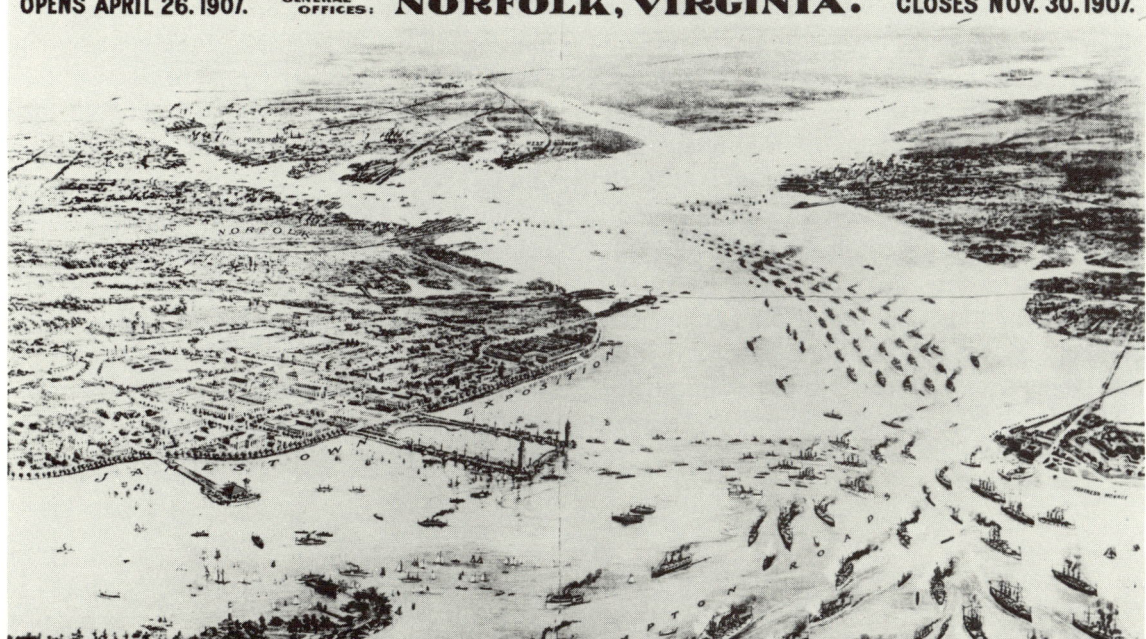

U.S. Navy photo

Jamestown Exposition was held in 1907 on Norfolk shore facing the Peninsula. In its Raleigh Square was a lagoon, terminated by a large friendship arch from Japan. The area was taken over as the Norfolk Naval Base before World War I.

Hamilton, Jefferson, Princess Anne, and Jamestown—all of 3,000 or 4,000 tons.

My acquaintance with the Old Dominion line was through its feeder line that operated from Newport News to Smithfield. Before I was born it had begun weekday sailings from Norfolk to Newport News, Battery Park, and Smithfield, at first using the ships Accomack and Pamlico. In 1909 it renamed its steamer called Hampton in honor of Smithfield and sailed it alternately with the Ocracoke. "Each made a daily run," writes Sniffen, "the one lying overnight at Norfolk and the other at Smithfield."

Sniffen mentions one of the Old Dominion's competitors, the tiny mail boat Oneita, which plied daily from Newport News to Smithfield. "The late United States Senator, Thomas Martin, feeling it advantageous that a regular midday mail leave Smithfield, secured a contract for Captain A.F. Jester to carry mail, passengers, and freight. This service was inaugurated about 1917 and continued until about 1931. . . . When the James River Bridge was built in 1928 . . . the knell of the boat service across the James was rung."

Captain Jester, who lived in Smithfield, also operated ferries at Jamestown and at Chuckatuck.

Those Old Dominion steamers could compete with railroads, but automobiles proved too much for them. When cars and modern hard-surfaced highways came along in the 1920s, coastal shipping died. Today few coastal ships except oilers and barges ply Hampton Roads or the nearby rivers.

15. *An Early High School Graduation*

THE spring of 1907 was busy on the Peninsula. The Jamestown Exposition opened at Norfolk, President Theodore Roosevelt had visited it, and Hampton Roads was alive with pleasure boats and excursions going to Jamestown and the exposition.

Then it was that the graduating class of 13 Newport News High School students took its place on June 6, 1907, on the stage of the Academy of Music, to receive its diplomas.

Professor Horace H. Epes was principal, and "The 13 Original States" was the theme. Annie Lash (later Mrs. Lewis Jester) was Virginia, and Agnes Epes (daughter of the principal and later to be Mrs. Lewis McMurran) was Connecticut. Guy Via, later to organize the shipyard's Apprentice School, was Georgia, and Jacob Harry Kerlin was Pennsylvania.

The other graduating seniors were Ellen Branch Ware (Delaware), Lucy Harrison (Maryland), Minnie Belle Harrison (New York), John Hughes (Rhode Island), Alice Evelyn Davis (New Hampshire), Ila Lewis (North Carolina), Amelia Virginia Godwin (South Carolina), Gertrude Loomis (Massachusetts), and Charlotte Selden (New Jersey).

Girls in the class outnumbered boys 10 to three, for most boys then went to work after elementary school. That changed after World War I.

I've read through the school magazine, "The High School Student," published in 1907 by the graduating class. It was loaned to me by a granddaughter of Ernest Shaffer, a 1907 student who drew the cover picture for this modest predecessor of later, more elaborate school annuals. Besides photos of the graduates, it also contains essays, poems, year-end awards at Central School (on the site of the later John W. Daniel School) and at School 2, School 4 and School 5. That was before Newport News began naming schools for people.

Fenno Heath, '09, wrote "Along the Shore in Old Virginia" in the magazine, while John Hughes endorsed "College Athletics as a Factor in Life." Marguerite Horne, '09, described "Tokio in a Jinrikisha," and Annie Lash wrote about "Immigration." ("We must not bar foreigners from our country. It is for the good of our nation that we admit them.")

Agnes Epes apostrophized Longfellow as "Our Fireside Poet," 1907 being the centennial of his birth. Margaret Buxton, '09, moralized on "Honesty Is the Best Policy."

It was a spartan magazine befitting a spartan town. The school had been organized about the time Newport News was incorpora-

An Early High School Graduation

ted, in 1896, on the third floor of a commercial building on 28th Street. Later it moved to the third floor of Central School building on 31st Street, which was to burn about 1911 and to be rebuilt as John W. Daniel School. For a few years after World War I, Newport News High School occupied the Walter Reed building in East End. It finally got its own building in the 1920s on Huntington Avenue, a half-block from Daniel School.

The rise of public schools was rapid in Virginia after Virginia's post-Civil War government in 1867-68 authorized them. The General Assembly in 1872 chose the Rev. William Henry Ruffner as first state superintendent. Newport News apparently got its first public schools—one white and one black—when it was incorporated in 1896. Thomas Temple Powell was the first local superintendent of schools, with a budget of $13,000.

Later school superintendents were E. W. Huffman, Willis Jenkins, Joseph H. Saunders (he held office in my day), R.O. Nelson, George McIntosh, Don Roberts, Oliver Greenwood, and Donald Bruno.

(So lacking was public education in Newport News before 1896 that a school for shipyard employees' children had to be provided by Collis Huntington in 1891, a year after he created the shipyard. It was at 34th and Washington, close to the yard. After public schools got going in 1896, the frame building became a

Daily Press

Newport News High School graduates in February 1916 were 16 girls and four boys. Classes were held in downtown school, later named John W. Daniel. The graduation program was in Newport News Academy of Music.

kindergarten for shipyard employees' children. I remember the building and kindergarten in the 1920s.)

The first public schools had a certain public prejudice to overcome. Since the beginning of Anglo-Saxon history, education had been the responsibility of the church. Public schools changed that, and some Virginians at first objected. They felt their children should receive religious instruction along with secular subjects. For a while after 1896, several private schools operated in downtown Newport News, including Mrs. W. W. Harwood's Female Seminary on 29th Street, Colonel E. W. Huffman's Military School on Lafayette (later Huntington) Avenue, and George Ben West's Newport News Academy on the Casino grounds.

But public schools gained, and the private schools finally died. In addition to Principal Epes, Newport News High had good teachers like Mrs. E. P. Griffith, Miss Nellie Kerlin and Miss Gertrude Davis, the latter of whom I knew in the 1930s when she was principal of John W. Daniel. (She played Sousa marches for us to march to.)

The high school in 1907 had fewer than 100 students and only a few teachers. This was the situation when its students published their 1907 magazine that I mentioned. In 1907 the town had about 10,000 people, living from Dawson City near the Boat Harbor to about 55th Street in the North End. It grew much larger in the two world wars.

The First National Bank, the city's oldest (now First and Merchants), advertised in the 1907 school magazine that it had capital of $100,000 and a surplus and undivided profits of $115,000. The American Tobacco Company advertised for "bright boys and girls to learn to make Little Cigars." The Old Dominion Land Company, housed in the Hotel Warwick, offered building lots for "easy payments."

Boys' suits for commencement were offered by Wertheimer's store from $1.50 to $8. Klor's Drug Store at 26th and Washington was pushing Dr. Klor's "Little Brownies" at "the best liver, bowel and stomach regulators on earth" at 25 cents a box. Charles C. Epes and Brother, stationers, advertised Kodaks and Brownie Cameras at prices from $1 to $20.

Gardens were then grown at most elementary schools. Central School reported in the High School Student: "Our sweetpeas and nasturtiums are ready to bloom. The corn and beans are growing nicely." School 4 was planting peanuts and cotton, "so that we will have something to look forward to and enjoy in the fall."

Another class reporter observed, "Several of our boys are going to make good farmers someday." I doubt that happened. Virginia was rapidly industrialized, as the North had done. Soon World War I would speed up the process. By the time of World War II, there were few farms left in Warwick or Elizabeth City Counties.

After World War I, high schools and colleges expanded even more rapidly. Vocational courses were added. Business and industry demanded workers with college diplomas. William and Mary and other colleges grew fast as a result.

By the time I entered Newport News High in 1931, it had grown far beyond Professor Epes' tiny school of 1907. It had more than 1,000 students, housed in a big tan brick monolith on Huntington at 31st Street.

Even so, the calibre of education in 1907 as I perceive it was not to be sneezed at. Reading through The High School Student of 1907, I judge by their writings that its thirteen graduates were fully as well-educated as today's. They had a discipline and a purpose that is often lacking in today's students.

It takes a lot more than material wealth to make a good school. They had it in 1907, and we need more of it today.

Excursion and sightseeing boats clustered at Old Point dock in 1909 when Teddy Roosevelt's 'Great White Fleet' returned from 18-month round-the world voyage. The president reviewed fleet aboard Mayflower off Fort Monroe.

16. *The Great White Fleet Returns*

BROWSING through the shops of Norfolk's Waterside recently, I came across an aged photograph that I recognized as an aerial view of Old Point Dock crowded with yachts and people. It turned out to be a shot made in 1909, when the "Great White Fleet" returned to Hampton Roads after a triumphal two-year voyage around the world.

It's forgotten now, but when I was a boy people still talked about the Great White Fleet and its voyage. It was Teddy Roosevelt's way of letting the world know that the United States had become a great naval power.

And what a success it must have been! The Navy had painted its 16 biggest warships white—to show that America wanted peace—and sent them to Tokyo to impress the Japanese. They made a lot of other political stops in South America, Europe, and Asia—all to "show the flag" and let the world know that America had become a world power.

My photograph of the fleet's arrival was taken from the old Chamberlin Hotel, which stood on the waterfront till it burned in 1920. It shows the Old Point dock surrounded by sightseeing boats, with larger ships anchored offshore. It was apparently taken on Feb. 22, 1909—the memorable day when the Great White Fleet sailed through the Virginia capes to be met in Hampton Roads by President Roosevelt aboard his yacht, the Mayflower.

The fleet's return was a sequel to the Jamestown Exposition of 1907, where the fleet had sailed on its mission with Teddy's waterside blessing. The exposition took place at the present Norfolk Naval Base waterfront from April through December of 1907. It celebrated the 300th anniversary of Jamestown's settlement in 1607. A few of the 1907 Jamestown Exposition buildings are still used by the naval base—some as admirals' quarters.

Teddy Roosevelt believed America needed a big Navy to help the British navy keep world peace. When he became president in 1901, he planned to "walk softly and carry a big stick." So he enlarged the Navy, which had just fought and defeated the Spanish in 1898.

The main object of the White Fleet's voyage out of Hampton Roads in 1907 was to show American strength to Japan, which had been angered in 1905 by Teddy's intervention in the Russo-Japanese War and by America's cutoff of Japanese immigration to California. Old Teddy tried to disguise the Navy's show of force by calling the voyage a "cruise around the world" and letting the ships stop at Trinidad, Rio de Janeiro, Punta Arenas, Valparaiso, the Philippines, Tokyo, and the Suez Canal. But the Japanese were impressed—for a while.

Newport News was involved in the voyage, for it had built two of the 16 battleships—the Kearsage and Kentucky—which made the cruise. Also in the fleet were six destroyers and several auxiliaries.

To greet the returning ships in 1909, Teddy sailed down from Washington on his presidential yacht, the Mayflower. With him were his wife, two sons, and two daughters, one of them Alice Roosevelt Longworth and her husband, House Speaker Nicholas Longworth. The Mayflower stood off the shore of Fort Monroe in order that the president could receive the 21-gun salute of the arriving ships. Shore guns at Monroe then fired to return the salute of each passing ship.

A witness that exciting day was William Breslow, a 15-year-old New Yorker who had come to Old Point with two teen-age friends to work on bumboats that would supply incoming ships with newspapers, magazines, ice cream, pies, and other items sailors had lacked at sea. Breslow later became a New York dentist. In 1971, when an old man, he wrote his memories of the event in a book called "Bumboater."

"The Mayflower stood in and anchored at the entrance of Hampton Roads," Breslow recalled in his book, "while the guns of Fortress Monroe boomed out a 21-gun salute to the president. At last the moment arrived, and from the massed crowds ashore, the shout, 'Here they come!' burst from thousands of throats. A few moments later the masts of the leading battleship came into view."

Sailing in a single file, 400 yards apart, the ships slowed to ten knots as they neared Fort Monroe. "I could see that the rails were manned by officers and men in dress blues,"

Hampton's volunteer fire department in 1909 stood ready for action. Horse-drawn hose and pumper wagons were replaced by motor-driven equipment after Henry Ford began making cars and trucks.

Syms-Eaton Museum

Breslow wrote. "The thousands lining the shores were cheering and shouting, but I stood silently near my bumboat. . . . As each of the ships came abreast of the Mayflower, it boomed out a 21-gun salute to the president, who stood at attention on the quarterdeck. . . ."

The ships, after their salute to the president, formed a double column and swung around till their bows faced the Fort Monroe shoreline. There they anchored.

The young bumboat salesman remembered that Old Point had been full of people that day. "The wharf at Old Point was a beehive of activity," he wrote. "Some 2,000 New York newspapers would arrive at the Fort Monroe Post Office (each day) to be carted down to the Wharf, where the local agent would distribute them to the bumboaters. . . . When local bakers could no longer supply the necessary pies, they had to be delivered daily from Norfolk."

Bumboats flourished in ports around the world in those days, before the U.S. Navy had developed more adequate means of meeting fleet needs. Alexander C. Brown, Newport News maritime expert, has written that "ships arriving from distant parts had been deprived of such shoreside amenities as newspapers and ice cream. These, together with souvenirs, pies, and other fresh edibles were the cargoes of bumboats—open craft propelled by oar or motor—which sailed out from port to meet incoming ships and offer their wares for sale."

After Teddy Roosevelt had greeted the Great White Fleet and congratulated officers and crews, he rushed back to Washington on the Mayflower. However, the fleet remained anchored near Fort Monroe and the Hotel Chamberlin for two weeks, enjoying shore duty and leave. Then all ships dispersed for four months to return to Hampton Roads in July for target practice.

During the fleet's Hampton Roads visit,

Syms-Eaton Museum

Marines in dress uniform come ashore at old Hotel Chamberlin in 1907. They were from Navy warships anchored offshore during Jamestown Exposition. The hotel burned in 1920 and was replaced in 1928.

wives and sweethearts of officers and enlisted men stayed at the Chamberlin and Monticello hotels, which were the center of fleet social life. The Navy had not yet established its Norfolk Naval Base, which began with America's entry into World War I in 1918. Those were great days for Old Point.

Barely two weeks after Teddy Roosevelt welcomed the fleet, he left office as president. On May 4, 1909, he was succeeded by William Howard Taft at inaugural ceremonies in Washington. And although Teddy was a Republican and Virginia was a heavily Democratic state, he remained highly popular in Tidewater. A lot of people in my youth liked to talk about the time "when I saw Teddy Roosevelt at the Jamestown Exposition" or "when I saw Teddy with the Great White Fleet."

Exciting days! Even a photograph catches a little of the excitement.

One of Newport News's big days was July 4, 1918, when three 1207-ton destroyers were launched at the shipyard. The war ended four months later.

III.
Years of the First World War
1917–1919

The Old Dominion Brewing and Ice Company brewed beer from 1901 until the 1930s in this Rhenish castle near 34th and Jefferson. It was used by the Army in World War I, then torn down.

17. *The Brewery: Victorian Curiosity*

NEWPORT News grew up in the Victorian age, but it has already lost most of its Victoriana. To be honest, most of it was so cheaply and hastily built that it didn't deserve to last. A few worthy exceptions like the Walter Post (Hiden) house at 56th and Huntington Avenue still survive. There are others scattered around.

The city's real Victorian jewel in my recollection was the big brick brewery at 36th Street and Warwick Avenue (now Terminal). It looked like a Rhenish castle, crowned by a cupola, turrets and crenelations like those used by medieval soldiers to fight off the Huns. It seemed born to be the background for some Gothic romance.

It's impressive to me to see how many other people remember the brewery, too. It was one of Newport News' landmarks, like the C&O granary, the original Warwick Hotel, the courthouse of 1892-1948, the casino building, the Academy of Music and the Norfolk ferry docks at the boat harbor.

The brewery was the most exotic of the lot. When you crossed 34th Street Bridge, it loomed up like something from a Douglas Fairbanks swashbuckler. It stood from 1901 until the year 1940, when it was torn down as unused and potentially dangerous. It had been built to supply beer and ice to the Peninsula, at a time when nearly every city had a brewery. Only recently has the growth of giants—Anheuser Busch, Miller's, Coors and Schlitz-Stroh—put local and regional breweries out of business.

The brewery was started by Theodore Reinecke of New York, and its officers were S.A. Wertmann, president, and H.G. Kimmich, general manager. The only English name was that of William H. Dodds, treasurer. The brewery began life as Warwick Brewing and Ice Company but changed to the Old Dominion after a year. Its two beers were Dixie and Wuerzberger, most of the brew being sold in barrels to be dispensed to saloons on draft.

Most Peninsulans in 1903 got water from wells, which made the water supply subject to infection. Kimmich exhorted Peninsulans to drink beer instead. "If the world would drink more beer, like 'Dixie,' " he pled, "and less impure and contaminated, treated or carelessly-charged mineral water, we should have more encouraging vital statistics." (And maybe more alcoholics?)

92 The Brewery: Victorian Curiosity

In the saloons that dotted downtown Newport News, Dixie beer at first sold well. Pat Laracy, who ran a saloon in his Huntington Hotel at 36th and Washington, remembered giving a free lunch to anyone who bought a mug of Dixie.

The Old Dominion followed Germanic practices, right down to the teams of Percheron draft horses that pulled its beer wagons. The brewery was handsomely built, with furnishings of copper, brass and stone. "The engine, refrigerating plant, the brewing vats, the cooling vaults and the bottling apparatus will be the finest possible construction," The Times-Herald reported. It made 500 barrels of beer a day and 60 tons of the "finest plate ice."

An unusual feature of the building was the "Time Ball," a doughnut-shaped device which was hauled up to the top of a flagpole and released at noon each weekday. That was before the shipyard whistle. It enabled shipyard workers to set their watches.

Apparently the brewery was too big for its britches, for it failed in 1907. It was blamed on the high cost of water, then provided by the Huntington-controlled Old Dominion Land Company. Efforts to sink artesian wells failed. Investors suffered, and 75 brewery workers lost their jobs.

The equipment was sold and the structure

Casemate Museum

A cow grazes along Fort Monroe's moat about 1900. Adjoining the flagstaff are the second Hygeia and the first Chamberlin Hotels, with Old Point pier beyond them.

was then used by the Army Quartermaster Corps in World War I and by Hiden Storage and Forwarding Company for tobacco storage afterward. It was razed in 1940 by its owner, the C&O. An important landmark disappeared.

Next to the brewery, I think the most exotic 19th century city structures were the two grain elevators which the C&O built about 18th Street in the 1880s. The Valley of Virginia then produced much wheat, some of which was milled by the Dunlop and Haxall flour mills in Richmond, and some shipped to Newport News and held in the C&O's grain elevators until loaded aboard ships.

Wheat-growing moved in the 19th and 20th centuries to the midwest, and the Valley of Virginia was no longer "the granary of the nation," as it claimed in the Civil War. I guess that's what killed our grain business.

I remember seeing one of the two grain elevators when my father took me about 1918 to see the Army's artillery horses penned in C&O corrals around the elevator, awaiting shipment to Europe. The first of the two elevators had burned but Elevator B remained a towering colossus until it was razed for lack of business in 1934.

Another Victorian casualty was Warwick County (later Newport News) Courthouse, built at the intersection of 25th and Huntington in 1892. When Newport News became a city in 1896, it became the ciy's courthouse until 1948, when it was razed and replaced by the present colorless building.

I often frequented the early courthouse as a reporter in the 1930s. It was rundown by that time, and overcrowded by the growing minions of the law. However, the building had pretensions to Victorian grandeur—a tall tower, purely useless and unused, and a church-like solemnity. It was built of shiny brown brick, popular in those days, and it had big arched windows like a church or railroad depot. Not beautiful, but hard to forget.

Judges and courts were then less ceremonious then than now. Some ludicrous and sometimes heated exchanges occurred in the courtrooms. You can get an idea by listening the phonograph records of Walter Kelly's "The Virginia Judge," which took off Judge J.D.G. Brown of Newport News police court.

Another memorable Victorian pile was the first Warwick Hotel, built by the Huntington interests in 1882-83 and the temporary abode of Collis Huntington when he came to town in the years 1883-1900. He wanted it to be as modern as any hotel of its day, for he hoped vacationers would ride the C&O to town and stay in his hotel. (Not many did.) The original Warwick was a wood building with a large, palm-filled lobby, a florid dining room, a big banquet hall (Rotary and Kiwanis met there till it was torn down), a landscaped park between the hotel and the river, and a Victorian casino building adjoining the park for games, lectures and entertainments.

Where are these buildings now? Gone with the wind. Newport News has little Victoriana left, but I hope it can preserve the best of that.

Daily Press

An observation plane and balloon of World War I are exhibited at early Langley Field. Langley continued the pre-war air training of Curtiss Field, started at Newport News' Boat Harbor in 1915.

18. *Daredevils of Curtiss Field*

NORTH Carolina was the birthplace of human flight, but Virginia did more to train flyers before World War I than any other place. A pioneer pilot program that was started at Newport News in 1915 antedated both the Army and Navy flight schools. Two or three major World War I aces trained right here.

All my life I'd heard people talk about the old flying field at the Boat Harbor, so I dug into Daily Press files to read about it. There I found the names of Newport News-trained aces like Billy Mitchell, Bert Acosta, H.M. "Buck" Gallop, Eddie Stinson, and other pioneers. I guess the field disappeared so rapidly in the city's World War I growth that it left no traces.

The only thing I remember at the early Boat Harbor besides the ferries to Norfolk were the Labor Day baptizings of Elder Solomon Lightfoot Michaux. Who could ever forget those glorious days?

But the story of the Atlantic Coast Aeronautical Station, as it was called, is full of drama. The field stretched from the tip of Jefferson Avenue, at the old ferry docks for a mile or so northward to Salter's Creek. It was chosen to serve both landplanes and seaplanes, for seaplanes were very important in early aviation.

When Europe exploded into war in 1914, many Canadians volunteered to fly with the infant British air service. Learning that Canadian and British air schools were overbooked, the Canadians then hastened down to the U.S.A. to learn to fly.

That's when Glenn Curtiss, a New York plane manufacturer, decided to move his flying school from Buffalo, N.Y. to the warmer clime of Newport News. He sent his friend Thomas Scott Baldwin, later an Army Air Corps officer, to the Peninsula early in 1915 to start it.

One of Baldwin's first applicants was a Newport News hellion named Buck Gallop. He had just married Maxine Finch, of the West Avenue Finches, whose nephew is William Allaun, an attorney of Newport News and Gloucester.

Gallop went from the local flying school into the Army, became an air hero in France, and was impersonated by Richard Barthelmess in the movie "The Dawn Patrol," which won an Oscar as the best movie in 1930. Many flyers thought Gallop was just as great as Eddie Rickenbacker.

Another star pupil of Tom Baldwin's was Major William Mitchell, an Army officer from Washington. Mitchell was so hot to fly that he boarded the Old Bay Line steamer each Friday from Washington, trained at the Boat Harbor on Saturday and Sunday, and sailed back on Sunday night to his Washington desk. Mitchell rose rapidly after the war to become a general, but he angered the Army so by his advocacy of an independent Air Force that he was demoted in 1927 to colonel.

Billy Mitchell then resigned in protest, but his hopes for military aviation were realized in World War II.

Another student at the Boat Harbor was Vernon Castle, who danced with his wife Irene on stage and in dance halls across the nation. Castle's wife lived briefly on the Peninsula while he trained here and took weekends off to fill theatrical engagements with her in Washington, New York, and other cities. Their specialties were the foxtrot, turkey trot, and other daring cheek-to-cheek steps.

When Vernon Castle graduated from the Boat Harbor school in February, 1916, he rushed to New York to sail for England and join the Royal Flying Corps, predecessor of the RAF. The slim, good-looking flyer was a devil with the ladies, and the Newport News papers daily reported his newest conquest or indiscretion.

When the United States entered the war in 1917, Castle resigned from the Royal Flying Corps and came home to Texas as a flight instructor. He was killed in a training crash. Irene married a Chicago millionaire.

One of Curtiss Field's instructors was Bert Acosta, who was to serve as pilot for Richard E. Byrd on polar expeditions. Another was Victor Carlstrom, who also performed as Curtiss's chief test pilot. In 1916 Carlstrom flew speed and endurance flights for Curtiss be-

Syms-Eaton

The Hampton Fire Department acquired its No. 1 fire engine before World War I. Solid rubber tires were later replaced by pneumatic ones. Military bases had their own fire wagons.

Daredevils of Curtiss Field 97

An early seaplane is beached at Atlantic Coast Aeronautical Station, at Newport News Boat Harbor, about 1915. Several World War I air aces learned to fly at the station.

tween Newport News and Fisherman's Island at Cape Charles, using a twin-engine Curtiss land and sea plane.

Carlstom's record-breaking speed test at Newport News was acclaimed by the Aero Club of America 1916 as "the most important aviation event of the year." As a result, Britain and Russia ordered $7,000,000 of Curtiss planes. That was a lot of planes then.

Carlstrom's career ended in a crash at the Boat Harbor with student pilot Cary Epes of Newport News, a brother of the late Perry, Horace, and Charles Epes and of the late Mrs. Lewis McMurran. The two men—Carlstrom only 32 and Epes only 25—were on a learning flight when a wing of the plane collapsed. It was Cary Epes' first flight.

An onlooker was Carlstrom's younger brother, Carl, who had just completed flight training.

Norfolk businessmen enviously eyed the flight school and tried several times to lure it across Hampton Roads. They offered use of the abandoned site of the Jamestown Exposition of 1907, fronting the water at Pine Beach.

At first Newport News resisted Norfolk's efforts, for it hoped to land several of the military bases which the Army and Navy were creating along the Atlantic. However, the Boat Harbor field was obviously too limited by its busy industrial surroundings to last long. In an effort to keep the field on the Peninsula, Tom Baldwin, its director, tried to buy another site near Buckroe Beach, but one key landowner wanted too much for the land. When the Armistice was signed in 1918, the field's days were over.

Several world records for speed and stunt flying were set in Curtiss's three years at the Boat Harbor. Instructor Eddie Stinson, who later manufactured the Stinson plane, set a record by looping the loop 22 times in succession. Such daredevil loops and dives were very big then, before training regulations outlawed needless hazards.

When Newport News businessmen learned that the Army would build aviation fields at Hampton, in Florida, and in California, they tried to get the Navy to take over Curtiss Field. However, the Navy decided in August 1917 to build its field on part of the Jamestown Exposition grounds, adjoining the new Norfolk Naval Base, now the biggest in the world. That was the end of Curtiss Field.

The Peninsula's aviation ambitions were soon rewarded by the Army's creation of Langley Field near Hampton.

Once the United States declared war on Germany on April 6, 1917, Newport News felt the overnight buildup of military bases it had hoped for. Tiny Curtiss Field was soon overshadowed by the rise of Army camps around Newport News—Camp Hill, Camp Stuart, Camp Morrison, and Camp Eustis. Five months after Congress had declared war against the Kaiser, the first of 200,000 American doughboys came to town on the C&O to encamp at Newport News and await transport overseas. The militarization of the Lower Peninsula has continued ever since.

Newport News' city fathers were embarrassed in 1917 by the gaudy houses of prostitution that had flourished almost since the town's beginning along old River Road, Eighteenth Street, and Warwick Avenue. People suddenly began to worry about the morals of the flyers and soldiers, though the city fathers had never been much concerned about the morals of the seamen who had come before them. So the city invoked a new federal law forbidding camp followers within five miles of a military base. That created hard times for Lula Ross and Kate Pleasants, who were the town's most celebrated madams. I wish Eddie Travis were here to tell me about it.

However you look at them, those were endearing years. You're bound to be impressed by the heroism of those early flyers. Curtiss Field helped give birth to the air age.

Buckroe Beach grew after trolley tracks were laid to it about 1900. Before World War I, bathers covered their limbs. The pavilion at left housed a dance floor and picnic tables. Syms-Eaton Museum

19. *Death on the Lusitania*

YOU can well imagine the concern in Newport News on the morning of May 8, 1915, when news of the sinking of the Lusitania appeared in the Daily Press. Aboard her were Albert L. Hopkins, president of the shipyard, along with Fred Gauntlett, a younger yard executive. Had they survived?

Terrible days of waiting followed. The four-stack British liner had been hit by a German submarine's torpedo as she crossed the Atlantic from New York, and the press reported many casualties. The passenger liner had gone down in only 18 minutes, leaving little time for the 1,500 passengers and crew to escape in lifeboats.

In a few days, the world learned that President Hopkins had indeed perished, but Gauntlett happily had survived. Also lost were 1,197 other people including millionaire Alfred Gwynne Vanderbilt.

Americans were incensed by the German act. Although the German embassy in Washington had advertised before the voyage that British ships were fair game for the German navy in the war, few people took the warning seriously. Besides, the Lusitania was a fast ship of modern, watertight construction. It was argued that she could outrun German submarines.

The year 1915 was a terrible one for President Woodrow Wilson. During his first term he had promised to keep us out of the war, but after 114 American lives had been taken in the Lusitania sinking, war sentiment in the U.S. intensified. "The Lusitania incident had much to do with preparing the way for U.S. entry," says the Columbia Encyclopedia.

Hopkins' drowning was described soon after the sinking in a memoir by Fred Gauntlett, sent to the U.S. consul at Queenstown, Ireland, where Gauntlett was landed by a rescue vessel the night of the sinking. He also sent a copy to James Plummer, New York representative of the shipyard, who sent it to Newport News for the benefit of Hopkins' associates.

"I was at lunch with Mr. Hopkins and Mr. S.M. Knox (president of New York Shipbuilding Company)," Gauntlett wrote, "when we were startled by a very heavy explosion, occurring on the starboard side of the vessel." The date was May 7, 1915, and the Atlantic weather was clear.

Hopkins and Knox rushed from the dining room, but Gauntlett lingered to instruct stewards to close the portholes. When he reached

The Cunard liner Lusitania was sunk by a German torpedo near the Irish coast on May 7, 1915. Of its 1,500 passengers and crew, 1,198 were drowned in the Atlantic.

the boat deck, he could find neither of the two older men. Gauntlett tried to board a lifeboat, but it was full. While being lowered, it went out of control and plunged into the sea. "The people were thrown either out of the boat altogether or into a struggling heap," Gauntlett wrote.

As the Lusitania listed perilously, Gauntlett went to his stateroom to look for Hopkins and his life preserver. He found Hopkins and his preserver gone and concluded he had already abandoned ship. Coming back on deck, he saw the ship was about to go under. If he delayed further he would be sucked down by the sinking hull.

"I slid down the deck," Gauntlett recalled, "and grabbed a boat davit to save myself from being thrown into the water, and climbing on the rail, swung myself by the fall from the deck and into a boat that was empty of people, and which no one had atempted to lower away."

The lifeboat deck went under before the boat could be released, and Gauntlett found himself swimming in the Atlantic. Thanks to his life jacket, he got to a collapsible lifeboat and managed to pull out his pocketknife to cut off its canvas cover. Then he and a ship's steward rescued Knox and 29 other survivors they found struggling in the sea. Soon their collapsible lifeboat was spotted and rescued by an Irish fishing vessel. Later that day, they transferred to a British tender, the Flying Fish, and were taken to Queenstown, Ireland, for medical treatment and rest.

Once ashore, Gauntlett frantically looked for Hopkins among the survivors being brought in. Eventually he concluded that

Hopkins was dead and had a handbill distributed in an effort to recover his body: "50 Pound Reward for the Recovery of the Body of Albert L. Hopkins, 1st Class Passenger. Age 42, Height 5 feet 10½ inches. Weight about 130 lbs., slight build, clean-shaven, dark hair."

To help identify the body, Gauntlett described Hopkins's clothes as "well-made, probably Rogers, Peet & Co. Tailors. Money and Papers in pockets, gold crest ring on finger." He requested the finder to notify him and the American counsel at Queenstown.

Gauntlett also chartered a tugboat and searched Irish coastal waters for bodies. At last on May 14—a week after the sinking—Hopkins' body was brought into Queenstown with 27 others recovered at sea by two British search vessels.

Gauntlett complained to the British about the slow search for survivors. A newspaper wrote that "Undoubtedly the vigorous protest put up by Americans, among them F. J. Gauntlett of New York and Newport News, is responsible for the collection of the additional bodies."

On receipt in Newport News of word that Hopkins' body had been recovered, the shipyard closed a half day. Hopkins' casket was returned to the United States and interred on June 5 at Glens Falls, N.Y., where the young yard president had been born and reared. At the shipyard, owner Henry E. Huntington named Homer L. Ferguson, who had been general manager, to be president.

Hopkins had spent most of his year as shipyard president in New York, close to Huntington. After Ferguson's accession, however, yard operations were firmly centered in Newport News.

Opponents of American involvement in the war questioned why the president of two American shipyards had been en route to Europe together on the Lusitania. One paper reported that the Newport News yard was

Youthful president Albert Hopkins, president of the Newport News Shipyard, was among Lusitania's casualties in 1915.

seeking contracts "to furnish the warring nations with armor plate." It was later revealed that Hopkins planned to visit Holland to examine Dutch submarine designs on which the yard had been invited to bid. It also came out that Hopkins had planned to confer with the German government on the status of two German liners that had sought sanctuary from British submarines in Newport News in 1915. They were the Prinz Eitel Friedrich and the Kronprinz Wilhelm, which had first been berthed at the shipyard before being tied up at Portsmouth Navy Yard. After the United States declared war against Germany in 1917, they became American transports.

Few shipyard veterans today remember the brief presidency of ill-fated Albert Hopkins. However, some give him credit for some of the yard's growth in his 21 years of yard service. He had come to the yard in 1894 as a government naval contractor, not long out of Rensselaer Polytechnic Institute. In 1898, he had joined the shipyard as assistant to superintendent Walter Post, who later became the yard's president.

In March 1914 Hopkins had succeeded Post as president—the fourth man to hold that position since Collis Huntington had started his Chesapeake Dry Dock and Construction Company—later Newport News Shipbuilding and Dry Dock—in 1886. His predecessors had been F.H. Davis, 1886-1888; C.B. Orcutt, 1889-1911; and Walter A. Post, 1911-1914.

As to Fred Gauntlett—the young man who survived the Lusitania—his is a happier story. Gauntlett continued as a ship yard Washington representative or lobbyist until he retired from the yard's service in 1938. He died in Washington in 1951, after countless interviews by writers reconstructing the Lusitania tragedy.

All his life Fred Gauntlett kept the pocketknife he had with him on May 7, 1915, when he cut the canvas cover from the empty lifeboat he clung to after the Lusitania sank. Often, when he came down from Washington to confer at the yard, he showed it to his coworkers.

"It saved my life," he said, and it was true.

Newport News Historical Committee

Payday at the shipyard each Friday brought long lines of workmen to pay windows behind administration building. Laborers preferred their pay in silver dollars.

20. *A Year that Changed the World*

In the annals of the Peninsula, no year stands as starkly historic as 1918.

I don't say that from memory but from the record. The year 1918 was the year of the terrible freeze that imprisoned all shipping for weeks in the Chesapeake. It was also the year of the great flu epidemic, which killed hundreds of soldiers in World War I camps on the Peninsula, plus civilians too. Finally, it was the year of the Armistice that ended World War I. That made America the world's most powerful nation.

I was three years old in 1918. My parents had just moved from Smithfield to a rented house on West Avenue, between Thirty-Second and Thirty-Third. The virulent flu nearly killed my mother, my brother Ran and me. Thanks to a local physician and a visiting Army doctor, we survived.

Apparently the cold 1917-18 weather helped to bring on the influenza and to worsen its effects, though the epidemic was worldwide. It was so bad in Europe that it influenced the Germans to throw in the sponge and surrender.

As a boy I heard old-timers talk so much about the Great Freeze that I feel I remember it. It started in the fall of 1917 and continued till the spring of 1918. At times you could walk across Hampton Roads or the James on the ice. Many daredevils tried.

My wife's grandmother was on her way from Urbanna to Norfolk in December 1917 to meet her Methodist preacher husband, but her boat was clogged in thick ice for several days off Lambert's Point. A government icebreaker finally got to it and rescued the passengers. Several were college students going home for Christmas.

Over in Gloucester, workers headed for the duPont ammunition plant at Penniman, just below Williamsburg, drove daily across the frozen York from Gloucester Point to Yorktown each day to get to work. Then, one day, the ice parted over the York channel and several workers and their car disappeared.

On the James River, in Charles City County, a similar disaster occurred. The car bore several workers headed for the day's stint at a Hopewell munitions factory.

Can you imagine Tidewater Virginia without drinking water? Pipes were frozen and nothing came out of city faucets. You had to find somebody who had a deep well.

One of the results of the freeze was the loss of the U.S. Navy collier, Cyclops. A new book about ship disappearances, "Without A Trace," describes how she loaded coal at Norfolk during the 1918 freeze, bound for the Caribbean. She had to break her way through heavy ice to get from Norfolk to the Capes, beyond which the ocean was clear.

The ship's crew reported that the strain on the Cyclops' hull could be heard as she broke her way out. That strain may have weakened her and caused her subsequent disappearance, somewhere between Virginia and the Caribbean.

On the heels of the freeze came the 1918 flu epidemic. Papers had described its ravages in Europe before it hit this country. Then, early in 1918, the Daily Press and the Hampton Monitor announced its outbreak in Peninsula camps.

Soldiers died so fast that coffins had to be made by hand for some of them. Many coffins bearing flu victims were shipped out each day on the C&O trains to the west.

Newport News was hemmed in during World War I by Army camps — Camp Morrison, Camp Stuart, Camp Hill, Camp Eustis. It also overflowed with shipyard workers, who had swarmed in from rural Virginia and North Carolina, living in crowded rooming houses. That helped create a real estate boom, leading to such projects as Hilton Village and Braxton and Perkins Courts.

It was real estate which attracted my father from Smithfield, before the United States entered the war in 1917.

Little Newport News was ill-prepared for such rapid growth, and it grew illogically. West avenue was the best residential neighborhood when the war started, but new-

Daily Press

The Red Cross aided soldiers departing Newport News in 1917 for European combat. Red Cross headquarters stood by the James at 24th Street, between the C&O depot and the city's Pier A.

A Year That Changed the World 105

Daily Press

Camp Hill stood east of Hilton in World War I to house soldiers in transit to or from Europe. After the war, barracks were torn down, but some Army warehouses remained.

comers who could afford it soon began to build on the Boulevard or the North End. The original city was soon hemmed in by the C&O, the shipyard, and the James River. It was poor city planning to build houses on narrow lots, as we now belatedly see.

I remember the close-packed black shanty area of Eighteenth Street and Jefferson Avenue, for as a little boy I once or twice accompanied my father when he collected rents from black tenants of Barrett Brothers, his real estate firm. Eighteenth Street had developed in the 1880s, when the C&O created the town. By 1918 white families had moved farther uptown, leaving it as a black rental tract, owned first by George Ben West and then by his heirs.

Ironically enough, Newport News' two most famous natives were born in such a transient black neighborhood in Newport News in 1918. They were Pearl Bailey and Ella Fitzgerald. And a third famous native novelist William Styron, saw the light that same year. He was born in Hilton Village.

Pearl Bailey tells in her autobiography "The Real Pearl," that she left Newport News as a baby. However, Ella Fitzgerald spent much of her youth here. Bill Styron lived here off and on till he finished college.

The flu diminished its virulence with the coming of summer in 1918. Hopes of victory in Europe rose that summer as our Yanks poured into France to swell General John J. Pershing's army. That's when General Pershing endeared himself to the French, announcing as he stepped ashore in France, "Lafayette, we are here."

Finally, on Nov. 11, 1918, came the news that Germany had sued for peace. I was a little over three years old, but I can remember the mood of elation that filled Newport News as the war ended. It was unfortunate that in 1919 the shipyard began a long, sad period of decline lasting till the mid-1930s, but most people overlooked that in their relief that "our boys" were coming home.

The doughboys' actual return wasn't until early 1919. That's the part I remember best. Newport News built the Victory Arch on Twenty-Fifth Street, and Governor Westmoreland Davis came down from Richmond to lead the applause as troops marched from their transports at the C&O piers up Twenty-Fifth Street, beneath the Victory Arch, to the waiting crowds along Newport News' streets.

A reviewing stand was built on the grounds of the Newport News Post Office and there Governor Davis, resplendent in cutaway, saluted the returning troops.

Photographs in the city's pictorial history *Endless Harbor* record the glory of that moment.

To see the soldiers and the bands, my father lifted me up on his shoulders. I was then only three and a half years old, but the memories of the parades, flags and band music are clearly etched in my consciousness.

Yes, 1918 is a year for Newport News to remember. If there'd been doubt before, it was clear in World War I that it was an important port. We survived the Great Freeze and Great-Epidemic to triumph in the Great Crusade.

By 1918 Newport News had become a name known around the world.

The Navy chose Hampton Roads as the base of its Atlantic fleet in World War I. Convoys sailed from the port, and destroyers from Hampton Roads patrolled Atlantic to destroy German submarines.

Daily Press

21. Memories of the First World War

WHEN I grew up in Newport News, World War I was a vivid memory. Four Army camps in the present city limits had to be demolished in the years after the Armistice was signed on November 11, 1918. Some Army barracks survived in town into the 1920s. A string of North End and Morrison warehouses, once leased to the Hiden Company for tobacco and other commodities, are still standing.

Easily the most interesting World War I holdover was the Hostess House at Camp Hill. The camp had occupied North End between 64th Street and the present James River Bridge approach on the river. The Hostess House stood close to the shipyard's new north entrance, at about 70th Street. In my youth it was used for dances and other civic events. Newport News then had few places for meetings.

The Army had built the Hostess House for wives and mothers of soldiers coming home from France after the Armistice. An old photograph shows the house as a sort of destitute House of Seven Gables, with wide porches. But I remember it as a pleasant nighttime dance hall, usually warmed by a hearth fire. It was torn down sometime around 1930 when the Camp Hill site was made into Huntington Heights, a residential area.

I was three years old when the Armistice was signed in 1918, but by the 1920s I ven-

Governor Westmoreland Davis and War Secretary Newton D. Baker sit in a reviewing stand by the postoffice building as troops return from Europe in 1919. Troop trains took them home.

107

Red Cross volunteers joined officials and military leaders in 1919 to welcome the 29th Infantry Division home from Europe. Newport News postoffice is in the background.

tured up Huntington Avenue from my house on 59th Street to play in the fields beside Hostess House. Further up Warwick Boulevard stood other World War I installations: Camp Alexander near Hilton, Camp Morrison near Oyster Point, and Camp Eustis on the James at Mulberry Island. It's the only one still going.

A fifth Newport News camp where soldiers awaited shipment overseas was Camp Stuart on Jefferson Avenue, near the Boat Harbor. Like Camps Hill and Morrison, it has disappeared.

Newport News was badly overcrowded in the war, and the terrible flu epidemic of 1918-19 was due partly to ill-heated barracks during that frigid winter (bodies of 37 victims were shipped on one train then). Shipyard workers increased from 7,000 in 1915 to 14,000 three years later. Many yard laborers had to rent bed space in downtown dining rooms or kitchens.

People need places to dance and play in wartime even more than in peace. A social center called the Tidewater Club was started in Braxton Court at 34th Street and the James River. Hostess houses were for social use of Camp Hill and Camp Morrison to entertain soldiers and their families. In the 19 months that the United States was at war in 1917-18, a total of 276,932 soldiers went through our town to fight in Europe. Many wives and mothers came to the posts to await their return, staying at Hostess Houses.

The buildup at the shipyard also required a lot of bedrooms. The War Shipping Board built the nation's first planned town at Hilton Village, spending $5 million to build 500 houses—nearly all still standing. The government also built the Shipyard Apartments from 46th to 50th Streets on the James. The yard provided barracks, tent colonies, and a few houses.

The yard in the war years turned out the battleship Pennsylvania and a half-dozen four-stack destroyers. (They were among 50 that the U.S. gave Great Britain in World War II, when Hitler threatened.) But the yard's major wartime task was to repair 1,000 U.S. and Allied ships, many damaged by German U-boats.

The Camp Hill Hostess House picture which accompanies this was taken in 1922, but I remember it as looking a lot better. Gazing out of its porch toward the James, you'd think you were in a Virginia Beach villa in those days. The living room had a gallery for dance chaperones, a large brick fireplace, and pine floors for dancing. Like all government wartime buildings, it had beaverboard instead of plaster. Personnel was apparently Red Cross and YWCA volunteers. The directress of the Camp Morrison Hostess House, Alice G. T. Sparhawk, wrote an account of her experiences after the war that reflects the problems faced by French war brides who had followed their soldier boys back to Newport News after the war.

"French war wives . . . have been sent to Camp Morrison in two installments," she wrote. The hundred French girls created "a gay and crowded Hostess House . . . they are now under the care of two Red Cross nurses, who have taken entire charge of them."

The last shipment was of 45 war brides, three babies fathered by GIs, and one determined French mother-in-law.

"The ship docked in the middle of a broiling July day," wrote Mrs. Sparhawk. "As the French girls stood together, . . . hot and perhaps depressed, . . . this comfortable elderly French woman sat in their midst, singing folk songs . . . and telling the girls how happy they would soon be in their own little American homes . . ."

The Hostess House staff had its hands full when a new and "lurid" shipment of women arrived. "The stories of the swift marriages and hurried departures from France were pitiful," Mrs. Sparhawk reported. "There are many tragedies among these ill-matched couples. Yet there are also many quiet and contented young wives who will make happy homes for their . . . husbands."

While the brides learned English at the Hostess House, their husbands were getting discharged at Camp Hill and or Camp Morrison. "The one excitement is when the husbands arrive from camp," the directress wrote. "Then there are shrill screams of joyful greeting as a trolley or taxicab brings a crowd of boys. The young couples are quickly mated, with the most open demonstrations of affection." Those mademoiselles from Armentieres had a way with them.

To welcome the returning American army, Newport News in 1918 built the handsome Victory Arch at 25th Street and West Avenue. (It was rebuilt several decades ago.) After a civic competition, an inscription by attorney Robert G. Bickford of Hampton was chosen for the arch:

Greetings with love to those who return:
A triumph with tears to those who sleep.

The Hostess houses were busiest in the months when the American Expeditionary Force returned. Transports landed 441,146 soldiers in 1918 and 1919 at Newport News. Many paraded up 25th Street under the Victory Arch, to be welcomed by Secretary of War Newton D. Baker and other officials on a

110 Memories of the First World War

grandstand alongside the Federal Building on West Avenue.

The whole town stopped work and people lined downtown streets as the soldiers marched.

The biggest day was May 25, 1919. On that day the 116th Infantry Regiment of the 29th Infantry Division—"Virginia's own"—debarked from the Navy transport Virginia and marched up 25th Street. Ahead of the regiment rode young girls on truckloads of flowers, which they strewed on the streets. Bands played, and the horses of the parade marshals threatened to bolt.

From the accounts of those who were there, it was an occasion never to be forgotten. Waiting relatives ran out into the street time and again to embrace sons or husbands

It must have been the happiest moment in all of Newport News' history.

Testimony of Newport News' pride was the Victory Arch built at 25th and West Avenue in 1919. Thousands of returning soldiers paraded through it on their way back to civilian life.

22. Songs of Lonesome Soldiers

SOLDIERS will do anything to kill time in camp. In 1918, when Newport News was full of homesick GIs, several poems and songs were written in World War I camps around the city which now and then come to light.

Geoffrey O'Hara was the best-known songwriter in town in those days. He wrote several World War I hit songs which crop up now and then. And recently the War Memorial Museum in Newport News showed me an amusing anonymous vilification in verse of my hometown, I had to clean it up for publication.

Now comes "Newport News Blues," a soldier's effusion published in sheet music in 1918 by Frederick V. Bowers Inc. of New York. The words are by Sgt. Hal Oliver and the music by Cpl. Willie Shifrin. It claims to have been "sung with great success by Frederick V. Bowers."

The cover of the sheet music is a night-time scene of Newport News' harbor, filled with warships steaming out of port under a full moon. The back sheet prints a photo of the supply division of Quartermaster Corps, Detachment 2, then stationed in Newport News. Apparently the songwriters belonged to that unit. They dedicated their song "to our Commanding Officer, Col. E. P. Orton."

"Newport News Blues" is no masterpiece. No wonder we've never heard of it! The first verse goes like this:

I've been around the world a bit, I seen 'bout all the sights,
I've heard a lot of melodies about the gay white lights.
But when I went to Newport News, I heard real Southern blues.
The blues is all that you can hear, down there in Newport News.

Then comes the chorus, with a slightly different tempo:

Oh! Newport News Blues is the latest fad,
Newport News Blues will surely drive you mad.
You start in to jazz, then you raz-ma-taz
Oh, way down South, in the land of cotton
Your Uncle Sam has not forgotten
You're away, away, far away from Broadway.
Newport News Blues is the fad down there.
They sing and dance that haunting melody.
Oh, when you're down in Newport News,
Why do they want to play that doggone blues?
The blues of Newport News.

The second verse suggests that Sgt. Oliver, who wrote the words, may have been an aspiring songwriter from somewhere up North. It goes thus:

I've travelled here, I've travelled there, from darkness to white lights,
But now I wish that I were back among the Southern nights,
For when I hear those darkies' voices chant that draggy blues,
I tell you, folks, I wish I were again in Newport News.

After that, the song repeats the chorus, "Oh, Newport News Blues is the latest fad," and so on. (I'm beginning to get enough of it already).

Bad as "Newport News Blues" is, it doesn't sound as direful as other wartime songs listed by Frederick Bowers. The cover of the song sheet gives one as "We're Going to Take the Germ out of Germany." If that isn't bad enough for you, how about "I'll Do Without Meat, I'll Do Without Meat, But I Can't Do Without Love?"

It gets worse. Bowers boasts he has published "Let Me Kiss the Flag Before I Die."

Daily Press

A troop transport docks at a C&O pier in Newport News to debark soldiers. In World War 2 another generation of fighting men went through the city to fight in Europe and the Pacific.

He also offers "Don't Trifle With a Soldier's Heart Unless You're Going to Love Him True." Another gem is "I'm Glad to Be the Mother of a Soldier Boy."

Just to show he wasn't partial to the South, I suppose, Bowers published a soggy ballad entitled. "I Wonder if She's Waiting in Her Old New England Town."

But "Newport News Blues" was on solid ground when it referred to black voices "chanting that draggy blues." For Newport News had a big black population, then as now, and blues music was widely sung.

When I grew up in those days, every up-to-date household in the North End had a piano—usually an upright but sometimes a baby grand. Most people also had a wind-up Victrola, and some had a newfangled radio so they could listen to Amos and Andy, Lowell Thomas and the Lucky Strike Hit Parade.

My own family was piano-centered. In our house on 59th Street, my mother whiled away a half-hour playing current hits or classical numbers she'd learned to peform as a girl in Smithfield or at Randolph-Macon in Lynchburg. "It's a way to relax," she used to say.

Those were the days of parlor favorites like "Fur Elise," "Traumerei," Chaminade's "Scarf Dance" and Fritz Kreisler's "Old Refrain." Mother also played popular things like "Maple Leaf Rag," "The Missouri Waltz" and music from World War I and the jazz era. The piano was covered with sheet music for songs like "Over There," "K-K-K-Katie" and "Yankee Doodle Dandy."

Mother's piano was an elderly upright my grandfather had given her many years earlier, and she loved it. Alas, mice loved it too. No matter how many traps we set, the little devils would hide out among the strings and hammers, nibbling away at the felt and glue that held it together.

In alarm, Mother called Gordon Weyburn, the piano tuner, "How can I get the mice out of my piano?" she pleaded. Gordon tried to help, but the mice continued to turn up their noses at traps and poisons. They preferred to eat piano glue.

Once a mouse died deep in the heart of the piano's bass notes. An awful stench spread over the dining room, but the corpse could not be found. We tried to stop breathing until it went away, but that didn't work. Other deaths followed. The piano became a mouse mortuary.

"Pauline," my father implored, "can't we get rid of that thing?" "No," Mother said firmly. "Papa gave it to me, and I'm attached to it." Besides, my three brothers and I by that time liked to bang away on its ancient keyboard. Mother had taught each of us the elements of piano before we studied other instruments.

The mice were finally evicted, and Mr. Weyburn repaired their damage. Then we younger Rouses began to perform music together, grouped around Mother at the keyboard. I sawed away at the violin, while my three brothers played saxophone, trumpet and drums. We dreamed of Ed Sullivan.

It was hard on neighbors, but they tolerated us. I suppose it was because many of their own children were studying music, too. Fifty-ninth Street at dusk sounded like Tin Pan Alley, for we had would-be vocalists in our midsts as well as instrumentalists.

But it was an affliction on husbands coming home from work and being assailed by such noise. "Sounds like 'Old Cow Died in the Mire,'" my father used to say, dismally.

When my three brothers and I went off to World War II, my mother had more time to play her piano. But when we got out of service after the war and came home to 59th Street, we found the old upright hopelessly out of tune. Mr. Weyburn had said it was so old that the strings would no longer hold their pitch. It stood there unused.

My brothers and I searched the classified columns, found a piano we could afford and bought it for Mother as a surprise. To avoid a return of mice, we chose a baby grand, reasoning that they couldn't climb up its legs to nest in the strings. It was a great moment. Mother again could whip out "Maple Leaf Rag." At 95 she's still playing, though less often and more briefly these days.

As it turned out, we Rouses never performed for Ed Sullivan, but others of our generation in Newport News achieved musical eminence. Even so, the pleasure we derive from music is worth all the lessons we took. I think I speak for many.

Yes, I miss a piano in the house. Sometimes I even have a loving thought for our dead musical mice. Obviously they enjoyed "The Maple Leaf Rag" as much as we did.

Daily Press

Sailors on the Government Dock at Old Point load sea stores for delivery to a warship in Hampton Roads. The tower of first Chamberlin Hotel, burned in 1920, is in background.

23. *Thomas Wolfe at Langley Field*

ONE of America's greatest novelists spent three months in Hampton Roads in 1918 and left an account of Hampton and Newport News. He was Thomas Wolfe, the Asheville, N.C., boy who was later to write *Look Homeward Angel* and other works which have immortalized him since he died in 1938.

Wolfe came to the Peninsula as a boy of 18 in June 1918 to work during his summer vacation from the University of North Carolina, where he had finished his sophomore year. He was in the same class with Paul Green and Jonathan Daniels. He later wrote about his experiences in "The Face of the War," a description of Peninsula events published in 1935.

Wolfe knew then that he wanted to be a writer. Turned down for World War I service for weak lungs, the 6-foot-3-inch beanpole decided to come to Hampton in June 1918 to get a civilian job at Langley. He spent a hot, uncomfortable month in the muddy wilds of rural, mosquito-ridden Hampton.

The highlight of Wolfe's Peninsula summer was his visit to a house of prostitution in Newport News. He described how he stood in line with soldiers waiting outside. He identified it as being "near the railroad tracks," presumably on 24th Street between Jefferson Avenue and Warwick Boulevard (now Terminal Avenue)—then the city's licensed prostitution area. Later the city closed the houses.

Wolfe had heard from former Chapel Hill schoolmates of high wages being paid in Virginia, so he set out, lured by "the fair promises of wealth. . . ." He wrote a friend of "the wait at Danville" in the railway station, "Richmond in the morning—Newport News—Ride across the sparkling bay," and the "electricity of war."

After visiting a North Carolinian who was serving in the Navy at Norfolk, Wolfe crossed Hampton Roads and got a job as a timekeeper at Langley, riding a horse around the field each day to record the work hours of laborers. After a few weeks' work at Hampton he became a supply checker on the C&O docks at Newport News.

"Meanwhile," writes one biographer, Andrew Turnbull, "he was fixing in his mind a variety of types from all over the country: Swedes from the Midwest, Jews from the sweatshops, Irishmen, Italians, Negroes, hunkies, Bowery bums." He wrote about them in his half-dozen widely-published novels.

After quitting his job at Langley on July 4, the gangling 18-year-old joined some Chapel Hill schoolmates for a weekend in Norfolk. He wrote this letter on the letterhead of the Atlantic Hotel at Norfolk (actually the YMCA) on July 6, 1918, to his mother in Asheville:

"Dear Mother,

". . . I have been working as time checker at Langley Field until the 4th. By that time I was consumed by mosquitos and bed bugs so, upon the persuasion of several of my school mates who are working here I decided to find more lucrative employment. Arriving in Norfolk day before yesterday, I went around to the Government Employment Agency. A young North Carolinian working there told me to go to work as a first class carpenter and told me if I would he would get me the job. So I start to work Monday at Porter Bros. who are building a big Quartermaster Terminal here. Will make about $7 a day if I can put my bluff across. Believe I can. Don't worry about me. I can always make a good living here. Whether I save it or not is a very great problem as everybody up here seems to have entered a conspiracy to see how much they can get out of you without making you squeal. It is rather hard to write home after ten hours labor but I will try to write one of the family once a week. I am sunburned to a tan from my sojourn at Langley Field. My stay there was a valuable experience and I made many friends who seemed genuinely sorry to see me go. My boss out there told me I could have a job any time I came back. . . ."

In his next letters Wolfe told of buying carpenter tools and working one day before his employer, Porter Brothers shipyard, found he had no carpentry experience and fired him. Wolfe sold the tools and went to work on the Newport News C&O piers, where troops and ammunition were being loaded for France.

While in Newport News Wolfe patronized a wartime house of prostitution. He wrote of "the waiting queue" outside. In an account that he published in 1935, he wrote:

"Over the bridge, across the railway track, down in the Negro settlement of Newport

Daily Press

Thomas Wolfe spent the summer of 1918 working at Langley and in Newport News, before he became a novelist.

News—among the dives and stews and rusty tenements of the grimy, dreary and abominable section, a rude shack of unpainted pine boards, thrown together with the savage haste which war engenders, to pander to a need as savage and insatiate as hunger, as old as life, the need of friendless, unhoused men the world over.

"The front part of this rawly new, yet squalid place, has been partitioned off by rude pine boards to form the semblance of a lunch room and soft drink parlor. Within are several tables, furnished with a few fly-specked menu cards. . . ."

"Meanwhile, all through the room, the whores, in their thin and meager mummers, act as waitresses, move patiently among the crowded tables and ply their trade. The men, who are seated at the tables, belong for the most part to that great group of unclassed creatures who drift and float, work, drift, and stare, are now in jail, now out again, now foul, filthy, wretched, hungry, out of luck, riding the rods, the rusty box cars of a freight, snatching their food at night from the boiling slum of hoboes' jungle, now swaggering with funds and brief prosperity—the floaters, drifters, and halfums, that huge, nameless, houseless, rootless, and anomalous class that swarm across the nation...."

"As for the women who attended them, they were prostitutes recruited, for the most part, from the great cities of the North and Middle-West, brutally greedy, rapacious, weary of eye, hard of visage, over-driven, harried and exhausted...."

Wolfe recognized one prostitute from Chapel Hill. She asked him derisively to give her love to the folks back home.

The young writer described in detail the C&O pier on the James in Newport News where he worked as a material checker. He wrote that its cargo was "crated woods containing food and shot provender of every sort—canned goods, meat, beans, fruits, and small arms...."

In September 1918, as school time approached, Thomas Wolfe took the C&O to Richmond and there transferred to return to Asheville before re-entering the university. His biographer says he was "matured and strengthened by his show of independence." Barely a month later came word that his beloved older brother, Ben, was dying of pneumonia in Asheville. Tom Wolfe was learning life could be hard.

Wolfe's play, "The Return of Back Gavin," was produced by the Carolina Playmakers in March 1919, soon after World War I ended. His writing then led him to Harvard and New York, where "Look Homeward, Angel," was published in 1929. In the next nine years he produced a torrent of novels and short stories. His death at 38 following an operation at Johns Hopkins in 1938 ended his meteoric career.

So far as Wolfe's biographies show, he never came back to the Peninsula. But his work greatly impressed young William Styron, the Newport News writer who, along with Hemingway and Truman Capote, shows influences of Wolfe's vision of the beautiful but tawdry world he lived in.

The dirigible Roma, bought by the Army from Italy, was reassmbled and based at Langley Field in the fall of 1921. She crashed and burned three months later at Norfolk, taking 34 lives.

Syms-Eaton Museum

24. *Washington Avenue in Wartime*

I REMEMBER nothing of World War I until the soldiers came marching home a few months after the Armistice. Then I recall being hoisted onto my father's shoulders so I could wave to the doughboys, above the crowd. Once peace returned, the shipyard slowed down and real estate went to hell—but that's another story.

It's hard to separate what you remember from what you've been told, but I clearly recall many events of the 1920s, after I started school. The James River was crowded with steamers in those years, waiting to dock at the C&O or to be repaired at the shipyard. About 1919 my family moved to 59th Street, but Washington Avenue remained the center of city life, and it sticks firmly in my consciousness.

Nearly every major Newport News store was on Washington Avenue, along with City Hall, the Academy of Music, and the town's first three banks—the First National, Citizens and Marine, and Schmelz Brothers. It was the place to be.

In memory, I can walk from Twenty-Fifth Street to the shipyard, along the thriving Washington Avenue of the 1920s. It was full of businesses and people. Most of the stores were locally owned, founded by men—Levinsons, Barclays, Motleys, Nachmans, Monfalcones, Epeses—whose enterprise built the city. Some have descendants in the Peninsula, though most of their stores have changed names or closed.

Those were the days of direct dealings. Store owners like the Nachmans were visible in their department store everyday. They knew customers and workers by name. I remember the Nachmans' son, Herbie, gassing with the blonde at Nachman's perfume counter. (Cosmetics salesgirls were always pretty, wore plunging necklines, smelled good, and looked like they'd just come from a party.) In Nachman's soda shop at lunch, you'd see many of Newport News' movers and shakers. Other tycoons ate at the Bide-a-Wee Tea Room or even Woolworth's, where one Navy admiral bellied up to the counter almost every working day.

Shipyard executives like Bill Blewett and Admiral Rawlings ate at a big table in the Warwick Hotel dining room. They rolled down like clockwork each day in the company limousine, joining their golf and poker pals to

Crowds jam Washington Avenue in Newport News in 1919 after 29th Infantry Division returned from Europe. Stores lining the avenue from the C&O to shipyard made it a shopping hub.

tease each other and talk politics over steaks. People called them "the Big Shots."

Washington Avenue seemed broad enough then, even though trolleys ran down the center and cars parked along its curbs. Besides, cars were few and went slowly. No need for stoplights till later. Most people came to work by streetcar, including Sam Plummer, president of First National. Mrs. Homer Ferguson, wife of the shipyard president, crept along in an electric car which glided quietly if slowly.

I remember Reyner's Ship Chandlery at 25th and Washington, for it had vegetable, fruit, and fish counters on the sidewalk in European style. Another such store stood at 28th and Washington. There you got your streetcar transfers. There also stood the First National Bank, where the shipyard kept its money. The Bide-a-Wee Tea Room was a few doors away.

In gloomy, ill-lit offices above the bank (60-watt bulbs were standard then) were the city's most prestigious lawyers. People spoke of "the First National crowd" and "the Citizens-Marine crowd," to designate rival banking and business groups.

Drugstores smelled good, and I remember Gorsuch's and Pennybacker's, especially. Milkshakes were 10 cents and made from real milk, ice cream, and chocolate. Mrs. Scott Copeland, who came from Richmond, complained to one Newport News soda jerk that milkshakes sold for only a nickel in Richmond. "Then you'll just have to go back to Richmond, lady," said the impertinent young man.

My favorite civic edifice was the schmalzy, ornate Academy of Music, which was pulled down about 1931 to make way for the art deco Paramount Theater, still surviving. The other theaters were the Palace, Rialto, Imperial, Cameo, and Olympic. I believe the latter was renamed the James, continuing to operate until recently.

Behind Epes Stationery store, Barclay's Jewelry, and the Broadway Shoe Store was

Newport News Historical Committee

Soldiers returning from Germany in 1919 parade up Washington Avenue, avoiding trolley tracks. Soon afterward the Army deactivated all wartime Newport News camps except Fort Eustis.

the Mennonite Market, whose entrance was on 30th Street. There Warwick County Mennonites in somber clothes each Wednesday and Saturday sold meat, produce, and eggs. Their stuff cost more, but it was worth it.

The sporting fraternity hung out at Monfalcone's News, next to Epes Stationery, and at Roy Charles' confectionary. The radio in Monfalcone's was always tuned to baseball or football games. It was the only Washington Avenue store to stay open on Sunday in that blue-law era. That was because it sold newspapers, a perishable commodity. Its stacks of the Daily Press and out-of-town papers were gobbled up soon after church, for most townspeople came downtown to worship. Monfalcone's was fortunately situated close to the Baptist, Methodist, Presbyterian, Episcopal, and Catholic churches.

Some parents wouldn't let their children read the funnies till they'd been to Sunday school and church. Even Episcopalians then viewed Sunday as a sombre day of quiet contrition. (Nobody was expected to work except black cooks, who came to work and prepared a big Sunday dinner for you before taking the afternoon off.)

Some of my earliest memories of Newport News center around the Casino grounds, which have now been largely built up. Billy Sunday held a revival there, and Fourth of July celebrations took place there. On Casino bluff you promenaded and gazed out on the busy James, crowded with ships.

Nearer shore were the Warwick Machine Company pier, about 27th Street, and Pier A, at 25th Street. The James River Line's day boat and night boat both docked at Pier A, as did the Smithfield passenger boat and Captain A.F. Jester's mail boat, the Oneita. Harbor tugs to assist James River ships also operated from Pier A, along with produce boats from Isle of Wight, Nansemond, Warwick, and other counties. I can just see the boatmen standing on their gunwales, handing up produce for inspection by buyers on the dock.

Except for the Casino, the only park in downtown Newport News was Washington Square, a half-block of grass on Washington Avenue between 25th and 26th Streets. I believe it was owned by Philip W. Hiden, one-time mayor and leading businessman, who later sold it for stores. When I was little it was a well-used square with a few shrubs, trees, and benches. On its 28th Street side was a kiosk for people waiting to transfer from one streetcar to another. That was because the line which operated to Hilton Village intersected there with the line which ran to Hampton and Old Point. That was cheap travel.

When I left Newport News for college in 1933, I suddenly learned that the hometown I thought so fine was disdained by others. A Southsider who lived briefly in our town liked to wisecrack that Newport News was the only place he knew "where people built slums by design."

It took awhile to get reconciled to the fact that my hometown didn't strike other people as the Parnassus I thought it to be. Its poor city plan and the auto age hurt it seriously when a great exodus left the downtown a ghost of its former self.

But Newport News remains one of the best ports along the Atlantic. With time, the downtown area can be redeveloped. Newport News has a future.

25. *Saloons and Bordellos*

UNTIL saloons were abolished by Virginia law in 1916, lower Newport News had its share of them. They catered to sailors from ships which called at our port, and they gave the town a garish reputation, even though most residents were staid indeed.

The saloons were concentrated along Washington and Huntington Avenues, between Twenty-Third and Twenty-Fifth Streets, close to the C&O docks. Along with them went the city's licensed houses of prostitution, which lined Twenty-Fourth Street from downtown over to Warwick (now Terminal) Avenue.

I've often heard old-timers talk of those days. What we got in its place was Prohibition, which got a bad name because of the lawlessness it bred. Finally, in Franklin Roosevelt's day, the nation made a compromise, which attempted to avoid either extreme. The resulting ABC system seems to me to work well, now that we have liquor by the drink.

Industrial America grew fast after the Spanish-American War. American commerce was expanding over the world, which brought us into competition with European industry. We needed a bigger navy and a standing army so that we could "walk softly and carry a big stick," as Teddy Roosevelt put it. Big business rode high, unhampered by income tax till Congress imposed one in 1913.

That was the era in which lower Newport News was a sailors' delight.

I suppose it was a consequence of the rough capitalism that Collis Huntington had brought here in 1881, when he built his C&O terminals and started a town where Civil War chaos had just been. Large numbers of freed blacks, first attracted to the Peninsula by federal military bases in the Civil War, were congregated in areas like Hell's Half-Acre, near Eighteenth Street, and Bloodfield, on lower Jefferson Avenue.

Hampton, Phoebus, and Yorktown had their shanty-towns in those days, too.

The C&O and the yard lured the ships to Newport News. The ships brought the sailors. And the sailors attracted saloons and honky-tonks. Actor James Barton worked in one bar on Twenty-Fourth before he became Jeeter Lester in "Tobacco Road" on Broadway. The Irish mimic Walter Kelly had a bar on Twenty-Fifth, where he developed his "Virginia Judge" routine for vaudeville. Saturday nights downtown were riotous.

Saloons and Bordellos 123

Syms-Eaton Museum

A sign on Mellen Street in Phoebus proclaims one of the area's many saloons before national prohibition in 1916 closed them. Many catered to seamen from ships in the area.

Those were also violent years on the waterfront. Seamen were sometimes robbed while ashore and drunk. Some were even shanghaied: carried unconscious to a ship to become a crew member, whether they wanted to or not.

Knifings were common, for pistols were few then. The old-fashioned straight razor was the weapon, aimed at the heart, throat, or carotid artery. Weekends were busy for the police and hospitals. The Daily Press each Sunday would describe last night's bloodbath.

Gradually, public opinion began to change Newport News. Churches and citizens began to try to improve things. One man who did a lot to improve it was Charles C. Berkeley, known as "Captain Charlie." He was a lawyer who served as commonwealth's attorney from 1908 till 1926. He died in 1949 at the Kencoughtan Veterans Facility.

Born in Staunton and educated at VMI, he went to Lincoln, Neb., to read law in William Jennings Bryan's law office. Like the "great commoner," Mr. Berkeley was always a friend of the underdog. After he served in the Spanish-American War, he came back to town and hung out his shingle.

Lawyers like William E. Carleton of Newport News and Judge Robert Armistead, who got their start in Captain Berkeley's law office, remember him well. He was hot-tempered, often vitriolic, and unconventional. But he had courage, and he never hesitated. He often rode a motorcycle. He was an ex-soldier, and he never forgot it.

To help get himself elected commonwealth's

attorney, he had to post two or three friends at each city ballot box in 1916 to keep the opposition from stuffing it against him. The opposition even brought over boatloads of men (women couldn't vote) from Norfolk and Portsmouth to vote against Captain Berkeley, but he won.

Berkeley believed in discipline. He made his children sleep with open windows in winter and sing "The Star-Spangled Banner." He loved military life and VMI. When a fellow lawyer remarked that VMI was "just a prep school," Captain Charlie nearly exploded. (He had played on the VMI football team, though slight, and was a track star.)

Once he and attorney J. Winston Read became so incensed with each other in Newport News Corporation Court that they jumped onto a table and mixed it up. It took four policemen to part them. Judge T.J. Barham fined each man $50 for contempt of court and proceeded with the case.

When Berkeley became commonwealth's attorney in 1908 he found the city exercised little control over the health of prostitutes in its licensed bordellos on Twenty-Fourth Street. So he had City Council push through a requirement that they be examined by the City Health Office on Twenty-Fifth Street each week. One resident remembers seeing the gaily-dressed floozies walking to their examination and waving happily to passers-by. They didn't mind publicity.

Newport News changed from a horse-and-wagon village to an automobile town in Berkeley's 18 years as commonwealth's attorney. Runaway horses were frequent when cars first began to travel city streets. A few businesses continued to make horse-and-wagon deliveries in the 1930s. I remember horse-drawn ice wagons, farm carts, and delivery wagons in North End in those years.

The adoption of the 18th Amendment by Congress in 1918 created huge law-enforcement problems in Newport News. The profits in liquor attracted normally lawful people to become distillers, bootleggers, and rum-runners. Makeshift stills operated around the city. As a boy in the North End, I often found active or defunct stills along Briarfield Road and in the Newmarket area, whose woods then attracted boys with beebee guns, like my brothers and me.

Commonwealth's Attorney Berkeley once

Coast artillery officers at Fort Monroe relax at the Casemate Club, created before 1893 within the moated structure. Many Army leaders of the World Wars were at Monroe during their career.

Casemate Museum

Saloons and Bordellos 125

Syms-Eaton Museum

When saloons were outlawed, some became soft drink bars. Lancer's Confectionery on Mellen Street in Phoebus offered sodas, candy, cigars, and a slot machine.

had to call on the Coast Guard to prevent Newport News tugboats from visiting rum-runners off the Virginia Capes, beyond the three-mile limit, to secrete bootleg liquor back to town. Berkeley learned of one such mission just before Christmas. He called the Coast Guard, and the jig was soon up.

Prohibition gradually tamed Newport News, as it did many other American towns—especially those serving sailors. By the time the 1930s came along, the saloons were gone and houses of prostitution were dying out. The enfranchisement of women undoubtedly had a lot to do with the improved public morality.

Newport News wasn't unique in this, for America in the 30s was giving up its old free-and-easy ways. Governor Harry Byrd had imposed severe fiscal morality on the state of Virginia, and Bishop James Cannon, a Methodist prelate, and a host of revivalists were denouncing liquor, beer, wine, card-playing, and even ballroom dancing. A few diehards even refused to read Sunday newspapers because they felt them a violation of the Bible's "day of rest."

I suppose one conclusion to all of this is that excess breeds excess, as they say in political science. Certainly mankind avoids the straight course to salvation, zig-zagging instead from permissiveness to puritanism and back again.

I'm glad Captain Charlie Berkeley and his generation helped clean up Newport News, but I still enjoy hearing about the town's wicked days. It was sinful, all right, but it was full of primal juices of life.

26. *Stars of the Academy of Music*

IT was curtain time in the Academy of Music. Into the orchestra pit strode the conductor, Professor Aage Schmidt. Down went the house lights and up went the asbestos curtain—a profusion of painted pink roses surrounding advertisements on Benson-Phillips, Epes Stationery, and other businesses.

Then, with the audience hushed and the Professor haloed in the Academy's spotlight, the overture began. While painted likenesses of Franz Schubert and Richard Wagner gazed down from the proscenium, the audience rapturously awaited the opening strains of "Blossom Time."

The scene was Newport News about 1922, but could have been Norfolk, Nashville, Grand Rapids, or almost any other American city in the early Twenties. For that was the heyday of theatrical touring, and Virginia's cities were part of a circuit radiating from New York into the stagestruck hinterland of America. Until the movies killed "the road" after World War I, no celebrities exuded a more potent magic than the great stars of Marilyn Miller's day.

Virginia, which never frowned on theatricals as early New England did, drew many touring shows. After the C&O was built to Newport News in 1881, the peninsula became accessible to road shows from New York via Washington, Richmond and other stops. At first they performed in Johnson's Academy of

Author's collection

'Blossom Time' at the Academy of Music dealt with the life of Franz Schubert.

Stars of the Academy of Music 127

Author's collection

A popular musical at the Academy was 'The Prince of Pilsen.' When talking movies came along in the 1920s, touring plays grew fewer and a movie house replaced the Academy.

Music at 2611 Washington Avenue, a primitive affair. But after the Academy of Music was built in 1900, the shows came there.

The ambitious theatre was built at Thirty-Third and Washington, where the Paramount Theatre now stands. It didn't look like much outside, but the inside was rich with red velvet, gilt and mural decorations. Built by Alfred Withers of Gloucester for $94,000, it held nearly 1,600 people on its main floor, balcony and peanut gallery. Like European opera houses, it was built to place viewers as close to the stage as possible. It was a genuine opera house, baroque and glamorous.

I remember the Academy well, for it was a lively place in the 1920s. I saw minstrels, magic shows, and a string of traveling dramas and musicals there. And I saw two early movie spectacles, "Ben Hur" and "The Big Parade," which had their own live orchestral accompaniment. Soon after that, talkies like "The Patriot" and "The Jazz Singer" put the Academy out of business. It was torn down in 1931 and replaced by a movie theater.

The Academy enveloped you in a rosy, make-believe world even before the show started. In a simple industrial town like Newport News in the 1920s, it was an oasis of elegance, in spite of all those peanut hulls that were scattered from the gallery at each show.

My first memory of that theatre was a performance of "King Lear," done by the Ben Greet Players, a popular New York company of Shakespearian players. Between the scenes of that somber tragedy, kettle drums pounded ominously in the dark. I can hear them now.

But most of my Academy memories were upbeat: performances of Victor Herbert musicals, magicians pulling rabbits out of hats, and comedies of the "Abie's Irish Rose" vintage. Sometimes I went with my parents and sat in orchestra seats. Sometimes I went with broth-

Author's collection

The stage of the Academy of Music resembled that of Richmond's Mozart Academy. The building stood at 33d and Washington and was Newport News's principal auditorium after 1900.

ers or friends to the gallery, where seats were ten cents to a quarter. The peanuts were extra.

The late Harry Reyner, mayor of Newport News, was a great Academy fan and rarely missed a show. His favorites were the minstrels brought to town by Al G. Fields and the Primrose-Dockstader company, which were celebrated troupes in the Academy's boom years. They would come into the C&O depot on Twenty-Third Street, put up at the nearby Warwick ("Most luxurious hotel south of Washington, D.C.") and then parade up Washington Avenue in the afternoon to work up enthusiasm for the matinee. Washington Avenue resounded to their sliding trombones, their brassy cornets, and their snappy drums as the high-stepping minstrel men strode from Twenty-Fourth to Thirty-Fourth Street.

Many stars came to the Academy in its 30 years. Hairston Seawell, who has written about it, says that such stars as Al Jolson, Maude Adams, Otis Skinner, Maxine Elliott, Eleanor Robson (late Mrs. August Belmont), Grace George, Nat Goodwin, Anna Held, DeWolfe Hopper, and Edna Wallace Hopper were among them.

Before the United States entered World War I, the German contralto Mme. Schumann-Heinck sang there. She began by singing "The Star Spangled Banner" for her son in the American army and then sang the German anthem for a son in the German army.

My memories of the Academy have dimmed a little, but I remember that you climbed two flights of broad stairs from the Washington Avenue entrance lobby to reach the orchestra level. In lieu of the elegant buffets and bars which big city opera houses offer for between-the-acts refreshments, the Academy had only a dinky confectionary which you could enter both from the street and the theatre lobby. That's where the peanuts were sold.

George B.A. Booker, the Academy's manager, was a good showman. He offered a popular Wednesday matinee for school children. It was scheduled to start at 3:05, which allowed downtown children a few minutes to get from school to the theatre. I can remember how we ran to get in our seats by curtain time.

The Academy had many memorable productions, most of them before my day. Fritz Leiber performed in "Julius Caesar," Chauncey Olcott in "Edmund Burke," and Madame Helena Modjeska in "Macbeth." In summers a stock company performed, with Charles Coburn as leading man and Edward R. Arnold as the heavy. Both later became familiar in the movies.

Eddie Travis, who covered theatrical events for the Times-Herald in those days told me later that when Fritz Leiber was rehearsing his "To be or not to be" speech for "Hamlet" one night at the Warwick Hotel, an irate guest called the night clerk. "Tell that guy to make up his mind whether to be or not to be," the guest shouted. "I need some sleep."

The minstrel shows that delighted horse-

and-buggy America were training grounds for talent. W.C. Fields, Al Jolson, Lou Holtz, and George Jessel all came to Newport News with those companies, performing onstage as blackface comedians in response to lines from the straight man, Mister Interlocutor. Jolson repeated some of his hits in his early talking movie, "The Jazz Singer."

Today blackface acts are ruled out as racist, but in those days blacks as well as whites flocked to them. The humor wasn't necessarily divisive.

When the red-nosed Fields was checking into the Warwick Hotel once, he shook up the desk clerk by making two fountain pens disappear by sleight-of-hand while signing the register—a trick he had learned as a magician. Then he calmly produced both pens from thin air and triumphantly signed "W.C. Fields."

One of the Academy's biggest nights was its premier of "The Birth of a Nation" in 1914. The last half of the film depicted the Civil War, and it attracted the last Peninsula survivors of the Confederacy. "They walked in, bent over their canes, and were given seats close to the front," Eddie Travis wrote. "Then, at the point where the action called for the orchestra to burst into 'Dixie,' the old boys forgot the canes. Cheering and yelling, they stood up on the seats during the entire sequence." For a moment they were young again.

After talking movies in the late 20s killed "the road," many academies of music in

The plain exterior of Academy of Music hid an interior of gilt, red velvet, and mural decorations.

America were converted to movie houses. Van Wyck's Academy of Music in Norfolk became the Wells Theatre, which has just been revived in downtown Norfolk. Unfortunately for us, however, the Newport News Academy was demolished. So far as I can learn, few photographs or playbills survive to tell of its 30-year life.

But for those of us who knew it, the schmaltzy old Academy will never die.

Daily Press

Paramount Theatre was built in 1931 in art deco style to replace Academy of Music. Gladys Lyle was its organist, providing 'sing-alongs' and intermission music.

Syms-Eaton Museum

After World War I, the nation became more militarized. Here the Navy's Atlantic fleet steams past Fort Monroe. Small ship at center is presidential yacht Mayflower.

IV.
A Calm
Between
Two Storms
1919–1940

131

Stonewall Jackson School at 47th and Huntington was an early Newport News elementary school, built in the 1920s. Marguerite Wilson was its long-time principal.

27. Hurrah for Jackson School!

TODAY's children, jammed into school buses twice a day, are missing a lot of the fun I had ambling to and from Stonewall Jackson School back in the 1920s.

Oh, I know many kids live too far to walk, but it seems to me that some can. In my day, getting to school was half the fun. Between Fifty-Ninth Street, where I lived, and Forty-Seventh Street, where Jackson School stood, you accomplished a lot of things. You chased girls, bought penny candy at North End Pharmacy, and put coins on the street car tracks to let the trolley wheels squash them.

Childhood has a romantic vision and you as an adult remember its details as bigger or better than they actually were. I realized how I'd romanticized Stonewall Jackson when I went back as a grownup. What a dinky place it was! The halls had narrowed and the rooms had shrunk. How could I ever have thought it so great?

Nowadays, almost 60 years after I first entered Carolyn Harrell's first grade in 1921, it seems unrelievedly rosey. Like a sundial, memory records only the sunny hours. There were lots of pretty girls, like Mary Diggs, Helen Hankins, Jane Wilton and Nancy and Frances Lee Parker. And there were marbles and fights and volleyball games at lunchtime.

After you ate your bag lunch (no cafeteria when I started) you could run over to Turner's Pharmacy and buy candy. If your chocolate was pink inside instead of white, you got a freebie. Mr. Turner was very patient as we big spenders decided how many Mary Janes, Tootsie Rolls, and cream mints we wanted.

Boys got crushes on their teachers, and I had a violent one for Eunice Harmon, who married Piggie Davis. But I gave her up in the fifth grade for Helen Smith, now Mrs. Stuart White. She taught us how to make five- and six-pointed stars, and she wore red dresses. I knew she liked me when she let me go outside and clean the erasers. A great moment!

After Carolyn and Lena Harrell, I advanced to Grace Jones, Viola Colonna, Pauline Miley, Mrs. Philip T. Marshall, Florence Mirmelstein, Lillian Todd and Hazel Wrench. But I can't remember my math teachers, and I hope they can't remember me.

Over this classy lyceum reigned Marguerite Wilson, the principal. I've learned to love her; but she scared the hell out of us in the 1920s. She had a saintly face and stern eyes, like an Indian. She was young but she meant business.

One year we had Ethel Taylor as principal. I

vexed her so much once that she grabbed my shoulders and shook me. "If you do that again, young man, I'll shake you," she said. All the time she was shaking me so my teeth chattered.

Wallace Hiden was the school cut-up. Once in class he used the word "bedraggled," pronouncing "BED-raggled." He reported that Martin Luther "irrigated" the Pope, instead of "irritated." Describing burials in India, he reported that "The wife is often inferred with the husband." He knew what he was doing, I think, but we laughed.

Supervisors often visited school to see how we were doing. Ella Hayes played Victrola records of Galli-Curci singing "Carry Meh Back to Old Vehjeen-ya," and Charles Hoster gave us calisthenics that stret-t-t-t-tched the muscles. Mrs. Allene Cox taught us Locker method writing, but I was left-handed.

The most exotic visitor was a low-slung New England lady named Idella Berry, who rolled up to school in a Franklin—a luxury car that went the way of the Pierce-Arrow, Packard and Durant. She had New England legs that were the same size all the way down, and a cultivated voice. She addressed us in a Bostonian baritone as "gulls and buoys." And she forbade teachers to call children by nicknames. She thought they degraded people, like Pretty Boy Floyd and Baby Face Nelson.

I wrote an article for The Times-Herald ten years later about her aversion for nicknames, and the Associated Press picked it up. Several editorial writers across the nation wondered in print why anybody named "Idella" wouldn't want a nickname. They had a point.

My big moment in Stonewall Jackson came when Eunice Harmon picked me as the bridegroom for the May Day parade of city schools about 1923. The bride was Reba Knox, who later moved north, and the rest of the class were bridesmaids, groomsmen and wedding guests. My mother made me a black suit and a black stovepipe hat.

I was still in Jackson School when Lindbergh flew to Paris in 1927 and Richard Byrd hopped the ocean. I remember the shipyard whistles that blew to celebrate their arrival. But I had gone on to the seventh grade at John W. Daniel when the stock market crashed in 1929. Those were rough times in Newport News, already hard hit by the scrapping of ships in the Washington Disarmament Conference.

Jackson School was next door to the North End firehouse, which served an area then developed to Sixty-Fourth Street. We loved to hear the fire bells clang and the big red fire engine roaring up the street. At lunchtime we boys would repeatedly examine the engine close up, hub caps and all. I had a big argument with Quincy Holt about how fast the engine would go. I claimed it went 60 miles an hour. "Impossible," said he. "That's a mile a minute."

We took history seriously. George Washington's portrait adorned classrooms, and we faithfully noted the birthdays of the founding fathers, especially Virginians. A lot of us helped plant a tree each Arbor Day, with the chorus singing:

> *I think that I shall never see*
> *A poem lovely as a tree.*

One of our learning devices was the Music Memory Contest, which Miss Ella Hayes put on every year or so. We listened to "The Bell Song" from "Lakme" and similar exotica so we'd develop musical taste. Then we went to the high school auditorium to hear live performers do them, unannounced, and to fill out a questionnaire identifying each. If you got them right you got a certificate.

Sex rears its head early, and it cropped up at Jackson in the way the boys chased and teased the girls. What James Thurber called "the war between the sexes" clearly starts with the eight-year-old male pulling the hair or stealing the bookbag of the eight-year-old female. It gets better.

This "courtship" flourished especially during our daily walks to and from school. We North End scholars streamed down Huntington Avenue each morning like Coxey's army, diked out in our wool caps, argyle socks, and Buster Brown shoes. Often boys ganged up on girls. A few girls fought back. I remember two or three charming ladies today, who could hold their own in any playground wrassle.

Boys also pursued girls by seizing their berets and hanging them up a telephone pole, forcing the indignant girls to climb up and retrieve them. A great little climber was Kay Aldridge, who came from Northern Neck. She had pigtails and skinny legs, and we called her "Village."

She became a top model for John Robert Powers' agency in New York and appeared on countless magazine covers before she married a Hollywoodite. Now Mrs. Richard Tucker of Camden, Maine, she returns now and then to visit friends. She owes a lot to her pole-climbing in Newport News.

I hate to think what today's kids miss on their long bus trips. Do they have the fun we did? As an old Stonewaller, I doubt it.

Casemate Museum

Football became the top school and military sport in the 1920s. Fort Monroe's team practiced on parade ground alongside barracks and ancient live oaks.

28. *The Gold Coast of the James*

SO the North Enders are banding together to save what's left of that Newport News suburb? I read it in the Daily Press, and it took me back to the days when people called Huntington Avenue "the Gold Coast," lined with the mansions of tycoons who helped expand the one-time village in the 1900s into Virginia's fastest-growing city.

It's slowed down now, but Newport News before 1945 seemed about to catch up in size with Roanoke and even Norfolk. I'm speaking of the busy years, when the shipyard was launching huge liners and aircraft carriers when F.D.R. saw that we might need to fight against Germany and Japan.

Those were days when Homer Ferguson ran the yard and Lloyd Noland Sr. was spreading indoor plumbing through the rural South. Saxon Holt—another North Ender—was lieutenant governor and a political power. Philip W. Hiden was a warehouse tycoon, and the C&O each night dragged long trains full of coal and cargo eastward through North End to its terminals, there to ship them abroad.

I was young and easily impressed, but North End then seemed bound to succeed. People had maids, and a few had chauffeurs (they called them "drivers.") Shipyard executives went to lunch at the James River Club in limousines after the club started in the early 1930s.

Today Huntington Avenue—North End's onetime pride—seems a banquet of leftovers. Gone is yesterday's confidence, born of the belief that America would prosper endlessly. In those years the Peninsula's wealthiest families lived in European-style mansions with porte-cocheres and the North End waterfront bulged with replicas of Berkeley and Westover plantation houses. We were blessed.

It's the people I remember best. Homer Ferguson was a figure of earthy charm, who could talk as easily to an illiterate welder as he did with Henry E. Huntington, who had succeeded his Uncle Collis as chairman of the yard and chief stockholder of the C&O. Like any good boss, Ferguson knew most of his workers by name or face. What's more, he could cuss with the best of them.

The Fergusons lived at 57th and Huntington and Mrs. Ferguson was often to be seen putt-putting down the avenue in her electric car. It had vases of artificial flowers inside. We kids used to run after it as it glided noiselessly under the sycamores.

Many people travelled by street car, whose tracks extended uptown to Hilton, running

Daily Press

Upper Huntington Avenue became wealthiest Newport News residential area in the 1920s. Houses faced the James River shore, where the shipyard later built atomic-powered ships.

along Virginia Avenue, now Warwick Boulevard. Sam Plummer, a gentle Carolinian who ran the First National (now First and Merchants) rode the nickel trolley with the rest of us. When somebody asked the name of his big house at Huntington and 60th, Sam replied embarrassedly, "Big Bluff," and it stuck.

In those days, nobody in North End went to private school unless he couldn't hack it in public school. Grammar school students ran breathlessly down Huntington to Stonewall Jackson school each morning (no school buses then), and in the afternoon they dawdled home. It was sport for boys to throw girls' caps up telephone poles and watch them shinny up to retrieve them.

Nobody minded walking to school, even though Jackson School, at 47th Street, was a long pull. Miss Marguerite Wilson, the principal, was a no-nonsense disciplinarian who kept us on our toes. In true American style, we Stonewall scholars turned up our noses at John W. Daniel School downtown and Walter Reed in East End. Americans thrive on local rivalries.

Nobody ever defined North End, but I take it to be the area north of 50th Street to about 70th Street, between the river and C&O Railway tracks. It was a narrow area, then plagued by coal soot, but it was paradise for kids. It had no park or playground, but it didn't need them. The James River—polluted but free to all comers—lay on one side and Briarfield Road and its bootleggers on the other.

Boys from North End could cross the C&O tracks after school to what is now upper Jefferson Avenue and Mercury Boulevard. There you could shoot your beebee gun to your heart's content, banging away at birds and rabbits. Now and then you might encounter a bootleg still in the woods, for the Noble Experiment was then in vogue, and "white lightning" was in demand. On Saturdays you could even hike out to Briarfield Road to Brick Pond on Joe Miante's farm, there to burn hot dogs over an open fire and to catch snapping turtles. Sheer ecstasy!

But the James River was North End's chief glory. Thirty years ago the shoreline was a green wilderness from 50th Street northward. A few ancient cypress trees—relics perhaps of pre-Jamestown days—stood near the shore at 58th Street. A couple of privately-owned piers served swimmers and boatsmen. There you could rent rowboats and buy bait for fishing. Otherwise the beach was left to soft-crabbers and nature freaks.

On summer nights it throbbed with romance, but that's another story.

We youngsters found the shoreline a Garden of Eden. In spring it bloomed with wild plum, and in summer with honeysuckle. The tides brought in a variety of objects to fascinate the young: dead birds, fish, and animals; exotic refuse from foreign ships anchored offshore; floating bottles, occasionally bearing messages; and occasionally a drifting rowboat or raft.

West of 64th Street, North End long remained an open meadow, marked by a few remnants of Camp Hill, which had stood there in World War I. For years after the war the camp's stucco Hostess House overlooked the James near 70th Street—a derelict dance hall. It was lit up for occasional Saturday night social events in Prohibition days, but they often ended in brawls, and the structure was finally razed.

Newport News Public Library

The Hostess House of World War I's Camp Hill remained in use in the north end of Newport News well into the 1930s. It faced James River near the present 67th Street.

Daily Press

The Chamberlin Hotel built this golf club at Phoebus when the sport became popular early in the 1900s. It later became the Hampton Country Club.

North End was an enclave of doctors' homes so long as Riverside Hospital stood at 50th Street. Once it moved up to J. Clyde Morris Boulevard, however, most of the medics moved north. About that time, big new houses sprouted along Museum Drive, which a new generation designated as "The Gold Coast." In time-honored fashion, North End lost out to New Money. It declined further when the shipyard extended from 50th Street almost to the James River Bridge. That ended the Garden of Eden.

Those who've lived in North End have been sad to see their old neighborhood decline as the tide of population moved west. Even so, many people prefer to live there, hemmed in between the C&O and the shipyard but still in view of the James. Their houses may have dropped in value, but they're home. Who can blame owners for wanting to stay?

In the long pull, North End's fortunes seem bound to rise again. Its residences will no doubt regain value as the city redevelops around them. In this age of fuel shortage, North End's nearness to transportation and jobs will save it.

Of course, we old-timers will prefer the suburb the way it was—bootleggers and all. But you've got to accept progress, whether you want it or not. That's America, and not even the Ayatollah Khomeini can stop that.

Passenger ships from Baltimore and Washington docked at Old Point in the early auto era. Travelers could go by trolley to Newport News and board James River steamers or the C&O.

29. *Life Along the Waterways*

NOTHING lasts forever, but a lot of shore dwellers around Hampton Roads wish we still had the boats that used to ply our waters before automobiles put them out of business in the '30s. I'm one who misses them.

If you lived in Newport News in the 1930s, the rhythm of each day was set by the arrivals and departures of steamboats and trains. The city then had a dozen or so shipping services which brought passengers and cargo daily or less frequently. They made the waterfront, from the Casino around Point Breeze to the Boat Harbor, an interesting place. You could see a lot of life at Pier A or at the C&O docks.

Living as I did in the North End, I was most aware of the James River shippers. There were two daily passenger services from Smithfield—the Old Dominion line's Hampton Roads and Captain A. F. Jester's tiny mailboat, Oneita. And every other day we could see the Richmond-to-Norfolk steamers as they passed our bluff at 59th Street. You could also hear the engine noise on a quiet dusk as the Pocohontas came up the channel from Norfolk.

What happened to them is what happened to all riverboat services in the auto age: they quit. Passengers abandoned them for quicker transit. For a while, a few shipping lines survived on freight alone, but that gave out too.

Many people remember traveling on those James River vessels, just as people on the York, Rappahannock, and Potomac do. Tidewater depended on boat travel. Shipping lines were arteries of news and commerce. They held us all together before bridges and highways came along.

And traveling them was fun. I can remember a trip from Newport News to Smithfield as if it were yesterday, though the Smithfield boat made that trip the last time in 1934, soon after the James River Bridge opened. By the mid-'30s, few Chesapeake steamboats remained in service. Some were sold south or overseas. Others rotted at moorings in creeks or on shoals. Their pictures are in the Mariners' Museum.

Both of the Smithfield passenger-boat services operated from Pier A, at the foot of 25th Street, and went to the Smithfield wharf on the Pagan River. (Condominiums now replace that wharf). Both sailed about 4:30 p.m. My family usually went on the Hampton Roads, which was bigger than the "Oneita" and had more space for children to roam.

My brothers and I were awed by the big black stevedore who wheeled and toted cargo

142   Life Along the Waterways

from the dock while the passengers boarded. We always spoke to the purser, who took our tickets, and to the captain—an important man. He was originally Gordon Delk of Surry, a first cousin of P.D. Gwaltney, whose peanuts and Smithfield hams the ship hauled to rail connections in Newport News and Norfolk. After his day, other captains came along: Schermerhorn, Harney, Gard, Matthews, and Winder.

We usually saw a lot of Isle of Wight people our parents knew on those trips to Smithfield. Women were usually returning from a day's shopping in Newport News or Norfolk, men from business trips. But sometimes they had been to the Academy of Music in Newport News, which offered touring stage shows, minstrels, magicians, and singers like Madame Schumann-Heinck.

After the "A-a-a-l-l aboard!" whistle had sounded, before we sailed from Smithfield, the stevedores threw off the hawsers, and the Hampton Roads headed into the channel. I remember passing the Casino grounds near Pier A, by Warwick Machine Pier, and the shipyard. The Hampton Roads had an airy white saloon with red cushions on benches and chairs. You could buy coffee or iced tea in the dining saloon, a pleasant room at the stern, near the waterline.

After moving up the James four or five miles, the Hampton Roads would turn away from the Warwick shoreline to enter Pagan River near the village of Eclipse, which Southsiders call Ee-clipse. From there on she moved slowly, for the Pagan was shallow, and at low tide the ship almost touched bottom. Low water made the ship tremble with engine vibrations.

My brothers and I clung to the foredeck, watched by our parents as we observed oystermen and shore birds. Red-winged blackbirds were thick in the marsh weeds. With her bullhorn sounding to warn boatmen around each bend, the Hampton Roads wound through the tortuous Pagan channel, banking

Hampton River became crowded with fish, crab, and oyster-buying houses in the 1920s and 30s. Today Hampton Yacht Club and several marinas add to the port traffic.

Daily Press

Life Along the Waterways 143

Daily Press

Watermen moor their vessels in Hampton River, close to the oyster and fishing grounds of Hampton Roads and Chesapeake Bay. Sailboats have returned in recent years.

so steeply sometimes that chairs skidded. I half hoped the ship would turn over, just to see what happened.

We stopped at Battery Park to exchange cargo. Passengers spoke pleasantly to those on the dock who'd come to see the steamboat. "How's the oyster catch?" "Fine." "Good size?" "We-ell, yes, but I've seen 'em bigger."

The landing in Smithfield was the climax. The ship blew her horn as she passed near Moonefield Farm, where my uncle and aunt, the Harry Dashiells, lived. And if the captain knew your daddy, he might lift you up on the whistle chain so you could blow for the landing.

Once a young mariner had pulled the ship's bullhorn for the necessary number of Boooops, he would rush out of the pilot house shouting, "Mama! Daddy! I blowed the wissel!" For such kindnesses the ship's captains are remembered by aging Southsiders.

Once the Hampton Roads hove in view, Smithfielders of all ages rose on front porches and sauntered down Wharf Hill to "see who's on the boat." That, I'm told, was a daily ritual in all wharfside Tidewater towns in the steamboat age. Nearly everybody knew the ship's crew. And everybody was anxious to see who might be coming to town.

The death of Smithfield's steamboats foretold the end of a gracious era in America. As Mark Twain wrote in *Life on the Mississippi,* it was a romantic time. People took care of each other. Then, when the auto speeded up our tempo, life became fast and less gracious.

The Hampton Roads was replaced by a smaller steamer in 1920. In 1929—a year after the James River Bridge opened—Captain A.F. Jester ended his mail boat trips on the brave Oneita. (Its roll usually made me seasick). In 1934, the ship which had replaced the "Hampton Roads" also gave up.

A few freight shippers continued to serve Newport News in the 1930s, but they faded fast. I remember the Merchants and Miners and a few other lines in the late 1930s, when I worked during summer vacations from college. In those days, shipping companies offered service to Newport News from New York, Baltimore, and Boston. That, too, soon ended.

Another victim of the auto was the C&O passenger ferry, Virginia, which operated daily from the C&O depot on 23rd Street to Norfolk. Peninsula people traveled it to enjoy the thrills of Norfolk's Granby Street. I remember early talking movies at Norfolk's Norva Theatre and meals at Colonel Consolvo's once-fashionable hotel, the Monticello. (Built for the Jamestown Exposition in 1907, it was pulled down in the '50s or '60s).

"Smokey Joe" made her last run decades ago, after C&O passenger service fell victim to the auto. In 1971 the C&O transferred passenger operations to Amtrak.

Other victims of the auto were the Chesapake Bay passenger steamers, which linked Old Point and Norfolk with Washington, Baltimore, and Chincoteague. Three shipping lines did a brisk business with the Peninsula for years. Their nerve center was the Government Pier at Old Point, where steamers docked daily. My family often drove to Old Point to see the big white boats, which had brought vacationers in earlier years to the Hygeia Hotel and the Chamberlin (replaced after a fire by the present Chamberlin).

But the lure of water travel is still alive. Several Atlantic coastal steamers bring passengers now and then to Yorktown, Winter cruises to the Caribbean and summer cruises to European and American ports are growing. Someday the Peninsula will regain its pleasure boats, if Newport News can become an attractive port once more. I hope so.

Many Hamptonians earn their livelihood from the seafoods of the Chesapeake and its estuaries. Hampton Bar outside the mouth of Hampton River is famous for its oysters.
Daily Press

30. *A Bridge to Southside*

ONE of the grand moments on the Peninsula was the opening of the James River bridge. It happened on November 17, 1928—a year before the stock market crash in October 1929, and it opened up a new world for a lot of people.

That narrow bridge livened up Southside as it had never been before. Over the years it created trade between the merchants of Newport News and the farmers of Isle of Wight. It brought to the Peninsula a lot of business which before 1928 had gone to Norfolk.

If you'd been there for the opening, as I was, you wouldn't forget it. The star was Woodroof Hiden, a shy girl of 18, dressed in peach silk. She cut the ribbon that opened the bridge, wielding a huge pair of scissors (wood, painted gold, with steel cutting edge). They're now owned by her widower. Wendell Hussey, who lends them out for big ribbon-cuttings.

The ceremonies took place around the toll plaza which had been built at the juncture of Warwick Boulevard and the bridge approach. Woody Hiden was "Miss Virginia," with a "court" of teenagers. The band played, and Governor Harry Byrd made a speech.

In Woody's entourage were a lot of teen-age girls. Elizabeth Copeland, who was Miss Newport News, is now Mrs. Fillmore Norfleet of Charlottesville. Mollie Masters, Miss Hampton, is Mrs. J. Britt League, Henrietta Chapman, Miss Isle of Wight, is Mrs. Julius Gwaltney, Eleanor Parrish, Miss Richmond, is Mrs. Robert Barton. Virginia Vaiden, Miss James City County, is Mrs. William E. Bowen. Cynthia Coleman, Miss Williamsburg, married Singleton Morehead and is no longer with us. Catherine Kearney, who was Miss Phoebus, married the late Rudy Kreibohm of Newport News. And Betty Johnson of Smithfield, whom I knew long ago, married a New Jersey doctor and lives at Virginia Beach.

The big moment was when President Coolidge pressed a button in the White House to raise the bridge span. It went 147 feet above the water—one of the highest bridges in the country.

When time came to hoist the five-foot pair of scissors, Governor Byrd helped Woody Hiden. Snip, snip, and it was all over.

Once the ribbon was cut, half of Newport News rushed to cross the river. The owners opened it free for the rest of the day, and traffic was bumper-to-bumper. Lots of my fellow Boy Scouts hiked over, but I rode in my

146 A Bridge to Southside

family's Model-T. We took advantage of a free trip to Smithfield to see relatives.

Those were days of big risks. Investors who invested money knew it was a long shot, and they were right. After the 1929 crash, times got really tough for the bridge. A lot of investors lost their shirts. Finally, the State bought the system in 1949, amortizing it with tolls. After the bonds were paid off in June 1976, the bridge was made free. (I don't see why they didn't do the same with the Hampton Bridge-Tunnel and Yorktown bridge, but I'm old-fashioned.)

The bridge was said to be the second longest in the country, spanning 4.9 miles and exceeded only by a bridge from Key West to the Florida keys. Everybody in those days talked about the $5.2 million it cost, though that seems a drop compared to what its replacement is costing.

A group of local businessmen had conceived the bridge and formed a corporation to sell bonds to build it. Philip W. Hiden, ex-mayor and father of Woodroof Hiden, who cut the ribbon, was one. Another was Albert Sydney Johnson of Smithfield, who became manager with an office along the bridge road at Earthlett in Isle of Wight, between the James and Chuckatuck Creek.

The corporation built smaller bridges over Chuckatuck Creek and Nansemond River to create a route from Newport News to Portsmouth and Norfolk. The James River span put Southside closer to Newport News than to Norfolk, and Smithfielders began coming to our town to shop, see doctors, and eventually to play golf and go to cocktail parties. (Early tolls discouraged such frivolous trips.)

All of that changed the pattern of life in Smithfield and Battery Park. The steamboat from Smithfield to Newport News and Norfolk went out of business after the bridge opened. So did Captain A. F. Jester's mail boat, the Oneita, and his car-ferry from the Boat Harbor to Chuckatuck. Instead of ship-

ping watermelons by boat to Pier A at Twenty-Fifth Street, farmers sent them over here by truck. A lot of Newport News people were partial to Smithfield-grown kale, turnip salad, sweet potatoes, side meat, and other edibles now low-rated by some people as "soul food."

(My friend Wesley Cofer, used to say that food tasted better from "the old country," as he called Isle of Wight and Surry. I think he was right.)

The bridge brought other changes. More Southsiders commuted to the shipyard and Peninsula bases. Shipyard traffic each afternoon loaded the bridge for an hour or so after

Mariners Museum

Building of the James River Bridge to Isle of Wight County in 1928 began Peninsula's growth as a trade center for Tidewater counties. This was the view from Huntington Avenue in 1946.

4 o'clock. It has become part of Tidewater's lifestyle since the bridge opened for people to live in the boondocks, where they can enjoy hunting and fishing and the outdoors when they get home from work. Some commuters plant a few acres, or raise chickens or even set a few traps for muskrats, as my Uncle Tom used to do.

Another benefit of the bridge was to enable young couples and retirees to buy houses on the Southside, where real estate and taxes in 1928 were cheaper than on the Peninsula. Today Southside is full of "come-heres," like all of rural Tidewater. Even Albert Sidney Johnson's old house on Smithfield's Church Street was bought by folks from Newport News. William and Mary professors also discovered the area and commuted to the college.

In time, the James River Bridge raised population, land values, and taxes in the Black Belt south of the James. Some may disagree, but I think the bridge did a lot more good than harm. The black people of Southside particularly benefited from the Peninsula job market and from the new money coming into Isle of Wight and Nansemond.

To appreciate the change wrought by the bridge, just compare Isle of Wight today with neighboring Surry County. Although Surry feels some effects of the bridge, its economy remains slower than Isle of Wight's, limited in part by the exasperating Jamestown ferry which ties it to the Peninsula. Many Surry folk I know want to keep it that way, and that's up to them, but I believe population and economics will eventually dictate a bridge near Jamestown.

As they say, trade is a two-way street. Both sides of the James improved after we got the bridge. Southside's politicos fortunately took the initiative in the 1940s to have the State buy the span and reduce tolls. The late Senator A.E.S. "Gi" Stephens had a lot to do with the State's purchase of it, and Delegate Mills Godwin of Chuckatuck, later governor, did a lot to reduce tolls, persuading the State to eliminate them first at Chuckatuck and Nansemond.

When Mills Godwin ran for Governor in 1961, he advocated elimination of the final toll remaining on the James River span, which was done at last during his second term in 1976. By that time tolls had paid off the indebtedness on the James River, Yorktown, and Rappahannock bridges, together with the Hampton Bridge-Tunnel.

It was a long wait, but a few of us who were present at the opening in 1928 have survived to enjoy the freebies.

No sooner was the James River Bridge toll-free than the State had to begin planning a new bridge to replace it. The old one was over 40 years old, and its aging skeleton was so expensive to maintain that the Highway Department felt a replacement was necessary.

I guess the moral of all this is that it pays to outlive a bond issue. I'm looking forward to another 50 years on the new bridge.

Daily Press

Familiar to Peninsula waters in the 1930s was James Adams' Floating Theater, which performed in Chesapeake towns. It was visited by novelist Edna Ferber for her novel, 'Show Boat.'

31. *Marching Through Daniel School*

FATE dealt me a cruel blow in 1928, when I was in the seventh grade of Stonewall Jackson School in Newport News. Miss Marguerite Wilson, the principal, announced at the start of the term that we seventh graders must move to John W. Daniel School downtown to make room for more first grade entrants.

John W. Daniel? We snooty Stonewallers had seen those kids each year at the interschool May Day (held, I seem to remember, at the high school athletic field, around maypoles of crepe paper ribbons.) Either from school spirit or snobbery, we disdained all other city schools except our own.

But move we did. And what a change! Instead of our tiny North End Elysium, we found ourselves in the city's oldest school building, extending from Thirty-First to Thirty-Second Streets, between Washington and Huntington Avenues. It was almost hemmed in by the growing city. Its hard dirt playground, unlike Jackson's, was surrounded by a fence. In those days, public schools were as utilitarian as jails.

We found the principal to be a formidable lady, Miss Gertrude Davis. She looked as serene as Juno in her rimless glasses, but she meant business. At recess and class-changes she stood in the hall, glaring at laggards. She ran her school in semi-military fashion.

Students at Daniel marched to rhythmic recordings, played by loudspeakers at recess, lunch, and assemblies. Miss Davis played Sousa marches on a Victrola outside her office door, and she sometimes clapped in time with

Daily Press

John Daniel School stood on 31st and 32d Streets, close to Washington Avenue. Shops and theatres attracted students after school.

the music. It was an oddly Hitlerian performance for a sweet, elderly lady who looked like a colonial dame.

I remember the Sousa March that we sang words to:

"And the monkey wrapped his tail around the flagpole,

'Round the flagpole,

'Round the flagpole.''

To my surprise, the kids at Daniel weren't such bad eggs after all. Except for the long trek to and from my home on Fifty-Ninth Street, the school suited me fine. We had four excellent teachers, who rotated daily between four sections of about 30 students each. They were Roberta Saunders, Florence Richardson, Myrtle Martin, and Amanda (Chubby) Gray, the latter very much alive today. A frequent substitute was Idalia Bland Minnigrerode, also still with us.

John W. Daniel had originally served as both high and elementary school, but Newport News High had been built in the 1920s to divide the load. It stood only a half-block from Daniel, on Huntington Avenue. The Newport News school offices remained in Daniel, housing Superintendent Joseph H. Saunders, Clerk Lively Tabb, Secretary Willie Rowe Nelms, and others. We had to be quiet outside their doors.

I had no idea who John W. Daniel was till years later. Then I learned he was a post-Civil War Lynchburg orator and U.S. senator, known as "the Lame Lion of Lynchburg" because of his limp. He made the oration when the recumbent statue of Lee was unveiled at Washington and Lee in 1872.

When recess or lunch rolled round, Miss Davis would come out in the hall and ring her bell. Then she would start her Victrola recordings of "Semper Fidelis" or "El Capitan." Class by class, we would thump down the metal stairs from the third floor to the basement restrooms. There you were on your own. Once you reached the toilets you could ignore Sousa.

Life on the Daniel school grounds was more competitive than at Jackson. Those downtown kids were street-smart, and fights erupted. The top gladiators were Joe and Bill Carpen-

Daniel School taught downtown Newport News students for nearly 50 years after 1900. Newport News High was built a block away, then one of two local high schools. Daily Press

ter, who became real estate tycoons. Joe was older, but Bill was quick and wiry. When they mixed it up, the teacher on duty would run to separate them.

"Boys! Boys!," she would say. "Aren't you ashamed of yourselves! Stop or I'll take you to Miss Davis." That ended it.

Next door to the school was the Elks' Lodge, while across Thirty-Second Street was the First Presbyterian Church. We often heard Mrs. Cofer, the organist, rehearsing next Sunday's anthems. Nearby was Rodef Sholom Temple, whose rabbi (or rabbit, as Ding Price would say) was then Jesse J. Finkel. Close to the temple was Watson-Gies auto repair shop, and nearby, at Huntington and Thirty-First, was a livery stable.

Washington Avenue was close to Daniel, offering quite a few excitements. Newport News wasn't booming in 1928, but the Main Stem looked prosperous to me in those days. It looked so even after the stock market crash in October, 1929, after I'd graduated from Daniel and gone to high school. You see, the Great Depression came early and stayed late on the Peninsula. We were used to being depressed.

The possibilities of Washington Avenue were several. If a good movie was on, you might persuade your parents to let you stay for a matinee after school. Or you could visit Mrs. Fox's Nut and Chocolate Shop to sample her fudge, divinity, or seafoam, crammed with black walnuts. Mrs. Fox was patient with nickel customers.

Nachman's Department Store had a coffee shop which also lured after-schoolers. The men's department then sold Harris tweed topcoats for $18 and Arrow shirts for $2. (I've grown accustomed to their price.) And Nachman's book counter and book rental library were a constant lure to me and Stella Ford Stephens and Bea Stratford, who could read a book a night.

We North Enders usually rode home by streetcar, which we boarded on Washington Avenue, but in good weather we could walk. I remember a tiny European bakery on Huntington which sold meringues for a penny. Sometimes I'd walk home and eat my carfare money.

There were few student activities at Daniel, for elementary schools then left such things to high school. Mostly we plugged away at English, arithmetic, history, civics, geography, and a dab of music and art.

I don't remember any sort of graduation at Daniel when I finished in February, 1929, and walked across the avenue to enroll at Newport News High, but I'd grown strangely attached to Miss Davis and John Philip Sousa. I suppose I am subject to what one writer has called "the melancholy of change." When a chapter of life closes, I am saddened by the consciousness that I can never recapture it.

Even today, a half-century later, I can smell the Varsol which coated Daniel's floors and the Lysol which enveloped its toilets. And when a band strikes up "The Washington Post March" or some other Sousa favorite, my mind goes unerringly back to Daniel School recess, where I lined up with Robert Saunders, Carolyn Richardson, and other classmates, poised like Hitler's Youth Corps, to march down three flights of steps to the waiting facilities in the basement.

And there in the middle of it all, stood dear Miss Davis, staring absently through her glasses as she gently beat out the rhythm:

"And the monkey wrapped his tail around the flagpole,
 'Round the flagpole,
 'Round the flagpole."

Every year, every day, every hour is unique. As the Greeks knew, time alone is irreplaceable; waste it not. I got my money's worth out of John W. Daniel. Every minute of it.

32. Model Ts and Sunday Drivers

THE Model T. Ford has changed life more than any other invention in my lifetime. Before Henry Ford's cheap cars began to take over the roads in World War I, America moved at the pace of the horse and carriage. But the Model T changed that. It led us on to hard-surfaced roads, bridges, and tunnels, and suburban living. How tempus does fugit.

Here on the Peninsula, the auto brought in military bases, the restoration of Williamsburg, and traveling for fun. It put people on the road at all hours of day and night, when they used to be home. It's been a mixed blessing.

My father bought our family's first car, a Model T Ford, about 1920, just before I entered Stonewall Jackson School. It was the standard black touring model, with the retractable top. It had ugly isinglass side windows that you installed in bad weather. My father had to crank it to start it.

On Sunday afternoons after lunch my parents would bundle us children in the back seat, and off we went to see the Peninsula. In summer we went to Buckroe or Grandview, which were small and quiet family resorts then. There we would swim and sometimes meet other families for a picnic supper. In fall and spring we'd drive up Warwick Road to Waters Creek (now the Mariners' Museum), or nearby to gape at Newport News's newly-created reservoir.

Warwick County Road was then a two-lane macadam strip that zigzagged up the Peninsula to Williamsburg. There it went up Duke of Gloucester Street and then on to Richmond. The road had been hard-surfaced by the Army in World War I, but it followed a dirt roadbed that went back to the 1600s. Much of it is now Route 60, one of the earliest routes in English America.

It was exciting to travel at 30 miles an hour, even though the road was bumpy. The roadside had a few county stores that had just added gas pumps. There you could also buy penny candy for children. And at Mrs. Smith's ice cream parlor in Norge you could get cones of homemade vanilla for a nickel each.

Sight-seeing was a Sunday ritual among families lucky enough to have a car in the 1920s. That's how I first got to see Williamsburg, Jamestown, Langley Field, Fort Monroe, and Yorktown. Sometimes we'd venture across Captain Ashe's Yorktown ferry to Gloucester or across Captain A. F. Jester's Jamestown ferry to Surry.

Do you remember the Burma-Shave signs

Model Ts and Sunday Drives   153

that sprouted along roadsides in the 1920s? They advertised men's shaving cream. The signs were four line verses, one line appearing on each of four signs about 500 yards apart. One set of them read: "I know he's a wolf,"/said Red Riding Hood,/"but grandma, dear/he smells so good!"

Another was "Angels who guard you/While you drive/ Usually retire/at sixty-five." More to the point was: "The bearded lady/tried a jar/She's now a famous/Movie star." After each poem came the Burma-Shave logo and commercial.

A favorite drive from Newport News was to the government dock at Old Point, now closed. Each evening between 6 and 7, the big white steamboats would sail in from Norfolk or from Baltimore. Three shipping lines used the dock: the Old Bay Line, the Baltimore Line, and the "Nip and N," or New York, Philadelphia, and Norfolk. I liked the Old Bay best.

It was pleasant to see the ships tie up to discharge their passengers, freight, and automobiles. Sometimes high winds and tides made landing difficult. Then the ship would back away from the pier and try again. Children stood on dock and waved to passengers on deck. I was tantalized by the view of the dining salon at the stern, just above the waterline. Through the round portholes you could see white-clad waiters serving patrons, with napkins on one arm.

We also noted the burly black stevedores. They tied the lines and hauled the cargo.

Fort Monroe was an attraction. The old moat surrounding the inner fort seemed to me to be spooky and medieval. (It still seems so.) We loved to see the casemate where Jefferson Davis had been imprisoned after the Civil War, now the Casemate Museum, thanks to Dr. Chester Bradley. We liked to get out of the car and walk around in the fort, finding the quarters where Captain and Mrs. Robert E.

Buckroe Beach Hotel, seen behind flappers, was a favorite object of Sunday outings in the family Ford. Note the girls' rolled stockings.   Virginia State Library

Newport News Historical Committee

Model T Fords park along 25th Street in 1912, alongside the Daily Press-Times Herald plant. Growth of cars and paved streets led to flight to Warwick and Elizabeth City County suburbs in the 1930s.

Lee had lived after their marriage. We discovered the house where President Lincoln had stayed briefly in the Civil War. We children had Confederate sympathies, but after all, Abraham Lincoln had been our president. People then admired presidents more than most of us do nowadays. (Whatever happened to hero worship?)

Downtown Hampton had many appealing old houses surviving from the post-Civil War years. (Every building in Hampton except St. John's Church burned in the Civil War.) I remember the Magnolia Tree Tea Room, a stately residence converted by several women to a popular eating place. The crab-picking houses that stood close to Hampton's center gave off an atrocious odor, entitling Hampton to the name of "Crabtown." (I still whiff that odor today as I speed over the Interstate through Hampton. It reminds me of Hampton in the '20s.)

Unfortunately, many of these fine old houses lay along Queen and King Streets, in downtown Hampton's center. As a result, many of them have been torn down. However, a few remain on Victoria and Mallory Avenues. Like so many other cities, Hampton has lost much of its character.

In those days, nobody I knew in Newport News had more than one car. People of all sorts went to work daily on the streetcar, which took you from North End to downtown for a nickel. You used the auto for church, parties, and trips. If you wanted to go by streetcar to Hampton, to Old Point, or to Buckroe, you transferred to the Boulevard run, at 28th Street and Washington Avenue. The best part of that trip was the track along the Boulevard between Newport News to Hampton. There it hugged the waterfront of Hampton Roads. However, the route was changed after the great 1933 hurricane washed out the Boulevard shoreline.

Kecoughtan Road was the first major hard-surfaced road between Newport News and Hampton, Shell Road and Briarfield came later.

After the Model T, it took Virginia many

decades to build bridges to connect our long-isolated Peninsula with its surrounding terrain. For years we depended on ferries. A ferry at the Newport News Boat Harbor took motorists to Sewell's Point near Norfolk, and another from Old Point took you to Willoughby Spit, near Ocean View. It docked close to the present Bridge-Tunnel beachhead. Then there was the daily C&O passenger boat from the Newport News train depot at 23rd Street to Norfolk, and Captain A. F. Jester's short-lived ferry from the Boat Harbor to Chuckatuck, across the James. My family traveled it in our Ford until the James River Bridge to Isle of Wight opened in 1928. Then the ferry quit.

Often my mother packed sandwiches for a Sunday auto outing. Sometimes we took a watermelon or bought fruit at a roadside stand.

Of the eight or 10 ferry services from the Peninsula in my day, only the Jamestown ferry is still in service. I understand it is one of only three state-operated ferries remaining in Virginia. Despite the recent addition of a new ferryboat, I believe its days are numbered. Ferries are too slow.

The year 1928 meant a lot to my family's Sunday travels. Not only did the James River Bridge open that year but the Rockefeller restoration of Williamsburg became public. Motorists swarmed to see "Rockefeller's folly." At first we ate at the Colonial Inn or at Bob Wallace's College Shop. But soon Greek eateries opened on Merchant's Square. Then the Restoration moved in the 18th century Travis House from Francis to Duke of Gloucester and ran it as a tavern. (It's now back on its first site.)

Model Ts were cold in winter, so we carried a carriage robe to wrap around our feet. Flat tires had to be changed with primitive equipment. Henry Ford built those first cars high off the ground, and people had trouble stepping up to the high running board to enter them. It was fun while it lasted.

The Ford Model A soon replaced the tin lizzie. I remember that secrecy and newspaper publicity when the first Model A hit the market. I saw it at a dealer's showroom on downtown Huntington Ave., near the old Newport News High School. By that time General Motors had got in the act, and my father traded our Model T for an Oldsmobile sedan. Not as exciting, but a lot more comfortable. It even had a built-in bud vase for flowers.

One by one, these artifacts of the past have gone. We live in a more complex world. But change isn't necessarily progress. I miss the people and the landscape of the '20s. I'm sentimental, I guess.

Daily Press

A winter storm in 1926 brought out storm windows on this Model T Ford, parked near Barclays' jewelry store.

33. *Building Boats on Hampton Roads*

ONE of the most elusive figures of the Peninsula in the 1930s was a wealthy playboy named Horace E. Dodge Jr., who ran a speedboat factory near the Boat Harbor for a half-dozen years before his debts caught up with him in 1935.

The son of the Detroit millionaire who originated the Dodge car, young Horace spent $2 million in 1929-30 to start his Newport News factory. Dodge became a tabloid celebrity of the 1930s and 40s for his half-dozen marriages to New York showgirls. In the process he spent his inheritance, estimated at $69 million, and died nearly broke in 1963.

The old Dodge factory now houses the Chase Bag Company at 1300 Marshall Avenue, overlooking Hampton Roads at Stuart Gardens.

Two ex-officials of the Dodge plant still survive. They are Earl Hatten of Hampton, who was plant superintendent, and John Berryman of York County, former materials supervisor and purchasing agent.

Berryman told me that Horace Dodge Jr. was an impetuous man who optimistically tried to sell speedboats to Americans at the depth of the Great Depression. His marriages

Mariners Museum

Earl Hatten and John Berryman led Dodge Boat and Plane Corporation in building speedboats in 1930-35.

cost him millions in alimony and legal fees. Less than a year after he opened his Newport News plant, he sent word to Berryman: "Start cancelling orders."

Young Dodge's enthusiasm for fast boats led him to start his first boat factory in 1925. Four years later he and a college classmate, William Horne, built a bigger factory at Newport News, called the Horace E. Dodge Boat and Plane Corporation. It produced 1,600 boats from 1930 to 1935. In 1941 the dormant plant was briefly revived to produce PT boats for the U.S. in World War II.

Berryman, one of Dodge's first local employees, was hired by vice president William Horne in 1930. After undergoing training at the Dodge boat plant in Detroit, he took over his Newport News duties. The Dodge factory was built by the Virginia Engineering Company (later Basic Construction) at the waterfront end of Marshall Avenue, near the World War I site of Camp Stuart. Later Stuart Gardens housing area was developed there.

"We produced good boats at low prices," Berryman recalls. For less than $1,000 a buyer could get a 16-foot mahogany outboard runa-

Mahogany speedboats await lifting by crane from Dodge factory near Boat Harbor into Hampton Roads. Depression of 1929 soon destroyed market for the luxury craft.

Daily Press

bout. The firm also produced runabouts and cruisers in lengths of 21, 25, 28, and 45 feet. All were double-planked with Philippine or African mahogany, and powered by Lycoming marine motors with a top speed of 30 miles per hour.

Horace Dodge's own succession of speedboats, which took part in major speed tests, bore the name "Delphine" in honor of Dodge's mother and sister.

The Newport News-made boats had such luxurious equipment as cigar lighters, Duesenberg-style steering wheels, and custom-made monel metal hardware. The Dodge trademark, the "Flying Lady," was a handsome nickel bow ornament designed by sculptor Russell Crook.

Horace Dodge Jr. was a friend of New York showman Earl Carroll, who in those years produced Earl Carroll's "Vanities" on Broadway, featuring beautiful showgirls scantily clad in furs and lingerie. Dodge's widely publicized marriages included several to "Vanities" showgirls, including the curvaceous Gregg Sherwood. His marital career was common fare in tabloids of the era, including the Hearst papers and the National Inquirer.

Says John Berryman, "The Dodge Boat and Plane Corporation in Detroit and Newport News built motor boats for about 25 years and played a big role in the rise of inboard speedboats. It pioneered in the industry, following assembly-line methods of construction developed earlier by auto manufacturers. The most modern methods were used."

When Dodge opened his Newport News plant, he credited his father for his industrial techniques. "It will be necessary for American boat builders to adopt the principles of efficiency and mass production which have made the automotive industry the world leader," he said.

The Dodge site spread over 100 acres, most of it formerly used by the Army in World War I. Dodge chose it because of its nearness to the C&O railway, highways, and Hampton Roads shipping lines. Its waterfront permitted sea trials for every boat built. Freshwater tests were made in the James River.

Though Dodge and his vice president, Bill Horne, expected to build seaplanes and amphibious planes, they apparently never built any.

An advertisement in a 1930 issue of Motor Boating magazine declared the craft were made "by modern methods of large-scale production at the great Dodge Plant at Newport News. Every one is tested . . . by expert drivers and mechanics in the salt sea waves of Hampton Roads."

Berryman is currently engaged in scientific plant research at a laboratory on Route 17 at Tabb. There he works in tandem with two scientists, Frank Perkins of Virginia Institute of Marine Science in Gloucester, and Martin Mathes, professor of biology at the College of William and Mary.

Berryman had helped build the Ford automobile assembly plant in Norfolk in 1929 before signing up with Dodge at Newport News. After resigning from Dodge at the end of 1930, he created the Tidewater Printing and Publishing Company and operated it on Washington Avenue. He later sold it to Raymond Brown of Newport News.

Boating fans from many places have responded to the Mariners' Museum appeal for participants and for the gift of memorabilia of the Dodge Boat and Plane Corporation.

34. Oystermen and Crabbers

MRS. Anne Darling Tormey of Hampton has given me a photo of the old Darling oyster pile that towered during the 1930s and '40s over Hampton's Queen Street, along Hampton Creek. It's gone now, but any Peninsulan over 40 is apt to remember it.

The oyster pile brings back the memory of J.S. Darling and Son, oystermen who competed with Norfolk watermen like J.H. Miles and Ballard Fish and Oyster Company. The Darling company has become inactive, and its shell-heap and docks have been replaced by new buildings. Founded after the Civil War by a New York transplant James Sands Darling, it was inherited in turn by his son Frank Darling, and grandson, J.S. II. Finally, it was run by George Bentley, one-time Hampton mayor, who lives on Chesapeake Avenue.

To Peninsulans in those years, Darling's oyster mound was one of the landmarks of the Peninsula. It disappeared about 1963, when the Darlings stopped shucking oysters and, for awhile, operated a marine railway in downtown Hampton. Now the railway has gone, too.

Like Crisfield, Md., today, Hampton was called "Crab Town" in my youth. Another Hampton come-here, James McMenamin, had started a crab-picking and shipping plant on Hampton Creek (next door to Hampton Yacht Club's present site) back in the 19th century. The late Judge Vernon Spratley worked there when a boy about 1900, folding price lists. McMenamin's sons, James and John, ran the McMenamin plant after their father. They later sold it to M.S. Quinn. The McMenamin site is now occupied by Blue Water Yacht Sales.

My memory of Hampton is colored by the vision of waterside crab factories we could see from bridges through the town in the 1930s. They were generally built on docks along Hampton waterways and painted red. They all had piers where crabbers could unload their catch and sell it. Inside each pierhouse was the picking room, where black women bent over piles of cooked bright orange crabs, separating meat from shell.

Besides the McMenamin plant, Hampton in those days had the Jarvis crab plant, operated by a black man at the foot of Queen Street. Another crab-plant owner was Howard Horseman, later Hampton's postmaster. William Evans operated a crab house up Sunset Creek, and the Cartwright crab plant flourished nearby.

Besides attracting lots of buyers to their

A mound of oystershells stood near Queen Street at the J. S. Darling oyster plant and boat works on Hampton River. It disappeared after World War 2, when the plant ceased.

wharves, the crab plants gave off a heavy stench of boiling crabs. We children held our noses and said "Whew" when our father drove through Hampton's streets on the way to Buckroe.

Other lost Hampton landmarks are the Langley Hotel on Queen Street, the Langley movie house across the street, and the Monroe Shop for ladies. It was run for years by the attractive Liz Hope Bentley. Queen Street in those quiet days had shops, two banks, the Central Restaurant, and lots of lawyers' offices.

The Fort Monroe bandstand was another 1930s landmark, for summer band concerts were big. It still stands in the greensward called Continental Park, close to the Government Pier and the Hampton Roads shore. The pier's newsstand and confectionery did big business when Bay Line steamers docked at Old Point, but the pier is quiet now.

An important site between Hampton and Newport News was the trolley-car barn of the Citizens' Rapid Transit Company on Victoria Boulevard. After the trolleys were abandoned in favor of buses (they were faster), the car barn became a bus-parking area and headquarters of the Citizens' Rapid Transit. It is now the office of Pentran, the government agency that bought up CRT and runs Peninsula buses today.

Another landmark in my youth was the

ferry dock at the Newport News Boat Harbor. Big ferryboats took you across Hampton Roads in about 20 minutes to land at Pine Beach, now part of Norfolk Navy Base. The Boat Harbor was a busy small-craft center, with the World War I sites of Camp Stuart, and the Curtiss flying field adjoining the ferry dock. The ferries were discontinued when the Hampton Roads Bridge-Tunnel was built.

An eye-catching sight on the downtown Newport News waterfront then was the first coal-loading pier built by the C&O in the 1880s at Point Breeze, next to the Boat Harbor. Before oil displaced coal as the world's favorite fuel (automobiles caused the shift), the C&O coal piers were always busy. Ships of all nationalities called there, awaiting their turn at the pier. Soon the C&O added other coal piers. As a boy, I watched them work as I fished in the James for croakers. The newest coal piers are said to be technical marvels.

A landmark of downtown Newport News until the 1930s was our red-light district—18th Street and River Road, down by the C&O docks. I can remember when the area was called "Hell's Half Acre" because of its bars, gambling saloons, and prostitution before the 1920s. There foreign seamen drank, made love, fought, and sometimes died violent deaths. But after World War I, prohibition ended the saloons. Then the bordellos moved to a controlled city area on Warwick Avenue till they too were closed by law.

When I think back of the Peninsula, I realize that the waterfront has changed most of all. I remember the huge C&O grain elevators that stood about at 18th Street, burned long ago. And I remember three city docks on the lower James in my childhood. One was the C&O passenger depot at 23rd Street. Another was the city produce pier called Pier A, at 25th Street. The third was the Warwick Marine Company pier jutting out from the Casino, owned by Hooper and Hardy.

Early Newport was poorly planned and

Syms-Eaton Museum

Fishing boats occasionally brought home to Hampton a big catch like this one. The photograph was taken by "Happy" Cheyne, who with his father recorded Peninsula history in early 1900s.

cheaply built as the city has learned to its great cost today. But I miss a few of those cheap early buildings, chiefly the Academy of Music on Washington Avenue, where the Paramount Theater now stands. It was ugly outside but fancy inside, decorated with paintings of muses, composers, and antique musical instruments. Its buff paint was livened by a

162 Hampton's Oystermen and Crabbers

crimson stage curtain and friezes of gold and colored murals. To an impressionable boy, as I was, the Academy was a taste of Broadway.

Another perished landmark is the old Warwick Hotel, built by Collis Huntington right after he created Newport News in 1881. The four-story wooden hotel stood between 24th and 25th on West Avenue, but most of it has been torn down. All that is now left is a brick section that was added later to the original, but it lacks the style of the original. The Warwick I liked had bay windows, potted palms, and a grand stairway. Stars like Al Jolson and W. C. Fields stayed there when they starred in shows at the Academy of Music.

Another landmark of the James River is Waters Creek, which was mistakenly called "Watts Creek" when I was a boy. It was bought by Archer Huntington in the 1930s as part of the land he acquired in order to create the Mariners' Museum. After it was dammed, it backed up to form Lake Maury, the central lake of the museum.

As a North End canoeist, I was sorry when the museum took away our wild waterland. After that, aspiring young explorers like Lewis McMurran, Perry Epes, and I could no longer paddle up the creek to see the shorebirds, wild ducks, squirrels, and especially snakes. Watts Creek was full of snakes, which we assumed were deadly moccasins, though I doubt they all were.

These are some of the memories of one Peninsulan. A lot of history took place between Jamestown and Old Point, and much of it is lost already.

Refrigerated trucks expanded marketing of Hampton crabmeat, pioneered by James McMenamin. Samuel Coston's crab factory on Hampton River in 1900 emplyed 36 crab pickers.

Daily Press

35. *Courtly Judges, Tipsy Lawyers*

AS a cub reporter on the Peninsula papers in the 1930s, I got my first view of courtroom life on Newport News' Twenty-fifth Street. Those days came back to me as I read Sclater Montague's *Memories of Hampton,* recently.

The General, an attractive and outspoken man, told of the many bibulous attorneys who graced the Peninsula bench and bar in the early 1900s, when he grew up. At the end, he added. "If I have wounded anyone's feelings, it was not my intention to do so, and I apologize." I guess any possible objectors were safely dead.

No doubt about it, those courtroom Ciceros were a colorful, high-living crowd. In those days, lawyers had a social cachet above most of us mortals. Judges and lawyers treated each other with old-fashioned courtliness, even addressing each other as "Esquire." Some of the wig-and-gown etiquette of stately old England rubbed off.

A lot of those now dead courtroom orators warmed up with a drink or two before court began. They explained that they thought better and spoke more forcefully with a little fire in the furnace. It didn't hurt some of them, though I don't think law schools advocated it.

One Newport News lawyer of my youth smelled so fragrantly alcoholic in the Justice of the Peace court one day that the judge summoned him to the bench. " 'Fore God, brother . . .," he whispered, "you smell so damn good I could eat you meat, bones, and all."

Another lawyer was so addicted to hunting that he brought his hunting dog to court. My fellow Times-Herald reporter, Eddie Travis, said that, all things considered, he'd rather be represented by the dog than the lawyer.

The air of disarray in courtrooms then was appalling. Judges and lawyers were forever continuing cases. Court was often late. In August, some courts quit altogether. And a lot of court clerks knew not to schedule cases in hunting season if the judge liked to hunt. That suited many lawyers too.

As Sclater Montague put it: "The practice of law in old Hampton was to a large extent a life of leisure. While there were exceptions, as a general rule a lawyer would come down to his office in the morning, and if he was lucky enough to prepare a deed, for which the fee in those days was $5, he had made about all the money he desired for that day. Quite often the lawyer would then spend the remainder of the day conversing with his friends in some bar room."

In his "Virginia Judge" monologues, in which he took off on Judge J.D.G. Brown of Newport News Police Court in the early 1900s, humorist Walter Kelly portrayed the judge as regularly rushing through the docket so he could get out and go hunting or fishing. One day the clerk whispered to the judge that the fish were running. "Bang," goes the gavel. "Court dismissed," exclaimed the judge, heading for the James River.

Daily Press

E. Sclater Montague was leading Hampton lawyer and legislator. He wrote his memories of Peninsula courts.

Newport News Historical Committee

Warwick County was briefly governed from this courthouse in Newport News in the 1880s, but the building became Newport News courthouse when the city was formed in 1896. It stood at 25th and Huntington.

When Colgate Darden was governor of Virginia, he expressed a concern about some of his fellow lawyers. "They come out of Charlottesville with a good education," he said, "and then they go back to the county and sit around, waiting for cases. Nothing to do but search a title now and then. No wonder some of them take to drink."

Sclater Montague tells the story of Judge J.W.G. Blackstone of the Eastern Shore, whose judicial circuit years ago included Hampton. A brilliant judge, he would often hole up for days at a time in what General Montague politely called a "sporting house," operated by Mamie Shafer in Phoebus. Lawyers whose cases Blackstone ignored grew indignant. One kindly lawyer frequently had to take the court orders and decrees to Mamie Shafer's sporting house so Judge Blackstone could sign them. An irate bar and public finally brought proceedings against the judge, and he stepped down.

Despite such high-livers, the bar drew a lot of fine lawyers and judges back in those free-wheeling days. I was fond of Judge T.J.

(Thomas Jefferson) Barham of Newport News Circuit Court, who once mistook me for my great-grandfather Holloway whom he'd known in Surry in the 19th century. His absent mindedness knew no bounds.

Another Newport News jurist was John B. Locke, who once heard a charge against J. Lynwood "Ding" Price, a fellow Times-Herald journalist, accused of shooting at a neighbor's dog. Eddie Travis, the Times-Herald's office cut-up, loved to impersonate Judge Locke, wagging a reprimanding finger and sorrowfully intoning from the bench, "You can't just shoot a man's dawg, Price." That became a byword in the city room when I was a reporter.

Judges often dismayed me by seeming to sleep on the bench. I remember old Judge Glasgow of Rockbridge County, a kinsman of Ellen Glasgow, snoozing with eyes closed at the courtroom in Lexington. But I was misled. The moment something struck his attention, he was all business. He reminded me of the sleeping lion in Aesop's fable who let the mouse play until he got close to hand. Then whammo! A dead mouse.

The practice of law has changed since Sclater Montague's youth. I am impressed at how hard most judges today work to keep their dockets current. Many lawyers tell me they miss the camaraderie of Sclater Montague's era.

Daily Press

Elizabeth City County's courthouse became Hampton's in the 1950s when city and county merged. The 1910 building has been expanded and other civic buildings added.

Daily Press

Begun in 1918 on Back River near Hampton, Langley Field was an early Army Air Corps training center. In 1930 its few buildings included few airplane hangars, but it grew in World War 2.

36. *Langley Rises from the Swamp*

AFTER World War I was over, Americans thought it could never happen again. We were wrong. I was at Langley Field one night in February 1939, when Colonel Walter Weaver expressed the view that Europe would be at war in 60 days. Sure enough, a month later Hitler seized Bohemia and Moravia, and World War II was underway.

I thought of that as I leafed recently through the picture book, *Langley Field, the Early Years,* which has been published by that base.

Langley was making history in the 30s. The Air Corps was still part of the Army, but aviation was feeling its oats. Americans knew that it would be the cutting edge of our military weaponry if we got involved in war. Bright Langley officers like Hap Arnold, Carl Spaatz, Elwood Quesada, Bob Stratemeyer, Ira Eaker, Frank Andrews, and Arnold Krogstad were showing what air power could do. All would become famous in the war.

And Langley itself made news. General Billy Mitchell, the outspoken air advocate, was often there in the 1920s, preaching the futility of battleships in a war with bombing planes. Mitchell himself led the air bombardment by Langley planes of a Navy ship in Chesapeake Bay, with General Pershing looking on. He showed us the danger to ships in an air war.

One of my Langley heroes was Colonel Robert Old, who, in the 1930s, led Langley flying fortresses on a series of goodwill missions to foreign countries—Brazil, Argentina, Colombia, and so on. Actually, they were trying to show off the Air Corps and impress the world with American might. Unfortunately, we didn't impress Hitler.

Airmen have flair, and Langley had its share of flair. Beirne Lay, who married Ludwell Lee of Hampton, was a good example. Besides flying, he wrote "I Wanted Wings," which became a smash movie. Langley's big flying fortresses and their crews starred in MGM's "Test Pilot" in 1938, along with Spencer Tracy, Myrna Loy, and Clark Gable. A few scenes were made at Langley, with the stars supported by enlisted men as extras.

The base then was small and nondescript. It had started only in 1918, when the U.S. decided it needed an airfield to serve both the Army Air Corps and the experimental National Advisory Committee for Aeronautics (NACA)—later NASA. After a long search, Army Captain Richard Coke Marshall came down from Washington and negotiated with Hamptonians Harry Holt, Hunter Booker,

Army airmen at Langley held an inspection of new planes in 1921. In World War 2 the Peninsula field became part of the newly independent U.S. Air Force and trained many flyers.

and Nelson Groome, who had optioned 1,659 acres along Back River to offer for sale to Uncle Sam.

To mislead other real estate promoters, the Army sent down secret investigators dressed as hunters and fishermen, to look over the prospective Langley site. A half-dozen old farms were included: Frank Darling's "Sherwood," John Kimberley's "Lamington" and "Tide Mill," and Robert Mason's "Downing Farm" among them. In the acreage was also "Chesterville," the historic house in which George Wythe had been born in 1726. All are gone now.

One of the workmen who worked to build the base was a big, overgrown, Carolinian named Thomas Wolfe. He wrote about it in *Look Homeward, Angel*.

Langley was a muddy mess for many years after 1918. One airman wrote that "Nature's greatest ambition was to produce in this, her cesspool, the muddiest mud, the weediest weeds, the dustiest dust, and the most ferocious mosquitoes the world has ever known. Her plans were so well formulated that she far surpassed her wildest hopes . . ."

It took many years to civilize the place. When I saw Langley in the late 20s, it still looked worse than other military bases, which is pretty awful. In those days officers at snooty Fort Monroe looked down on Langley as a disaster area. Stately old Monroe had age, tradition, comfort, and picturesque architecture. Langley had only temporary hovels, mud, and mosquitoes.

But things got better. The rise of aviation

was inevitable. As one of the Army's first airfields and as the seat of the prestigious NACA, Langley attracted not only daring young men in their flying machines but also skilled scientists and designers.

We locals at first regarded the bearded NACA wizards as weirdos, up to no good. They dressed and acted like kooks, and they worked at mysterious jobs. But years later, when that research produced trips to the moon, we had to take it all back.

One of their leaders was Eastman Jacobs, a handsome, bearded scientist now living in California. We called him the mad genius.

The most interesting craft at early Langley was dirigibles. In the early days of air travel, both the Army and Navy experimented with lighter-than-air craft, which Count Zeppelin had pioneered in 1900 in Germany. The big zeppelin hangars at Langley attracted many Sunday visitors. I remember the smell of chemicals and rubber in those vast halls—a very different smell from the banana oil and gasoline of the airplane sheds.

I suspect that the crash of the Langley-based dirigible Roma had something to do with the decline of such experiments at Langley. Billy Mitchell had urged the Army to

Casemate Museum

Dirigibles were based at Langley in the 1920s while the Army tested their usefulness for observation and transport. Four were photographed over the landing field in 1921.

buy the Italian airship in 1920, after the Army had been unable to buy a German zeppelin. The Roma was bought and disassembled in Italy, then sent to Langley by ship in 1921. But she was a headache all the way. Her fabric was found to be mildewed and required 84 repair patches. Her Italian engines had to be replaced.

Finally, the big pachyderm took off from Langley to test her new engines on a February day in 1922. Her nose began to buckle almost immediately. When she reached the Naval Air Station at Norfolk, her box-kite elevator slipped. That jammed her controls, and the great ship crashed at Norfolk's Army piers. As she fell, she struck high voltage wires which ignited her hydrogen. Suddenly she was a pillar of fire, visible all the way from Hampton and Newport News.

Thirty-four of her 45 crew were killed that day. Some jumped from her gondolas and were killed by the impact. The city of Newport News held a memorial service on the Casino grounds. One casket was carried in the procession, symbolizing all the dead. During the service, Langley flyers overhead swooped down and dropped roses. It was an unusual—and unnerving—tribute.

Pearl Harbor changed Langley and the NACA into big operations.

When World War II burst, Langley was the crest of its wave. My friend Colonel Weaver became a general and head of the vast Army Technical Training Command. (His aide for awhile was Delk Simpson, a fellow Smithfield native and Times-Herald staffer, who rose to become a colonel). Many of those fly-boys I'd known as captains, majors, and colonels moved up to three- and four-star generals. Langley was the mother of it all.

The war expanded the Army Air Corps into the United States Air Force, a new service.

Yes, the exciting aerial action today has moved to outer space. In the 65 years since Langley started, the military plane has become as old hat as the battleship. We take it for granted. Where do we go from here?

By 1934 Langley was growing rapidly. This Army dirigible was berthed in hangar at rear of landing field. Langley also became base of the National Advisory Committee on Aeronautics.

Daily Press

37. *The Crabber-Typhoon Rivalry*

EVERY time I drive by old Newport News High School, now no longer used for that purpose, I suffer from nostalgia. It's no beauty, God knows, and its neighborhood has sadly declined, but to generations of graduates it holds memories.

Who can forget those fierce Newport News-Hampton rivalries—the Typhoons against the Crabbers—that absorbed us? Or the critical year-end football game which ended in bloody noses and broken goal posts? We were a typical segment of pre-World War II America—full of school spirit and churning ambitions. Winning games and going on to college, riches, fame, and marriage were our modest goals.

Seriously, though, I believe Newport News High School did more to unify and direct community spirit than anything else in those days. Newport News was a new and shapeless city, lacking unity, civic spirit, or a due sense of its importance. People from older towns like Hampton, Williamsburg, and Norfolk thought the upstart industrial center which Collis Huntington had started in 1881 lacked culture. (Some still do.) We tried to show them they were wrong.

When I entered the school in February 1931, it seemed huge. Actually, it had only about 1,000 students, but it dwarfed Stonewall Jackson and John W. Daniel, which I previously attended. (Confederate names then graced many Newport News schools, white and black.) When the corridor bells rang to change classes, the halls instantly filled with noisy, darting teen-agers, for you had only five minutes to get to your next teacher.

Those halls were unforgettable. They reeked of Varsol and Lysol, for cleanliness was next to godliness in public schools. Football trophies and Latin mottoes around the hall walls urged us to "live up to our capacities," as Principal Fred M. Alexander exhorted in Monday morning assemblies. I remember that one motto read "Ad astra per aspera," which my Latin rendered into "To the stars through hope," or something.

High school was the great middle-class opportunity, and most Typhooners took it seriously. Oh, we had schoolyard fights and cheating on tests, but decorum and the honor system generally prevailed. When teachers like Margaret Sayre or Annye Burbank saw us loitering in the halls, they strictly reprimanded us and sent us scurrying. Teachers had authority. We feared it.

If you were really bad, they sent you to "the

office," where Fred Alexander or Assistant Principal Lamar Stanley talked with you, or sent you abjectly home. Girls who offended had to see the dean of women, who was Mary Wynne Jones and, after her death, Ethel Gildersleeve.

I'll never forget the morning at high school when Miss Jones died. The high school orchestra was rehearsing, under Eleanor Sherman, when a messenger interrupted the Barcarolle from the "Tales of Hoffman." Miss Sherman read the note inaudibly and dropped her face in her hands. Then, with tears in her eyes, she told us Miss Jones had just died in school of a heart attack.

Our heroes in those blessed years were the stars of our Typhoon teams. Those jocks wore varsity sweaters knitted of gold and blue. Girls worshipped them. Guys like Bird Hooper, Cootie Almond, Horse Hallett, and Charlie and Bob Spangler were far more important to us than Calvin Coolidge or Herbert Hoover, loafing around up there in the White House. If you made the winning touchdown against those Crabbers, you could have a job in the shipyard for life.

We non-athletic fellows, deprived of varsity letters, wore smelly brown buckskin jackets and dirty white buck or brown-and-white saddle shoes. Girls fancied sweaters and skirts. If their clothes were too low-cut or too short, the dean of women would call them down. We must be ladies and gentlemen.

By modern standards, the high school was undemocratic and "elitist." It had no blacks, for they all went to Huntington High. And we Typhooners were clearly divided into pre-college, commercial, and industrial arts candidates, which some souls today would condemn as derogatory to non-collegiates. But I don't think it was or is.

Ours was the twilight of the liberal arts, and we pre-college hopefuls got heavy doses of English, history, algebra (ugh), geometry (ugh), physics, chemistry, Latin, and modern languages. The English department especially was notable for talented teachers like Anne Perkins Scruggs, Mae Marshall Edwards, Anne Victoria Parker, and Annye Burbank. "Miss Annye" polished us up so well in senior English that William and Mary made her a Phi Beta Kappa for her good works.

In fact, Newport News graduates were recognized at William and Mary as among the best-prepared students they got. One reason was that the Newport News system, under Superintendent Joseph H. Saunders, paid teachers better than most Virginia towns, thus drawing top teachers from other localities. Even so, the salaries ranged around $2,000 to $5,000—good in those days. Many elementary teachers in Virginia then made less than $1,000 a year.

Most colleges required Latin for admission, so I struggled through Caesar, Cicero, and other bores with teachers Mabel Barham, Elma Free, and Willie Shelton. Latin was believed to help you with English, French, history, and God knows what else, but it seemed to me a hard way to acquire "culture." The best day in class was when Jimmy Bond, a tough amateur prizefighter, lifted little Wallace Hiden up by the scruff of his neck and the seat of his pants and deposited him in the shrubbery outside our first floor classroom window. Miss Barham fortunately wasn't looking.

"Activities" played a big role at N.N.H.S., and everybody was supposed to "go out" for something. I played a quavery violin in Eleanor Sherman's orchestra, and I remember every note of the second violin part of "Our Leader," which we played as the recessional when Howard Scammon's class graduated, about 1933. An emotional fellow, poor Howard burst into loud tears as he led his classmates up the aisle, in cap and gown, after Fred Alexander had fulsomely bestowed diplomas

Newport News High School was that city's only white high in 1929. It was closed in the 1970s. Based at 31st and Huntington, its Typhoon football team annually played season's finale with Hampton's Crabbers.

and his blessings. Howard has since told me it was my sensitive violin playing that undid him, but I doubt that.

My chief extracurricular interest was the Beacon, the high school paper, which chose me as editor the last year. When I wrote one editorial filler that said "What this school needs is less principal and more interest," Principal Alexander called me in for a heart-to-heart talk. Boys will be boys.

Some teachers had a tough, no-nonsense approach which upset students and parents, but I guess it was good for us. When I turned in to Annye Burbank a rewrite of a paper from an earlier course, her indignation knew no bounds. She threatened to put me out of class. And when I made a bright remark in physics class to Dr. Cornelia Segar, she responded: "Young man, there's only one funny person in this room. That's me. Understand?"

Most of us had difficulties with math, for the subject wasn't taught then as well as the "new math" is today. Poor Lily Saunders, Ethel Gildersleeve, and Herman Levy of the math department really struggled with us dolts. I never could fully get the hang of it, so my checkbook is chronically out of balance even today. But I still doubt the utility of algebra and geometry to most students.

At last, in February of 1933, came the day when I too marched up the farewell aisle, as Howard Scammon had done, while Miss Sherman's orchestra scraped and puffed away at "Our Leader." Unlike Howard, though, I felt no great sadness at leaving all those math theorems, those Latin conjugations, and those tables of kooky elements in Dr. Segar's physics. Still, life has often reminded me since that there was more to Newport News High School than met the eye. (Or the nose.) I wish I'd learned to do math better, for one thing.

That's why that forlorn building is a sad sight to see. It is filled with ghosts and memories of youthful ambitions for my generation.

38. 'Happy Am I' Elder Michaux

IF I were asked to name the most unforgettable character I've known, I'd pick Solomon Lightfoot Michaux.

Elder Michaux was a black evangelist who was born at Buckroe about 1895, began to preach in Newport News in 1919 and carried on a mighty "War Against the Devil" over national radio for 40 years before he died in 1968.

But the Elder wasn't your ordinary, run-of-the-mill preacher. No, sir. He was a showman who led massive parades of rhythmic, white-clad followers down Jefferson Avenue every Labor Day. His huge "baptizing" at the Small Boat Harbor drew thousands, both white and black. His "Happy Am I" theme rang out over the CBS and Mutual networks for decades.

The Elder was a product of the Peninsula. Even after he became rich and lived in style in Washington, he and his wife kept their house at 505 Ivy Ave. Several times yearly his chauffeur would drive him here from D.C. in his Cadillac. His Gospel Spreading Church, which he founded in World War I, still stands at 19th Street and Jefferson Avenue.

Some people questioned Michaux's sincerity, but to me he seemed a godly and kind man. His church did much to help blacks and it continues in 14 locations today, from New York to North Carolina.

Elder Michaux has been criticized for the amusement park which stood on the Colonial Parkway near Jamestown. I'm one who objected to it, but I can understand Michaux's desire for a memorial to those first Africans brought to Virginia in 1619. Fortunately, the Park Service has now leased the area and is restoring it to nature.

Another of the Elder's projects died soon after he did. That was his projected "Francis Lightfoot Lee Residential Colony," which he announced in the 1960s in Charles City County. The 636-acre tract was sold recently and a riverfront estate is being built there by Walter Robertson Jr., Richmond tobacconist and son of a World War II diplomat.

I knew Mr. Michaux in the Newport News of the 1940s and '50s. He was a stocky mulatto spellbinder with a gift for gab. He had dignity and a gravelly voice of great power. He proclaimed himself "General of the International Forces of Right Against Wrong," and made you feel that the devil was a living person—a diabolical communist.

The Elder had the orator's ability to put

Daily Press

Elder Solomon Lightfoot Michaux was a widely known evangelist who began his career in Newport News.

things in dramatic terms. He made World War II a battle between a free enterprise Jehovah and a communist devil.

"Happiness in God" was the Elder's favorite theme. Though he shouted and gesticulated as if he were angry, he didn't try to frighten his congregation with visions of hellfire. His God was a loving father to his wayward children. "Is everybody happy?" he would ask in his sermons. "This is Elder Lightfoot Solomon Michaux, the "Happy Am I" preacher, with glory in his soul. Glory means praise and I am filled with the praises of a mighty God."

Michaux called his listeners "my precious ones." But despite his faith, he grew a little pessimistic in old age. "People the world over have left God," he said before he died. "The world is not getting better. We're in an awful condition . . . The communists in Russia represent the devil and there can be no compromise with the devil."

The Elder had powerful friends. One of them, Eleanor Roosevelt, persuaded F.D.R. and Harold Ickes that Michaux's projected 1,000-acre Negro historical park near Jamestown was compatible with the Colonial Parkway. As a result, the Park Service had to let Michaux's ferris wheel and merry-go-round occupy the James River shore. Though that has now ended, Michaux's organization continues to operate a dairy farm nearby.

What sold Eleanor Roosevelt on Michaux was his work with the New Deal to build cheap housing for blacks in post-Depression Washington. His Gospel Spreading Association created more than 1,300 low-income apartments, some with FHA money. His association still runs these.

Michaux in old age came to be regarded as an "Uncle Tom" by militant young blacks, but he remained popular with many old people. In his last years he attacked Martin Luther King for his strikes and demonstrations for black rights. "I don't approve of King's manner in defying local government," the Elder said.

Such gradualist views pleased moderates, including many whites, no matter how they displeased King. Michaux was often a guest on shipyard trial trips and often in demand to speak to workers at the yard and the Smithfield meat packing houses. He was a good moderator.

Michaux claimed credit for the idea of the Colonial Parkway, but that concept really went back beyond him to the Yorktown Sesquicentennial of 1931. It's true, though, that Michaux bought his Jamestown acreage before the parkway was built.

It's also true that he told Park Service Director Arthur Demaray in the 1940s that the Park Service should rebuild the 17th century road which led from Jamestown to Williamsburg by College Creek.

"Happy Am I" Elder Michaux

The Park Service did just that and paid Michaux $10,000 for his river frontage.

The Elder claimed kin to the proud Lightfoot and Michaux families of Virginia and he was probably right.

As a boy he fished for a living at Hampton and he came to see himself as Jesus' disciple, Peter the fisherman. He held his first tent meeting in 1919 at 19th Street and Jefferson Avenue, converting 150 hearers. Then he started a charity store at Bloodfield, a black area near the Boat Harbor, where blind people and invalids could eat free and others at cost.

When I lived in Newport News Michaux was at his height. His only rival as a black leader was Bishop Grace, a Portuguese whose House of God for All People had competing revival meetings.

Daddy Grace was the more impressive figure of the two—tall, mustached and with long hair and curling fingernails. He had an air of mystery, but in the final analysis, the Elder got a bigger following. Nobody could beat his radio exposure and his War Against the Devil. Nobody had friends like Eleanor Roosevelt and Harold Ickes.

Once you saw the Elder leading the army of the Lord down Jefferson Avenue as I did, you couldn't forget him. He brightened Newport News life.

Daily Press

Elder Michaux, at right, was welcomed to the podium at a Washington service. Eleanor Roosevelt admired his Gospel-Spreading Association, which built low-rent apartments for blacks.

39. *Stores on Washington Avenue*

THE Peninsula's big shopping street in the 1930s was Washington Avenue in Newport News. But since then, both old Hampton and old Newport News have lost business to surburban malls and roadside shops.

To main stem of the Peninsula today is Warwick Boulevard. It's become very popular with doctors, lawyers, and realtors. Mercury Boulevard is easily the Peninsula's retail hub, more a part of Hampton than of Newport News.

Old Washington Avenue was a lively place from Spanish-American War days till the end of World War II. It saw its share of military parades, ship launchings, and war bond rallies. It was never beautiful—too narrow and lacking handsome buildings and vistas—but it was *the* place to have your store. People came from Gloucester, Williamsburg, and Smithfield to shop there.

The key intersection was Twenty-Eighth and Washington. There the north-south trolleys met the east-west trolleys. There you could transfer to go to Hampton, Old Point, Hilton, or wherever the lines went. For a few years in the '30s, pleasant little Washington Park offered a pavilion and a grassy plaza for those waiting for streetcars. It was later built up.

Cater-cornered across from the park was the First National, the city's oldest and richest bank, with four or five floors of lawyers over it. It had been founded by the Huntingtons in 1889, a few months before George Ben West and a few locals created the competing Citizens Marine Bank. They were hot rivals, for Mr. West and his board resented the power of "the shipyard crowd."

The early avenue was lined with locally-owned businesses. Most of these later gave way to chain stores, which sought the trade of shipyard laborers. Many local shops were killed by the chains; others moved west. Thus, as the suburbs grew, an early exodus of business began. It has led to the virtual end of downtown as a shopping area.

Below Twenty-Eighth Street the social tone of our main stem from the city's first years was tarnished by proximity to the waterfront. On lower Washington were many saloons before prohibition stopped them. Some were dives, not much better than those on River Road and Hell's Half Acre. By the 1930s, when I knew the avenue, restaurants like Lohse's and the U.S. had replaced the saloons. Even so, the area had its low-life rooming houses and prostitutes.

At Twenty-Fifth and Washington was George Ben West's Citizens Marine, later merged with the Jefferson, also topped by lawyers' offices. On another corner was Levinson's market, which had sidewalk counters to display fish and vegetables. Streetside displays were common in those days. I remember another such emporium at Twenty-Eighth and Washington which had a roof over its sidewalk. You see that often in Caribbean and Mediterranean markets.

Chain drug stores in the '30s were few. We had Gorsuch's, Pennybackers, and Falconers. All had round marble-top tables where you drank your sarsaparilla, cherry smash, or root beer.

I remember a Richmond lady objecting to the ten-cent price for a milkshake in one of these emporia. "I've never paid more than a nickel in Richmond," she told the soda jerk. "Well, I guess you'd better go back to Richmond," said the jerk, saucily.

My favorite store was Epes Stationery, the town's only book and stationery shop. It also sold cameras, developed film and framed pictures. That was the day of Wallace Nutting and Maxfield Parrish. I spent a lot of time looking over Mr. Epes' Tom Slade and Tom Swift books, but he never objected.

Next door to Epes' was Monfalcone's, which called itself a newsstand but did a heavy trade in cokes, coffee, and sports gossip. After church on Sunday, everybody went to Monfalcone's for the New York Times, which then cost 25 cents. A few diehard Republicans—there weren't many of them in town—insisted on the Herald Tribune.

Across the avenue from Epes' was Ferguson's Music Store, which had a large plaster dog in its window, listening to "His Master's Voice." Wind-up Victrolas were new then, and you went to Ferguson's to get Paul Whiteman, Al Jolson, Nat Shilkret, and Rudy Vallee records. If you were into opera, you went for Galli Curci or Caruso.

Ferguson's rival was Gemmell's, about Twenty-Seventh, which was big in musical horns. Gordon Weyburn and others taught instrumental music in upstairs rooms. On summer days, they left the windows open, and the shoppers got an earful—good or bad.

Mr. Rosenbaum, a pudgy emigre from Germany, had the town's biggest hardware store, about Twenty-Sixth Street. He added china, glass, and decorative objects as time went on and ended up as a small conglomerate. A lot of ladies then painted china, and he catered to them. I remember buying oil paints and toy soldiers there. A competitor further up the avenue was the China Place and Gift Shop, also owned by German emigrants.

The biggest store on the avenue was Nachman's. I was first aware of its existence at about Thirtieth and Washington, but it built a bigger store and moved to about Thirty-Second and Washington. It was a well-run, friendly place that dealt kindly with its employees and creditors in Depression days. Next to Richmond's two top stores, it then did the heaviest business of any department store in Virginia. The good-looking young ladies at the cosmetics counter dressed in low-cut black, as if they were going to dance at 9 a.m., and they smelled to high heaven. Needless to say, they drew a lot of attention from swains from the Apprentice School and the high schools. Herbie Nachman had to keep a close eye on the merchandise.

The town's movie palaces were a glamorous touch in an otherwise working-class city. Even their names—Rialto, Olympic, Cameo, Palace—evoke pleasure. The Gordon brothers did a good job of promoting their aging Palace against the chain which operated the others. The confectionary next door to the Palace sold the best orange snowballs in town.

Stores on Washington Avenue

Lunch hour on working days was a social occasion. Most bank and legal tycoons went home to lunch. Some people even "dropped down" to sleep for a half-hour or so after lunch, a now-dead Southern amenity.

There never were many good eating places on the avenue, and people probably couldn't have afforded them if they had existed. So Woolworth's lunch counter, Nachman's soda shop, Day's Drugstore, and the United States Restaurant got the business. If you were well-heeled, you'd go to the Bide-a-Wee Tea Room on Twenty-Eighth or to the faded elegance of the Warwick Hotel dining room. It was patronized daily by a limousine full of shipyard executives.

I remember several stores for their good products. Mrs. Fox had a candy store near Nachman's which sold the best chocolates and salted nuts you ever ate. And the Florida Orange Store, across the avenue from Nachman's, was the best produce store the town had. Its owners came to Newport News from Florida and decided to show us what tree-ripened oranges tasted like. They succeeded.

The area around the shipyard, on upper Washington Avenue, was another world, frequented by shipyard workers. Several European families who sold five-cent hot dogs there did well. It's impressive to see how many family fortunes on the Peninsula have grown from little enterprises that started in my day on Washington Avenue. That's America, and I'm all for it.

Daily Press

Washington Avenue in 1931 was the Peninsula's shopping hub. Clock at right marked First National Bank at 28th Street. Across the avenue was Washington Square, where Hampton and North End trolley routes crossed.

The shores and creeks of the Peninsula began to attract home-builders in the 1930s, leading to an exodus from the two downtown cities. Alexander C. Brown took this scene of workboats on a James River inlet in those years.

V.
The Beginning of the Suburbs
1930–1940

Daily Press
Hampton Mayor J. G. Crenshaw turned first shovel in 1952 to widen Victoria Boulevard to six lanes as state and local offiicals watched. Growth of traffic led to wider streets and new bridges.

40. *The Flight to the Suburbs*

SINCE World War 2 automobiles have lured most ex-residents of downtown Newport News and Hampton, to live in the suburbs. We're really one big, loose confederation now.

It was simpler when I grew up in Newport News in the 1930s. Then the Peninsula had a few well-defined towns and cities: Hampton, Phoebus, Newport News, Yorktown, and Williamsburg. The rest was woods and farms.

But the flight from downtown Newport News and Hampton in the 1930s and '40s has peopled the shores of the James and the York with waterfront subdivisions. Some commute daily from Williamsburg to Norfolk or Richmond. Gloucester and sunny Isle of Wight County are also gaining many Peninsula commuters. We're a more complex society than we used to be.

How different all this is from the years 1921 to 1934, when I was going to public schools in Newport News. Then the city was made up of clearly identified sections: West Avenue, downtown, North End, East End, the Boulevard, and a few others. Woods and fields separated Hampton and Newport News. The counties of Elizabeth City and Warwick competed with the cities until Hampton took over one and Newport News the other.

My world at Stonewall Jackson School in the 1920s was the orderly small world of North End. North End ran from about 50th Street westward to the city limits at 64th Street, and from the shipyard on the south to the C&O tracks on the north. But even North End was divided into neighborhoods.

Hilton Village was a different place, built as a World War I workers' town. It was part of Warwick County, so its children went to county schools, including the high school at Morrison. We didn't mix much because you stayed mostly in your own sanitary district. We didn't have many cars.

I and other North End kids went to Stonewall Jackson, close to Huntington Avenue and 48th Street. It was a nondescript building (now torn down, I think) next door to a fire station. Close by were Calvary Baptist Church and Turner's Drug Store, which we students haunted for candy and Coca Cola at lunch. Jackson school originally carried you through the 7th grade, but in my era the 6th and 7th grades were moved to John Daniel school downtown.

North End was what you'd call "upscale" then, but there were social gradations within North End which a child could feel. For one thing, houses got bigger the higher you went up Huntington Avenue. I mean, it was tonier to live on 64th Street than on 45th or 50th, though that didn't seem to bother most Jacksonians. Very few people had what you'd call "big money," and most of those who did have it tried to act like they didn't.

Throughout North End were gangs of children who played together because they lived close by each other. For example, around 53rd Street were the Samuel Buxtons, Caleb Wests, A. A. Applewhites, Henry Marshalls, T. J. Hundleys, Edward Siegels, and P. F. Halseys. I saw a lot of many of them.

Close to 55th Street were the Nortons, Wheelers, Bivins, Hutchens, Hidens, and Fergusons. I went to 55th Street to put pennies on the trolley rack and to pick them up after they'd been mashed flat.

In my 59th Street neighborhood we usually congregated on the James River bank or went down a steep dirt path to swim or crab in the river below. At various times the participants included Rouses, Epeses, Holts, Richardsons, Garys, McMurrans, Huffmans, Seneys, Hopkins, Pughs, Watkins, Longakers, and Amorys. I also have memories of other children whose families moved away early, like Atkins Spencer, Nancy Rice, and Roger Lord. What became of them?

By the time my younger brothers, Dashiell and Bill, came along, the teen-age action had moved from 59th Street to about 64th. On or near that street lived the Logan Harrises, Downings, Marables, Mabrys, Sneads, Stuarts, Overtons, and others. By that time Huntington Heights was building up beyond 64th Street, and new families were coming in too fast for me to know.

It was a sad day for Jackson School when its enrollment outgrew the building. (It had started out with eight classrooms but doubled in size in the 1930s). I believe I was in the first Jackson 6th grade that had to be sent downtown to attend John W. Daniel School, between Washington and Huntington Avenues and between 31st and 32d Streets. We 6th graders felt like we were being deported to Devil's Island, but it didn't turn out to be so bad.

Going to Daniel opened up a new world. My family had lived in 1918-19 downtown on West Avenue, near the school, when we first moved over from Smithfield, but I was too young to know downtown (I was three years old). However, I found some virtues in Daniel School. For one, you had a bigger choice of stores after school. For another, it was next door to the Palace Theater.

When my class entered Newport News High in 1930, it was easy for me because John W. Daniel School was located just across Huntington Avenue from it. (Rodef Sholem Synagogue and Watson-Gies Auto Repair stood between them, but you could see one school from the other.)

High school at first overwhelmed me by its size. It had about 1,000 students, which was double the number at Jackson School. Most of them in 1930 came from the East End and had gone to schools like Woodrow Wilson, Bankhead Magruder, and Walter Reed. After a while I liked them as well as the classmates I'd grown up with at Stonewall Jackson.

I found that East Enders had groups too. In high school I saw a lot of what we called the Orcutt Avenue crowd, the Oak Avenue crowd, and the Boulevard crowd. Although we fussed about it, Newport News High was a good school. We had fewer luxuries to distract us than today. Drugs were unheard of in school. Certainly we had the advantages of a spartan spirit in that work-oriented blue-collar day. That was before the integration of blacks and whites, which has changed education greatly.

When I drive through downtown Newport News today, I look for the houses of ex-schoolmates. But most of the houses are torn down. Much of West Avenue, downtown, and the East End have simply disappeared. Most of North End and the Boulevard have thus far escaped the axe. I hope they can survive, for some of those old houses have charm and happy associations for many people who grew up in the past 60 years.

There's been a steady flow of households westward since the year 1881, when the C&O railway came in and Newport News started as a town. At first the town's homes were on 18th Street. Then householders fanned out along trolley lines following the James River and Hampton Roads. Now the waterfront is filled, and interior areas are filling up. We'll be one big community someday.

All this makes life complicated. The Highway Department says we'll need a second bridge across the York in no time. And if we're smart, we'll replace those ferries across the James at Jamestown with another bridge or a tunnel. Highway traffic grows from 2 to 4 percent a year, and it doesn't take long to develop gluts like the current one on the Hampton Roads Bridge Tunnel.

All this underlines the wisdom of efforts to improve downtown Hampton and Newport News and draw residents back there to live. If everyone commutes, we'll have more traffic than we can handle. And cities need hefty real estate revenues to offset highway and police costs. That's why I hope the Newport Centre plan in my ex-hometown will succeed.

Children growing up need a sense of belonging. The Peninsula must always have its neighborhoods, its school rivalries. We need local attachments to give us roots.

Cars destined for Newport News ferries to Norfolk traversed Jefferson Avenue in the years before Hampton Roads Tunnel was light. The avenue is major center of black commerce.

Daily Press

41. *Pearl Bailey and Ella Fitzgerald*

WHEN men begin reminiscing about how hard they worked as $10-a-week helpers at the shipyard in the old days, I feel left out. I earned my summer keep instead at the C&O terminals, and later at the Times-Herald, when it was printed on Twenty-Fifth Street.

As a boy in the North End, I was a neighbor of James Carr Baker, who was superintendent of cargo piers at the C&O, and he gave summer jobs to my brother Ran and me. It was hard work for $1.50 a day, but that was good then. And the piers were an international world of ships, trains, and exotic cargo. They smelled of tobacco, coffee, and other things. The banana boats brought big tropical spiders.

In those days, River Road ran from Pier A, at Twenty-Fifth Street, past a motley collection of crew outfitters' and ship chandlers' shacks down to Eighteenth Street and Hell's Half Acre. By 1936, when I was 16 and permitted to work for the C&O, sinfulness had largely disappeared from Hell's Half Acre, worse luck, but a few sinners were still left. They added to the excitement of an otherwise proper city.

At Eighteenth Street and along River Road were low-class eateries, ex-saloons, and faded "houses of ill-repute." The lurid past of the area when Newport News was decried in the press as a "wide-open" port still gave the city a bad name. To a squeaky-clean Baptist kid of 16, as I was, Hell's Half Acre in my youth seemed gloriously sinful.

Jimmy Baker hired me at $9 a week to work at night, checking freight. It came off the coastal steamships and my job was to get it onto freight cars. I went to work about suppertime, after the ships had come in each day, and labored till 2 or 3 in the morning, when the big C&O engine pulled our long line of loaded freight cars and empty gondolas up the tracks through Richmond, Huntington, W.Va., and on to the west.

If the weather was good, I walked home then to Fifty-Ninth Street to save a 50-cent taxi ride.

Night people live in a world of their own. The C&O docks bred a camaraderie of loneliness—busy men working against the clock to get ships unloaded and the train made up. Each of us checkers had a gang of six or eight freight handlers—burly black men who were as awed of me as I was of them. By summer's end, though, we were friends.

I nearly gave my boss a heart attack when I misloaded a barrel of rat traps on a freight car to East St. Louis instead of a barrel of sugar.

Pearl Bailey and Ella Fitzgerald   187

In those days the C&O handled lots of bauxite ore, which came from the Caribbean to make aluminum. The most fragrant cargo was tobacco, packed in hogsheads on its way to the British Isles. Much of that leaf, alas, has now moved to Carolina ports.

Other cargoes which we handled—on daytime shifts rather than at night—were coffee and rubber. But the U.S. doesn't import much rubber any more, I believe, now that tires are largely synthetic.

In the darkness of summer nights, foreign crews—Lascars, Chinese, Japanese, Indians—looked ominous. In fact, many killings had occurred on Hell's Half Acre in the World

Newport News Historical Committee

Pearl Bailey was born in a poor neighborhood near Jefferson Avenue in 1918.

They looked alike, but at the end, I had a telltale extra barrel to account for. Too late: I found a bill of lading which read "1 bl rat traps." It was life's darkest moment.

(I can see in my mind that storekeeper in East St. Louis prying open a barrel to scoop out sugar. Damnation! Rat traps!)

You couldn't hear yourself think on those piers. Noisy tractors pulled lines of heavily-loaded dollies from shipside to loading docks. Sometimes the men sang as they worked—gospel or work songs, I suppose, but I couldn't hear much in the din. When the supper whistle blew at 11, we sat on the dock and ate from paper bags or lunch boxes. No finger bowls.

Newport News Historical Committee

Ella Fitzgerald was born within a month of Pearl Bailey in nearby Bloodfield.

War I era, but they had subsided when my work days came along.

In his memoirs, Walter Kelly, who became the "Virginia Judge" of vaudeville fame, wrote of the terrible fights in the saloons of Hell's Half Acre and of Twenty-Third and Twenty-Fourth Streets in the years at the beginning of this century. Kelly, who came to the yard in the Spanish-American War, was himself a big Irish brawler, and he had plenty of fights of his own before he became a man of property and quieted down. He opened his own saloon, learned to ape Judge J.D.G. Brown of Newport News police court, and went on the stage to become a worldwide hit.

Hell's Half Acre was known for its bordellos in those permissive years. Several flourished on Eighteenth Street, which had briefly became Newport News' "bon ton" section after the C&O began to change that little fishing village into a city in 1881. But soon proper families moved westward to the Casino, along West Avenue, to escape the onslaught of rail workers and ships' crews. It was the beginning of the urban flight which today afflicts too many cities.

Those "houses of ill-fame," as the police called them, spread in the 1890s and 1900s over lower Newport News, catering to ships crewmen on the prowl. The late Eddie Travis wrote of Kate Pleasants, a local madam, who flourished undisturbed by police for many years on Eighteenth Street. A civic reform administration in the early 1900s, sparked by the Rev. E.T. Wellford, alas, finally did poor Kate and her sisters in. Prohibition in 1919 helped to douse the flickering flames of sin in our erstwhile "Sin City."

Another gaudy area was "Bloodfield," which adjoined Warwick and Jefferson Avenues for about 40 years after Newport News started in 1881. Saturday nights at Bloodfield, Dawson City, and Hell's Half Acre regularly brought dozens of murders, brawls, and razor cuttings in the years before World War II. As I've said, when Newport News moved northward and eastward, these early areas became slums, occupied by poor blacks. The crime rate was horrendous.

I became acquainted with Hell's Half Acre in the 1920s, when I walked with my father on his weeky rounds to collect rents for his uncle, William E. Barrett, who had bought or inherited much of Eighteenth Street from George Benjamin West when Mr. West died in 1917.

I well remember the little "fice" dogs which yipped loudly around those slatternly houses, long gone.

Bad as those days were, they brought better things. For one thing, both Pearl Bailey and Ella Fitzgerald were born in the Bloodfield area in 1918, at the low point of our civic righteousness. Today they're among America's most famous musicians. And Solomon Lightfoot Michaux started his preaching in that area during World War I. He went on to become an important black leader, whose influence continues many years after his death.

No, I'm not ashamed of Newport News' early years, for they help explain our nation's greatness. They were the price our area paid for the Civil War—for the despoiling of our Peninsula, the relocation of uprooted black families, and the birth of a rapacious, no-holds-barred industrialism. We're overcoming them all, but it takes a little time.

42. *'Live Up to Your Potential'*

WHEN I was in high school, it was considered unAmerican not to have school spirit and not get involved in student activities. That's why Newport News High in the 1930s was a mass of would-be actors, athletes, journalists, musicians, and what-have-you.

"Motivation" was the name of the game. Principal Fred Alexander harangued us constantly about "living up to our potential." If you didn't try to Be Somebody, you weren't with it.

I guess that's how I got so deeply involved in the Beacon, the four-page weekly that I helped put to bed each Thursday afternoon at Franklin Printing Company, on Twenty-Fifth Street. It also explains my efforts to become a violinist in Eleanor Sherman's high school orchestra and those adolescent effusions I had to write and read for the long-suffering members of the Writer's Club.

Some teachers used to complain then that "activities" were crowding out classroom studies at the high school. Sometimes it looked that way, for Newport News High allowed a 50-minute "activities period" each morning, to work at your chosen pursuit. Many of us also stayed after school to rewrite, rehearse or try to make some team. We were an ambitious lot, pressed onward by the Protestant ethic.

The football players took top place in our hierarchy. Jimmy West, Horse Hallett, and their contemporaries were the envy of everybody. Then came the actors, who shared a touch of Hollywood's glamor. Dorothy Crane, who directed the plays, was a lady of verve and authority. She taught a lot of would-be Barrymores between her vacations in New England, where she worked in summer theatres.

Tilden Davis was the school's matinee idol. He was said to be a preacher's son, and he had a dark defiant look that won the ladies. He starred in a melodrama about a condemned man, "The Valiant," in which he wowed us. I remember his brave lines as he faced the electric chair, or something: "Cowards die many times, but The Valiant die only once."

Miss Crane's plays attracted pretty girls who were also, in some cases, cheerleaders. I remember Daisy Moore, Sally Moss, Olive Carleton, Nancy Applewhite, and a few others. Once or twice, I think, Miss Crane and her fellow teacher Eleanor Sherman would produce an old-fashioned musical. I remember being in the chorus of something about Rip Van Winkle. We performers took ourselves so seriously you'd have thought we were at the Metropolitan Opera.

Miss Sherman was an effective director of the orchestra and band. She took over from Melba Brustuen, who deserted scholarship in the 1930s to marry Sam Hoyle, business manager of the Daily Press and later city treasurer. Eleanor was a no-nonsense lady who could crush you with a glare when you hit the wrong note.

Several excellent high school violinists in my day made the competition for orchestra places keen. One was Howard Boatwright, who teaches music now at Syracuse University. Another was his cousin, Layton Goodman, who was lost when the submarine he commanded disappeared in World War II. Another was Irving Berlin, now a Peninsula physician. And then there was a tall girl named Sudie Jones.

With all that talent, I could only be a second violinist. But at least I was responsible for showing all the other second violinists when to attack the music and how to bow. Uniform bowing is important in an orchestra, for it looks bad if the violinists don't move their arms up and down together.

My deskmate was a cute girl named Lucille Moseley, now Mrs. Charles Epes. My standing joke with her was: "Lucille, if my G-string breaks, please take over." It had some basis of fact because the four violin strings, E, A, D, and G, sometimes break in the heat of combat. Even Itzak Perlman has lost his G-string now and then.

All of us string players sat to the left of Miss Sherman because we made up about half of the orchestra. To the right were the brass, woodwinds, and the tympani. The brass boys were a lively crew, if ever I saw one, most of them precocious jazz band performers.

They were sufficiently sold on Miss Sherman to form the first marching band in her era back in the 1930s. I have a photo of it because my brother Ran was a charter member. So were a lot of others, like Robert Saunders, Charlie Epes, Marx Eisenman, Louis Perzekow, Mabry Minter, Rouzee Givens, and Otho Givens. They were an innocent looking bunch, dressed up in their simple capes of gold and blue.

Our orchestra played for countless assembles and graduations. We were pretty good on upbeat things like "America the Beautiful," Sousa marches, and our alltime favorite for academic processions, "Our Leader." But we didn't tackle demanding music, like Bach or Beethoven.

The club to belong to was Mae Marshall Edwards' Literary Club, which had no stated requirements. If Mrs. Edwards like the cut of your jib and sensed you had "literary" interests, she asked you. We talked about books and a lot of things at meetings, but the real incentive to belong was the annual outing on a yacht up the James to see the plantations. It was an all-day bacchanalia.

We were at the age of courtship, and many a romance began to simmer as we putt-putted up the river in the June sun. Mrs. Edwards, whom we called "the General," ran the trip like a benign Captain Bligh, dispensing fried chicken and devilled eggs to the faithful, between rounds of "truth or consequences." It was one of the few benefits I've ever derived for being literary.

Equally high-minded was the Latin Club, whose annual bash was a Roman dinner. We dressed in bed sheets and arranged ourselves on low benches around a square table so we could lounge like Romans as we ate. Grapes were very popular because the Romans had no knives or forks but ate with their fingers. Even so, the advisor (Miss Mabel Barham, Miss Elma Free, or Miss Willie Shelton) had arranged a few other dishes of ancient times.

We skipped the wine, which was the heart of those Roman orgies.

Unlike the noble Romans, we never tickled our tongues to induce regurgitation so we could continue to eat. The menu was so unappealing that I often wondered upon what meat doth this, our Caesar feed that he hath grown so great. Recumbent eating must have kept old Julius lean and hungry. Hard on the hiatus hernia, too.

Another group I got into, for some reason, was Miss Harriet Smith's speaking chorus. I took her public speaking course, and she needed a baritone like me to balance the girlish sopranos. One of our big numbers was Vachel Lindsey's poem, "The Congo." I had two solo lines, which came at the end of each stanza, as a refrain:

Then I saw the Congo, creeping through the black,
Cutting through the jungle with a golden track.

The line demanded a majestic Paul Robeson or some deep-voiced black bass, but I pitched my voice down in my belly and tried to be an African chieftain. It wasn't exactly what Miss Smith had in mind, but our school was segregated and we had no Paul Robesons.

In lieu of the chapel sessions held in church schools, we Newport News High Schoolers had a weekly assembly each Monday morning in the auditorium. It gave Principal Alexander a chance to urge us onward, and it was a showcase for ambitious students and for clubs which had worked up some project. Once I wrote for an assembly a one-act mystery melodrama, "Dirty Work at The Crossroads," which drama students produced. I was so nervous about it that I stayed home from school that day.

Looking back, I realize those were golden

Richard E. Byrd was a Virginia hero in the 1920s for his polar and Atlantic flights.

days. The United States was struggling with a prolonged Depression, but that added to our incentive to excel. In any case, it seems to me that my high school contemporaries by and large have proved a credit to their alma mater. We may not have reshaped the world, but we surely enjoyed it.

There's a lot to be said for trying to live up to your potential.

Early churches in downtown Newport News included First Baptist and Trinity Lutheran, top, and St. Paul's Episcopal, First Presbyterian, and Trinity Methodist, below.

43. *Sundays and Blue Laws*

No aspect of life has changed more than church-going. The Peninsula of the 1930s was a community of small churches, mostly Protestant. They exerted over their members a strong hold, even determining whether you could drink beer, play bridge, or go to the movies.

Things are different now. We're more sensible about separating religion and recreation. But being Southerners and traditionalists, we Peninsulans still go to church, even though church is rapidly losing out as the influence it used to be.

When I was little, there seemed to be more important ideological differences between Baptists and Methodists, who predominated, and the more intellectual Episcopalians and Presbyterians. (In those innocent days I didn't know much about Lutherans, Disciples of Christ or other sects.) And there were then few "off-brand" denominations—gospel, rock, Seventh Day Adventists, and born-again denominations that flourish today.

Even Roman Catholics were few in Tidewater until after World War I. Baptists, Methodists, Presbyterians and Episcopalians were the South's "popular brands." Anything else made me uncomfortable.

The nearest thing to a pope in Newport News was the Rev. Edwin Taliaferro Wellford, who guided the First Presbyterians like a pillar of fire. The First Presbyterian was the city's most influential clerical stronghold, for it had a highly literate congregation, attracted by Dr. Wellford's erudition and energy. He was tall, thin, and even looked a little like a Renaissance pope, minus the biretta.

A few Scottish shipbuilders who had emigrated to the shipyard helped make up the Presbyterian congregation, along with shipyard executives. (I mention that because the yard had great civic and social influence in those days. It made Newport News a "company town.") Many shipyard officials were Northerners, trained in ship design at Cornell, and other Northern engineering schools. Some had been Congregationalists. The nearest things to Congregationalists in Newport News were Presbyterians.

But Baptists were surely the most numerous tribe on the Peninsula. The First Baptist Church on Twenty-Ninth Street was one of the first downtown churches to be built after Collis Huntington breathed life into Newport News in 1881. We went there because my father was a Baptist, and husbands usually chose the family church in those days.

We prided ourselves on our simplicity and democracy. Our most memorable minister was the Rev. Alfred Dickinson, who had the Baptist skill of packaging eternal verities into simple pulpit anecdotes. I remember some as if they had been holy writ.

Mr. Dickinson insisted that the Baptist faith was simply what the Bible said man should be, requiring no further elaboration. That's why most Negroes were Baptists, he told us, because Baptist beliefs were simple and readily understood. "If you find a Negro who isn't a Baptist," he used to say, "somebody's been fooling with him."

Early in life, my brothers and I began to rebel against the negative morality of some fellow Baptists, especially the "hard shell" kind from the deep South. They were hell-bent against dancing, Sunday pleasures, and card-playing. As we got older, their sentiment against beer and whiskey bothered us more. When I married, I lapsed into a more permissive Episcopalianism. But to be fair, I think the Baptists have moderated greatly.

"Hard shell" Baptists could be unbelieva-

Old Dominion Land Company built rowhouses in early Newport News. This row adjoined First National Bank on 28th Street and housed the popular Bide-a-Wee Tea Room.

bly narrow. I remember one First Baptist parishioner insisting to my mother, who'd been born a Methodist, that total immersion was the only form of baptism God recognized as valid. (I don't know how she knew.) The alternative, she said, was hellfire. I hope such sentiment has abated today; certainly hell is going out of style, at least in Williamsburg's tolerant theology.

Baptist revival preachers and their hellfire and damnation sermons also worried me. There's a puritanism in some religionists that's only happy when it is forbidding the social pleasures of life, like parties and dancing. Revival preachers would come to our church and excoriate these basically innocent pleasures, making all us teen-agers feel condemned. It was an era of intense Calvinism and puritanism, now thankfully in retreat.

One visiting Baptist evangelist even led a revival parade in the 1930s down Washington Avenue, to our acute embarrassment, making "war on the devil." The band marched to a hymn titled "He Died For Me" whose music was the Hawaiian chant, "Aloha O." I was dismayed by such jazzy showmanship.

The Methodists' chief Newport News citadel in those early days was Trinity Church on Twenty-Ninth Street. I never got to know many of its preachers, because the Methodists moved them in and out of town too fast. But Trinity usually had a strong preacher—one of Newport News's best.

Episcopalians had a hard time in the steamy fundamentalism of early Newport News. They seemed a little un-American, as some Southerners today still regard Roman Catholics. They had an aura of elitism, for they suffered the opprobrium of latent anti-British feelings that had held on in some parts of the United States from the Revolution to the 1920s. Thank goodness we finally made up with the poor old Britons during the two world wars.

Life was prosperous for the downtown churches so long as Newport News' population remained south of Fiftieth Street, as it did through most of World War I. But the city's population explosion in the age of autos and streetcars in the 1930s took people away from the downtown churches and created new suburban rivals. Soon the new suburban churches had outgrown the old ones. Downtown life and its participating churches began to wither, and that remains a problem today in Newport News as in other cities. It's sad to go back downtown now.

Sunday school picnics were popular then, too. Every church went to Buckroe, Grand View, Bay Shore, or some place each summer. It was a great outing, and it was as important to individual salvation as was the Fourth of July. The practice has largely subsided, though many old churches still have periodic homecoming services and picnics, especially in the country.

Syms-Eaton Museum

American Theatre brought movies to Phoebus in 1920s. Renamed the Lee Theatre, it became an adult film house in the 1980s but was closed after lengthy litigation.

44. *Movies of the 1930s*

OLD movies like "Casablanca" have become cultural artifacts of the 30s, and they're repeated endlessly on TV. But I wish those culture arbiters would consult me now and then, for my choices are very different and often, I suspect, better than theirs.

(It happens that I never saw "Casablanca," having been so remotely situated on a Navy ship in the far Pacific during World War II that no decent movies of that era ever got close to us.)

I got my first talking movie thrill from Al Jolson in the 1920s, in that old tear-jerker of the Movietone era called "The Jazz Singer." The highlight was Al Jolson in blackface, for some fool reason, singing to Jackie Coogan in a woe-begone knitted cap the theme song, "Sonny Boy."

"When there are gray skies,
I don't mind the gray skies,
I'll still have you, Sonny Boy."

It sounds mushy, but in the 20s that was dynamite music. Charlie Boy Epes and I used to play the record endlessly on his parents' windup Victrola on Fifty-Ninth Street, almost weeping at the devotion of old black-faced Al to sadeyed young Jackie.

Another early landmark was "The Virginian," a cowboy movie made from the novel by Owen Wister. As I remember it, the Virginian's only good line was "When you call me that, pardner, smile." It was the beginning of the craze for cowboy movies. It was remade two or three times. Randolph Scott, a Virginian himself, was starred in the role.

Another cultural landmark was "The Scarlet Pimpernel". As I remember it (probably very erroneously) Leslie Howard played the role of a rakish duellist, always arriving in time to save the virginity of the heroine. (Saving virginity in those days was almost as important as saving money.)

Just as the dastardly Sir Clarence de Greiff was about to force the distraught heroine to accede to his bestial tastes, Leslie Howard would step out from the arras, draw his sword, and save another virgin for God and England.

Somewhere during these proceedings, the Pimpernel would spout poetry, rhythmically matching his swordsmanship with rhyme, like this:

"Is he in heaven?" (stroke of sword)
"Or in hell?" (another stroke)
"This demmed, elusive Pimpernel?" (He kills the villain)

It was enough to make you want to give up

Stonewall Jackson School and rush off to Lower Slobovia, or wherever womanly virtue was being jeopardized. We admired the Pimpernel because he seemed to have no designs of his own on the ladies. (Actually, I was crushed later to learn that Leslie Howard was one of the lustiest womanizers of his time.)

I also loved dear old Barry Fitzgerald, who played Irishmen in dramas of little old New York. My favorite sequence was of Barry watching from a school window as a group of uniformed Catholic girls in the schoolyard below were skipping rope, while Barry mumbled an old jump-rope jingle:

> *"In comes the doctor,*
> *In comes the nurse,*
> *And in comes the lady*
> *With the al-li-ga-tor purse."*

Sadness was a dominant mood of many of those movies. You could hear the audience weeping forlornly when the theme song subsided, and even boys joined in the tears, if they didn't think girls were looking. I was torn to shreds by post-World War I German melodrama in the 1930s at the Palace Theatre, called "Four Brothers." It described the tragedy of four German boys who served the Fatherland in World War I and got killed on the battlefield.

As I had three brothers, I couldn't help but identify with poor Rolf, Kurt, Helmut, and Eric as they one by one bit the dust. Unfortunately, my companion in the Palace was my schoolmate, Wallace Hiden, who was a stolid Anglo-Saxon, devoid both of sentimentality and brothers. He went back to John W. Daniel School next day and announced to class 7B under Miss Amanda (Chubby) Gray: "Never go to a movie with Parke Rouse. He cries so loud you can't hear a thing."

But the saddest movie was "Back Street," from a novel by Fannie Hurst. It played for a week of torrential tears at the Palace, attracting a lot of women who had read this grim warning of what sex can do—or rather, undo—for the working woman. Irene Dunne was the heroine, and she was a secretary to some Daddy Warbucks-type executive. After she took his dictation all day, poor Irene went home to her flat on a back street and became his after-hours mistress.

The picture had Irene working her charms to the bone, making everything shipshape for old Warbucks. He'd breeze in after a day of big deals, have his kicks with Irene, and then go off to his French Provincial chateau in nearby Grosse Pointe, to enjoy the evening with his snooty wife and French Provincial furniture.

The whole thing seemed unfair to Irene, and everybody wept at the injustice of it. On maturer reflection, I realize now that she was a damned fool to let herself get locked into a no-win deal like that. But of course those were Depression days, and a girl had to turn her hand to anything to keep herself in hairnets and silk stockings.

One of the heroic film episodes of the era was the chariot race in "Ben Hur," which was the story of an up-and-coming Jewish boy in the wicked days of Rome. Ben raced this Mafia crowd in the Coliseum for some fat prize, like the Golden Fleece. The Mafia was out to get Ben, and its chariots kept sideswiping his, pulling off its wheels and enmeshing Ben in their horsewhips.

But Ben was made of the right stuff, and he beat the Mafia at its own game. God was on his side because his heart was pure.

As you can see, "Ben Hur" had everything. You don't have to drink, smoke, or be a Gentile to win if you know the Ten Commandments. But you do need a strong pair of chariot wheels.

Movies didn't try to be realistic in those days, and that made them better. In the musical "Flying Down to Rio," a bevy of girls danced on the wings of an airplane as it flew from New York to Rio de Janeiro.

And in Jeannette MacDonald musicals, Nelson Eddy would always ride onto the scene on his faithful Mounted Police horse in the Canadian Rockies. All of a sudden a 120-piece orchestra would coalesce out of the blue to supply the harmonies for "Stout-hearted Men" or "When I'm Calling You, OO-oo-oo, OO-oo-oo."

You also had to be impressed by Nelson Eddy's horse for the beast didn't bat an eye when Nelson started bellowing about "Stout-hearted men" and the 120-piece orchestra began to rev up, kettle drums and all.

When the Paramount Theatre replaced the Academy of Music on Washington Avenue in the early 1930s, one of its first features was the Time-Life documentary, "The Birth of a Baby." Lewis McMurran and I were then about 14 or 15, and the subject seemed to merit our attention. We decided to invest 25 cents apiece, or whatever it cost, and get at the bottom of life.

I'm sorry to report that our outing was a failure. There is nothing romantic about the ordeal of birth, and before long I was ready to leave. The only trouble was that I had been reared in the Protestant ethic, which dictated that you had to stick through anything to the end, no matter how bad, for your character's sake. This was true of books, school courses, movies, and even of marriages, though it has changed, thank God.

Lewis stood it as long as he could. Then he told me he was going out to the lobby because he didn't feel well. I would have gone, too, but I was so Protestant that I couldn't bear to waste the unused ticket.

When I finally got to the lobby at the end of the show, Lewis was beginning to show a little color again. We were finally able to take a streetcar home.

After that experience, I stuck to romantic movies, where I could laugh or cry to my heart's content. They gave me a lot more to think about at night than the birth of a baby.

The circus came to Newport News each summer, pitching tents on Virginia Avenue (now Warwick Boulevard) near the shipyard. This side show came with King Brothers' Circus in 1954.
Newport News Historical Committee

45. *Newspapering on 25th Street*

THE Times-Herald city room of 1931 was no beauty, but it was a good place to observe changes in life from the Depression until the onslaught of Franklin Roosevelt and the New Deal in 1933. America was threatened within and without. There were bonus marchers, hunger marchers, and the rise of Hitler and Mussolini in Europe. Dangerous times!

I spent part of those years as an apprentice Times-Herald reporter, just out of high school. The Peninsula's newspapers were crowded into a narrow shoe box of a building on Twenty-Fifth Street, between Washington and Huntington. It was a spartan environment of metal furniture and linoleum floors. On the street around it were hot dog stands, grocers, shoe repair shops, and empty stores papered with displays for circuses and minstrel shows.

I went to work in February, 1933, after graduating from high school. The Peninsula was sunk in the Great Depression. The shipyard was at a standstill. Real estate wouldn't sell, and the stock market hadn't revived since that "Black Friday" in 1929 that destroyed so many businesses and hopes—and men.

I'd set my heart on the job every since Mr. Pugh, a North End neighbor, and part-owner of the papers, knew I'd been elected editor of the high school Beacon and had offered me a job on graduation. However, Raymond Bottom had since come in as boss, and he told me he didn't need me. My spunky mother fixed that. I was hired at last, but at a learner's wage of $2 weekly.

The papers clung to that tiny building to be close to Newport News City Hall, courts, and police department, all in the same block. And were we packed in! On the first floor was advertising, the presses, the circulation people, and Eugene Pugh's photo studio. On the second floor were the news staffs and composing room. The third floor housed the top brass—Major Bottom, Captain William Van Buren, Sam Hoyle, and Arthur Brown.

Your first job isn't easy. As a teenager you've got to learn to deal with older people. The papers had a military tone, imposed by its two top men, and it made me uncomfortable. Yet jobs were so scarce you'd do almost anything to hold one. We news staffers spoke in awe of the "open door policy"—either you liked your job or you could walk through that door onto the street. But people were patient and appreciative.

I guess that's why I enjoyed my stint.

Everybody went out of his way to teach you the business. Nobody seemed to begrudge my job. (Maybe they knew my salary.)

Instead of starting in the city room, I was given the job of reorganizing the advertising illustrations. I was dismayed by huge stacks of unorganized matrices going back several years. The lights were so dim I had to buy glasses, but I got a lot of help from N.R. Hoyle, the advertising manager, and veterans like Helen Reams and Helen Siegrist.

I must have done all right those first months, for Major Bottom offered me $10 a week as a relief reporter the next summer, when I came home from my freshman year at college. I moved up to that select elysium on the second floor, the city room, and the most hilarious crew I'd ever met.

It's hard to believe how tough times were. Major Bottom used the reverse side of junk letters to write his decrees from On High. One set of desks and typewriters had to serve both staffs, we Times-Heralds slaving from 7 to 4 and the Daily Press crowd from 4 to 1 the next morning. It was a sort of fruit basket turn over.

You were bound to hate the Daily Press man who took over your seat at 4, for he always changed your typewriter settings. You had to hide anything you were working on for fear of its getting in The Other Paper.

When I see the staffs which produce today's papers, I wonder how five or six of us could produce a Times-Herald six days a week. Every afternoon at 3, when the presses below the city room began to groan with their first

The C&O passenger ferry Virginia crossed Hampton Roads to Norfolk twice daily. It was a feature of the busy waterfront scene that faded after the advent of the auto.

Newport News Historical Committee

birth-pains, Managing Editor Ding Price and some of his minions would rush to look over the first papers. Sometimes we'd catch a terrible gaffe (we often blamed it on the composing room) but usually we could let 'em roll.

Like most papers then, we went heavy on wire and "canned" copy and short on local news and feature stories. One obvious shortcoming was proofreading. We usually had a woman college graduate of recent vintage read the galley proofs in the city room. But the poor girl had to read so fast she missed terrible bloopers.

Frequently Major Bottom, upstairs in his command quarters, would tear out some error, encircle it with pencil and send it down to Ding Price, marked "How come?" or "Explain this. **R.B.B.**"

We tried to help our lady proofreader, especially in such arcane specialities as sports or the stock market, but errors persisted. Sports reporter Stanley Kennon wrote a kind of Damon Runyonese, then very popular, which avoided any simple and usual word in lieu of a slangy, Brooklynese substitute. Our young Westhampton college graduate would give poor Stan a hard time about his bizarre language, and sometimes the fur would fly.

"Well, why can't you just say 'batted the ball,' for heaven's sake?" she would shriek.

When the noise level got too high, Ding would remind us that Major Bottom would surely hear the fight and come down and fire us all. Beside, added Eddie Travis, such altercations weren't appropriate for Dr. Lynwood Price's Finishing School.

From the opposite side of the room, glowering through her prince-nez, Society Editor Margaret Flannagan tried to ignore all that and to stay above the fray. Eddie Travis had designated her "dean of women" in Dr. Price's Finishing School. When voices were raised, he sometimes mischievously tried to involve her.

"I think this is a matter for the dean of women," he would say. "Margaret, don't you want to come over and settle this?"

Mrs. Flannagan was too astute for that. So she would tell Eddie in a few well-chosen words to leave her alone, and he would let up. Although she could hold her own in finishing school, Mrs. Flannagan was too busy to get involved.

Once or twice the lady proofreader and Margaret Flannagan had a set-to of their own. Wedding accounts were then filled with minute details of the bride's gown, the bridesmaids' dresses, and even the bride's going-away dress. Often this description involved esoteric French words which would drive any proofreader mad.

"Listen to this," the proofreader would yell across the city room at Margaret: "The gown was made of peau de soir.' But you misspelled it 'peu de soir.' That's not right! I studied French in college. It's 'peau de soir.' That means skin of silk."

"I copied it exactly as the bride's mother brought it in," Margaret would explain, patiently. "If it's wrong, don't blame me. Change it. That's your job, for goodness sake."

I'm sure visitors to the city room who heard our finishing school in session must have thought we were nuts. Actually, it was as harmless as Alice in Wonderland. When 4 o'clock came and those Daily Press fellows came in to take over the hot seats, we Times-Heralds felt a kinship that comes from hardships shared and dangers overcome. We were like survivors of the Alamo.

Strange to say, I missed Lynwood Price's Finishing School when I finally came to leave Newport News for a bigger world. It had taught me a lot of things about life—and even a few about newspaper work. I hadn't earned much, but I had a lot of memories.

46. Hampton's Biggest Trial

THE most sensational murder trial ever to erupt on the Peninsula was the Kane case, heard in Elizabeth City Circuit Court in Hampton in December 1931. I was in high school and followed it avidly through the *Daily Press,* which devoted at least a page a day to the trial, from December 9 through 12.

It was a dramatic and powerful story, reminiscent of Theodore Dreiser's novel, "An American Tragedy." A Hilton girl, Jenny Graham, had married Dr. Elisha Kent Kane III, a well-born Pennsylvanian who was chairman of the romance languages department at the University of Tennessee. While visiting Mrs. Kane's parents in Hilton on September 11, 1931, they had gone to Grand View to swim at the lighthouse near Back River. Jenny Kane had drowned, and the Commonwealth said her husband had done it.

I still remember how newspapers sensationalized the story. Jenny Kane was pretty, and her husband was prominent. He was the son of a surgeon, Dr. Evan O'Neil Kane, of Kane, Pennsylvania. Young Kane was described in the press as "wealthy," "handsome," and "aristocratic." Jenny was depicted as the poor girl he had married and then grown tired of. The prosecution hinted that he loved another woman. It seemed the old triangle.

Presiding in the trial was 39-year-old Judge Vernon Spratley, a scholarly, experienced Hampton jurist with a no-nonsense approach. Arrayed before him in the courtroom were a half-dozen skilled criminal lawyers, reporters from a dozen metropolitan papers, and a courtroom full of spectators.

Professor friends of Elisha Kane came from Knoxville and Chapel Hill to defend his character and deny difficulties between him and his wife. Another witness was his father, the surgeon, who had earlier got national press attention when he had removed his own appendix. He testified that Jenny Kane suffered from a heart ailment, which might have contributed to her death when she jumped from the lighthouse rocks into water over her head.

The trial was a field day for lawyers. Roland Cock, Elizabeth City County commonwealth's attorney, was assisted by three who were retained by the Grahams. They were Harry Smith of Richmond and Frank and Ross Kearney of Phoebus. Defending Kane was the well-known J. Winston Read of Newport News, plus Percy and Macy Carmel of Hampton. They were good strategists.

Jenny Kane's family thought Kane had murdered her, they said, because of several odd circumstances. For one, Elisha Kane was a strong swimmer and should have been able to pull her safely to shore. For another, they thought Kane had wasted crucial time in going for his car in order to take his wife's lifeless body to Dixie Hospital; they thought he should have lifted her from the shore to the car.

There were no witnesses, but offshore clammers saw Kane from a distance pull his wife's body from the water. Their testimony added little.

After the drowning, the professor stayed with his in-laws in their Hilton house until the funeral several days later. Two hours afterward, as he was about to leave Hilton, he was arrested, handcuffed, and taken to Elizabeth City County jail on charges of murder. He was released on $15,000 bail until the grand jury arraignment and the trial, two months later. The charge was deliberate and premeditated murder.

After testifying in the crowded Hampton courtroom, the mother of the drowned woman burst into hysterics as a photographer tried to take her picture. The next day her daughter-in-law smashed a press camera in order to avoid a photograph.

Even the defendant, normally cool, grew indignant when one of his wife's kinsmen testified he was profane and called his German police dog "Jesus Christ." "Allegations of profanity made by relatives of Mrs. Kane caused him to leap from his chair and rush to Judge Spratley's bench and shout denials," the *Daily Press* reported on December 12. Then Kane turned to the judge and apologized, "Pardon me, Judge. I've had to stand so much."

Lewis T. Jester, reporting the case in the *Daily Press,* commented on Kane's restraint. "Question after question was fired at him by prosecuting attorney Harry M. Smith," Jester wrote, "some of them confusing and most of them apparently designed to get under his skin. But the professor kept his head and bridled his tongue."

The prosecution also tried to have Judge Spratley admit as evidence letters which had passed between Dr. Kane and a woman identified as Betty Dahl, in an effort to impugn his fidelity, but Spratley refused to permit them to be introduced. The defense then asked the judge to dismiss the case for lack of evidence, but again he declined.

Throughout the five days of the trial, the prosecution tried to portray Elisha Kane as abusive to his wife, at odds with his in-laws, and profane. Kane was also charged with having packed his wife's jewels to take with him when he was about to leave Hilton after his wife's funeral.

The trial ended Saturday afternoon, December 12, and the jury of 12 men retired at 8 p.m. after a long day in court. It returned at 11:45 and announced its decision: not guilty. The crowd broke into loud applause, which the judge halted. The accused professor was overwhelmed by friends. He told the press that "It was a terrible ordeal, and I was mighty uncomfortable at times, although I am innocent and believed that the jury would so find." The Daily Press next morning carried a streamer headline, "Dr. Kane Is Acquitted."

Even so, Elisha Kane's ordeal wasn't over. He had resigned his professorship in Tennessee when he was indicted, but neither it nor any other institution rushed to hire him. Wrote Douglas Freeman in the Richmond News Leader:

Dr. E. K. Kane doubtless told the grim truth when he said on the witness stand that he had spent 'three months in hell.' His family has been compelled to raise $12,000 for his defense. Wherever he goes hereafter, gossip will follow him and sharp-tongued persons will whisper, 'You know, he was tried for killing his wife.' Unless the verdict of twelve jurors and the opinions of 90 percent of the spectators are entirely at fault, society has done the professor a great wrong.

In retrospect, it seems clear that the trial of an innocent man might have been averted at the grand jury level by more careful examination of evidence and motives of those preferring the charges. Under the circumstances, however, Judge Spratley and the jury had reached a fair and prompt decision.

Out-of-town newspapermen wrote the judge a letter before leaving Hampton, concluding that "We have never seen a trial conducted in fairer, more impartial, or more dignified style."

From a hotel in New York, a chastened Professor Kane a few weeks later also wrote Judge Spratley "To your integrity and sense of justice I owe my life or—what I prize more—my freedom," he declared.

Justice had been done, but Elisha Kane would never be the same. It was an American tragedy indeed, but not as Theodore Dreiser told it.

Syms-Eaton Museum

Elisha Kent Kane, Tennessee professor, was the defendant in a dramatic murder case in Hampton in 1931. Kane, left, and attorney Macy Carmel walk to courthouse in this photo.

47. *Judge Spratley and Fair Trials*

THE Peninsula has produced a lot of good judges, but the most celebrated one in this century was Claude Vernon Spratley, who rose through judicial ranks to be a justice of the Virginia Supreme Court from 1936 until he retired in 1967.

Two important cases at Hampton in the 1930s spread his reputation and led Governor George Peery to appoint him in 1936 to Virginia's high court. The first case was the trial of Dr. Elisha Kent Kane III in 1931 on the charge of drowning his wife. The other was his decision in 1933 that a black man could not be barred by color from voting in a primary election.

It's hard to believe such flagrant racism as that existed so recently, and we're indebted to fair-minded jurists like Judge Spratley for helping to end it. As for the judge, he had no hesitation about his decision, though he knew it would be opposed by many Virginians. As he saw it, "I couldn't see any more reason for a man to be denied this right because of brown skin than because of brown hair."

A lot of us revered the jaunty judge. He lived to be 94, dying in October 1976 after having retired at 85 from Virginia's high court.

He kept his wits and lively humor to the end. I'll never forget how packed St. John's Church was with statesmen, judges, and Hamptonians at his funeral, conducted by Bishop John Bentley and the Rev. Francis Hayes.

The voting rights case was brought by L.E. Wilson, a well-regarded black man who worked for a Hampton building and loan association after election judges had refused to let him vote in a primary on August 1, 1933. They were simply following the usual Southern practice. They argued in their defense that "party plans of the Democratic party limited the right to vote in the primary to white persons only."

Wilson then brought suit against Democratic officials. He said he had met all conditions of residence and poll tax payment. He was represented by J. Thomas Newsome of Newport News and A.W.E. Bassette Jr. of Hampton. When the case was heard by Judge Spratley in circuit court, the judge concluded that Wilson had been entitled to vote. As he put it:

"I held that the primary was being held in accordance with statutory provisions; that the expenses thereof were paid from the public

Daily Press

Vernon Spratley, attorney and State Supreme Court justice, stands outside Hampton courthouse, where he was once a circuit judge. He was the Peninsula's best-known jurist.

funds; that the statute itself prescribed the qualifications for a right to participate therein and did not exclude a person by reason of his color; that although the primary plan of the Democratic party provided only for participation in its primaries by white persons, the provision was in conflict with the law and the law prevailed; and that, therefore, a negro could not be denied the right to participate in such primary merely because of his color . . ."

As expected, Judge Spratley's decision provoked wrath. "It was thought by some political sages at that time that his career as a judge was finished," said his friend Thomas B. Gay, of the Richmond firm of Hunton, Anderson, and Gay. But others felt the judge was right. The New York Times ran the story on its front page, headlining it "Negro Vote Ruling Surprises Virginia."

Most Virginia newspapers applauded the decision. Attorney Ben Jacobs of Newport News wrote to one paper that Judge Spratley's "just and courageous ruling" had been handed down in a Virginia court, without pressure or agitation. He felt the decision "pointed the way to proper adjustment of race matters" and had "not left any bitter after effect."

Although Hampton Democrats asked party authorities in Virginia to appeal the decision, they failed to do so. When the issue of black voting came to trial in other Virginia localities, all the other judges followed Spratley's lead.

In his 31 years on the State Supreme Court, Judge Spratley wrote an opinion for the majority in 664 cases and for the minority in 74 others. In his entire judicial career he made or took part in 7,000 opinions. Governor Lindsay Almond, himself a lawyer, praised their "crystal clarity" and "marked erudition."

Although he remained an independent spirit, Judge Spratley was a strict constructionist. He felt the Supreme Court had no power to reshape laws passed by Congress or the Assembly. In one dissent, he wrote that "We have nothing to do with the wisdom, policy, or expediency impelling the makers of the Constitution in drafting the fundamental law. Whether the law, as written, be harsh or unjust, contrary to 'ancient jusage,' or contrary to expediency, as we view it, we cannot correct same, or relieve against it.''

Judge Spratley's humor endeared him to me and many other people. In his office he usually wore a green plastic visor, like an old-fashioned pool player. Like many men of his era, he liked to chomp on a cigar, while he worked. Often he wore in his lapel a sprig of azalea or a rose from his yard on Hampton's Columbia avenue, cut from the garden planted by his wife, the former Annie Woodward of Hampton, who died in 1948.

The judge was born in Surry in 1882 of an old county family. He graduated from William and Mary in 1901, aged 19, and taught math and Latin in Hampton and Newport News schools to save money to enter the University of Virginia law school. He said he made his first dollar folding crabmeat price lists for James McMenamin, a crab-packing operator.

He began law practice in Hampton in 1906 and became Hampton's city attorney in 1912. He held that office until appointed judge of the circuit which included Hampton, Elizabeth City, and Newport News. A good friend was Judge T. J. Barham of Newport News Corporation Court, who had also been born in Surry.

I began covering the law courts of Newport News in that era, and I remember Judge Spratley and his contemporaries. They were an interesting lot, including such colorful courtroom pleaders as J. Winston Read, Allan D. Jones, Thomas Newsome, Charles C. Berkeley, A.L. "Allie" Bivins, Charles E. Ford, Lee Ford, Sclater Montague and Fay Collier. Of more sedate style were R. M. Lett, Philip Murray, W. B. and Shep Colonna, Fred Skinner, John Marshall, Herbert G. Smith, Sinclair Phillips, Billy Carleton, Frank Blechman, and some younger men who are now seniors or retired.

One of them is E. Ralph James, who, like Judge Spratley, came to Hampton from Surry. He remembers how Judge Spratley welcomed him his first day in court: "All good things have their beginning either in Surry or at William and Mary," the Judge said. "You came from both, so you're doubly blessed. You'll get along all right."

What I liked about Judge Spratley was his boyish enthusiasm, even in his 90s. He loved parties and repartee. A fellow Hamptonian once listed his hobbies as "golf, canes, gardens, loud-barking dogs, week-end visits, buttonhole bouquets, social intercourse and entertainment, and snappy ensembles in dress." I can vouch for the snappy ensembles.

And he adored circuses. Said an old friend, "He would have adjourned the Kane murder case to go to the circus." That was Judge Spratley.

Judge Vernon Spratley in retirement tended his rose garden on Hampton's Columbia Avenue.

Daily Press

48. *Hampton's Crabs and Terrapins*

THE Peninsula has had colorful people in its day. One whom I'd like to know more about was Albert T. LaVallette, who lived on a houseboat on Hampton's waterfront for several decades until 1937 and raised diamondback terrapins. People in those days loved to eat terrapin stew.

What's more, LaVallette's houseboat was furnished with objects of interest from the USS Constitution, one of the Navy's first men-of-war. For the terrapin farmer was the grandson of a famous father, well-known in Navy history as a contemporary of Stephen Decatur and other Navy greats.

I first heard of LaVallette from Admiral Ephraim Holmes, the Navy's retired Atlantic Fleet commander, who lives in Williamsburg. He remembered the LaVallettes' houseboat as being moored on Hampton's waterfront back in days before World War II. Thanks to Hampton friends, I've learned a little about an unusual man I'd never heard of.

Albert LaVallette died at Kecoughtan Veterans' Hospital in 1937. I've learned that when the great hurricane swept the Peninsula in August 1933, 71-year-old LaVallette was injured trying to save his LaSalle Avenue houseboat and his waterfront seafood plant. He lingered four years.

The plant is shown on Captain LaVallette's business letterhead of 65 years ago, a copy of which survives. Advertising "Genuine Diamond Back Terrapin," it also depicts a crabmeat factory and crab-shedding basin, both operated by LaVallette on the Boulevard until the 1933 hurricane hit. After that, LaVallette was out of business.

The objects and papers from the Constitution had come from LaVallette's grandfather, Captain Elie LaVallette, when he commanded the Constitution from 1825 till about 1828. A navigator's protractor used aboard the Constitution was given to the Mariner's Museum by his grandson's widow in 1947, after she left Hampton to live in New York City. She had also served as sponsor for the destroyer LaVallette at its christening in 1919.

I was unable to learn much else about Hampton's terrapin supplier, but I've seen a letter he wrote to the Navy from Hampton in 1917 about his grandfather. "I am in possession of his private papers, books, letters, and various other records," the grandson wrote. "Also a very comprehensive biography in manuscript, which has never been published," he informed the Superintendent of Naval Records and Library in Washington.

An obituary in the July 14, 1937 Daily Press

210 *Hampton's Crabs and Terrapins*

Albert T. LaVallette lived in Hampton houseboat and sold diamondback terrapin and softcrabs. But 1933 hurricane injured his health and forced him to give up the business.

At Pier A and joining 25th Street in Newport News, watermen hawked seafood and farmers sold watermelons and other produce. The Casino and Federal Building are visible in background.

records the death several days earlier of Hampton's LaVallette. "Captain LaVallette, born in Pennsylvania, owned and conducted a terrapin farm on the Boulevard a number of years until it was demolished in the 1933 hurricane," it reads in part. "At the time he received serious injuries."

Though called "captain," the younger LaVallette never rose above the rank of lieutenant when he served in World War I in command of a Hampton Roads pilot boat on patrol off the Virginia Capes. After the war, he left naval duty to return to his seafood and terrapin business.

The elder LaVallette first sailed as a ten-year-old "captain's clerk" in 1800 on board the US frigate Philadelphia, commanded by Captain Stephen Decatur, soon to be a hero in the wars with the Barbary pirates. The youngster liked sea-going, so after many merchant voyages, he signed up for the Navy as a career in 1810. He advanced to command the Navy's Mediterranean Squadron in 1857, retiring as a commodore in 1862 after 52 years of service.

Whatever became of the Constitution's furnishings and records owned by grandson LaVallette on his houseboat in Hampton? Except for the navigator's protractor at the Mariner's Museum, they went to the LaVallette heirs, no longer in Hampton. I'd like to know where they are now.

Daily Press

Picking crabs by hand is slow and tedious, but buyers prefer it to machine-picked meat.

49. *Big Ships for a Big War*

THE Peninsula was shocked in 1940 when Archer Huntington announced that he planned to sell the shipyard. He had inherited it from his parents, but he had left its operations to others. Even so, we wondered how the yard would fare without a rich and powerful patron.

The sale took place in New York on May 10, 1940. Several dozen Wall Street underwriting firms paid $19 millions for it and then sold stock to the public.

The sale came at a crucial time, for the yard was already building several major carriers for the Navy, and others were on the way to defend the United States against the growing threat of Germany and Japan.

Newport News was an exciting place to be in the years leading to World War II. I was present at the birth of several of the famous aircraft carriers that went to war against the Axis after Japan blasted Pearl Harbor on December 7, 1941.

I was a senior in Newport News High School in 1933 when Franklin D. Roosevelt became president. FDR had been second in command of the Navy in World War I, and he saw the need as soon as he entered the White House for more ships. He moved decisively.

Five months after he became president, Congress authorized two big Navy carriers, the Yorktown and the Enterprise.

That was the beginning of Newport News's famous succession of aircraft carriers in World War II. They helped to crush the Japanese navy.

I was in college on October 3, 1936, when the first Enterprise that Roosevelt ordered was christened at the shipyard.

I was still in college, when the yard finished the Ranger (christened by Mrs. Herbert Hoover), the first Yorktown (christened by Mrs. Roosevelt); and the Enterprise. I was working on The Times-Herald by the time their sister ship, the Hornet, came along about 1937.

Then, on December 7, 1941 the Japanese attacked Pearl Harbor. After that the shipyard worked round-the-clock. Do you remember the allnight clangor? And the stories of "hot beds" in rooming houses crowded with workmen?

In those years, the Peninsula grew rapidly with temporary housing. By V-J Day, the city of 35,000 people I'd left in 1941 was much bigger.

When I witnessed the birth of those famous

warships, the yard was still building them on old-fashioned inclined shipways. Launchings were more exciting than nowadays, when big ships are built in graving docks.

When launching time came, powerful rams began to put pressure to move the big hull. Riggers and shipwrights knocked out blocks to release the hull, chanting in unison. On a shipway larded with tallow (to ease the slide into the James), the great hull began to move. The tallow burned from the friction of the sliding steel.

Captain Roger Williams, the yard's vice-president, always helped the ship's sponsor bash the champagne across its prow. A net of twine encased it so glass wouldn't cut anybody.

The sponsor was usually the wife of some Washington biggie. She was dressed to kill, with a big bouquet. As the big moment came she'd hand her flowers to her maid of honor.

Then, crash! The foaming champagne spattered the ship. Whistles throughout the yard blasted the air. The band played, and another Newport News ship was on its way.

I saw many famous people on those launching stands. Navy Secretary Claude Swanson came, along with Admiral Emory Land, head of the shipping board. New Deal brain truster Tom Corcoran came, too, along with Joe Kennedy, ambassador to Great britain. Rose Kennedy, his wife, christened one ship. Mrs. Kennedy was at her prime, a dark-haired woman with the patrician features which she passed on to her children.

I went in the Navy in 1941, so I wasn't around when the last of the shipyard's first Roosevelt-era carriers was delivered. She was the first Hornet, called CV-8, which was turned over to the Navy on October 20, 1941.

I kept up with Newport News-built ships as I fought in the war in the Mediterranean and

The main Shipyard gates disgorged hordes of workmen at day's end before World War 2. Many boarded Washington Avenue streetcars, shown at right, later replaced by buses.

Newport News Historical Committee

Newport News Historical Committee

Two Newport News-built liners, America and United States (berthed) served as World War 2 transports. Aircraft carriers also were docked at shipyard, in this photo, with the Casino at right.

the Pacific. Whenever I went aboard a Navy ship, I'd look for the marker's plate near the quarterdeck to see if she'd been built in my hometown.

The USS Essex, CV-9, was the fourth big carrier to be built by the yard in Roosevelt's administration. She was delivered to the Navy on December 31, 1942, and became the "fightingest ship" in the Navy. I suppose she was the most celebrated U.S. warship in World War II.

Beginning with the Essex in 1942, Newport News delivered eight Essex-class carriers in the record time of 27 months—an average of one every 15 weeks. After the Essex, they were the second Yorktown, (known as the "Fighting lady" and the subject of a splendid movie); Intrepid (called "the most hit ship in the Navy"), Hornet, Franklin, Ticonderoga, Randolph, and Boxer. Nearly all played a major part in the Pacific carrier war. Several were sunk.

The yard built the Franklin in the record time of 13 months and 24 days. The United Press wrote of the Franklin's terrible trials that "no other ship in American history survived a like ordeal."

Because the shipyard built such excellent carriers, the Navy gave it a contract in 1941 to design and construct an advanced type ship, even bigger than the Essex class. The delivery of the first of these in 1945—USS Midway—turned a new page in carrier history. She was the largest warship going. Since then, it has built even bigger ones.

Altogether, the yard built 185 warships that fought in World War II. My favorite—a sentimental choice—was the USS Dover, originally the gunboat USS Wilmington. She was built in 1897 for the Spanish-American War. She fought in three wars.

The shipyard also built 243 merchant ships in World War II. These were constructed at the yard's subsidiary, North Carolina Shipbuilding, at Wilmington. This company, which closed after V-J Day, was started in 1941 with Homer Ferguson as chairman, Captain Williams as president, and P. F. Halsey as vice president and general manager. A lot of my high school contemporaries played a part in the yard's achievements.

If we must build warships, Newport News is a good place to build them.

50. *German Sailors in Hampton*

GERMAN agents along North Carolina's Outer Banks? Those rumors kept bobbing up in the grim years of World War II. And they were true. At least one German U-boat tried to send spies ashore in April 1942, just four months after the Japanese had attacked Pearl Harbor and brought the United States into the war.

Wartime censorship kept the news out of the press, but today it can be told.

It's the story of the German U-boat U-85—the first enemy submarine to be destroyed after Germany had declared war on the United States on Dec. 11, 1941. Evidence of the attempted sub landing is provided by 29 gravestones in Hampton National Cemetery. Each bears only a German name, without date or other detail.

Buried secretly 39 years ago, the Germans' story has gradually leaked out over the years. As a newspaperman in Newport News in 1942, I first heard rumors of the burial.

Yes, the Navy admitted, they had buried those bodies at night, but they could say no more. National security was involved. Now the Navy has lifted most of the secrecy. What emerges is an almost successful German submarine landing on the Carolina coast in the early morning of April 14, 1942. But for the vigilance of an old four-stack destroyer, the USS Roper, some of those 29 Germans would have got ashore to infiltrate the United States as intelligence agents for the Fatherland.

Unlike the Roper, the U-85 was the newest and largest type submarine the Germans had launched in their bitter undersea war against Atlantic shipping. Masterminded by the brilliant Adm. Karl Doenitz, Germany had sent out nearly 1,000 submarines to sink American ships and cut off aid to Germany's British and French opponents.

Chesapeake Bay sea-lanes were haunted by Doenitz' wolf packs, as they were called. Offshore sinkings were often visible from the Outer Banks, which Carolinians called "Torpedo Alley." Debris from sunken ships and from vanished crewmen often floated ashore onto the quiet beaches that extend from Virginia Beach south to Cape Hatteras.

Lacking new destroyers, the Navy had pulled World War I four-stackers out of mothballs and set them to work combatting Doenitz' undersea fleet. That's how the USS Roper happened to be steaming south from Norfolk on the night of April 13, patrolling the coast southward from Cape Henry to Cape Hatteras.

At midnight a new watch took over. The

215

Author's collection

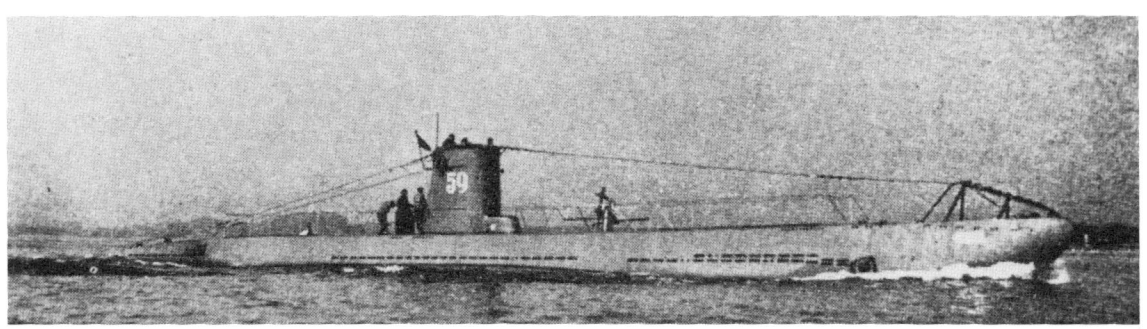

German submarines like this menaced Hampton Roads shipping in World War 2. The Nazis' U 85 was pursued off the Virginia Capes early in 1942 and destroyed.

spring night was clear and starlit. The sea was almost calm and glints of phosphorus brightened the ship's wake. To starboard, men on duty could see Wimble Shoal Light off North Carolina's Outer Banks.

Then, at six minutes past midnight, the Roper's radar showed an object bearing 190 degrees true at a distance of 2,700 yards. Lt. Cmdr. Hamilton Howe, the captain, decided to investigate. The Roper's underwater detectors soon picked up propellor sounds which confirmed the radar.

Howe increased speed to 20 knots and bow lookouts began to spot the wake of a small vessel running away at high speed. As the Roper closed on her prey, Howe sounded battle stations and ordered all weapons ready to fire. As the Roper gained ground, the invisible object changed course radically. The Roper changed too, pulling up to within 700 yards of the unknown adversary.

Suddenly a torpedo sped toward the Roper, narrowly missing. The destroyer had a U-boat on the run.

The USS Roper, a four-stack destroyer built in World War I, pursued and claimed the first of the war's German u-boat casualties in April of 1942. Many enemy submarines menaced Hampton Roads.

Author's collection

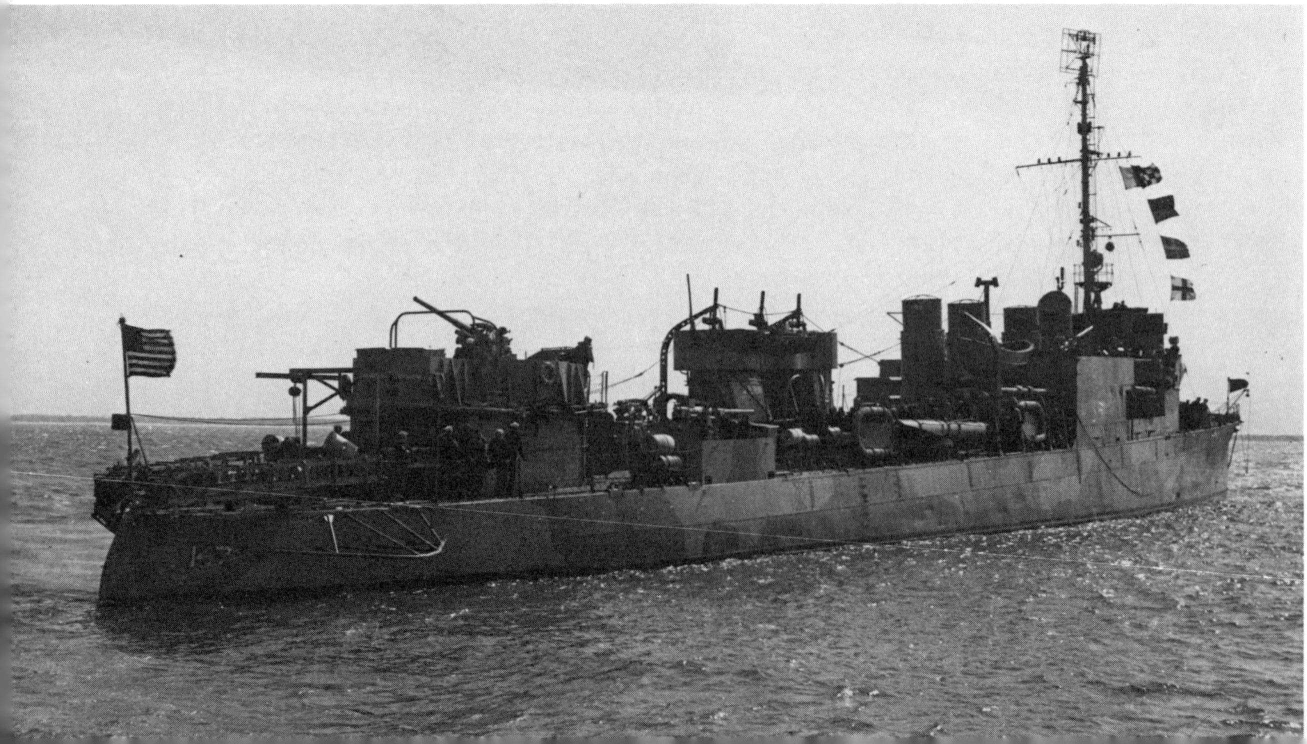

"When the distance had been reduced to 300 yards, the fleeing vessel cut sharply to starboard," Howe reported to his Navy superiors.

"At this instant, using the 24-inch searchlight, she was identified as a large submarine moving on the surface. The searchlight was held on her and fire was opened first with the machine guns and the three-inch battery. The machine guns cut down the submarine personnel rushing to man their guns."

At that moment, young Coxswain Harry Heyman, manning Gun 5, scored a direct hit on the U-boat's conning tower. It was his first shot in combat. The Roper's crew saw water begin to pour into the ruptured submarine.

In the glare of the Roper's searchlight the German crew scrambled wildly out of the disabled sub as she began to sink. Screaming and shouting, they plunged into the waters, some without life-jackets.

Howe ordered a torpedo fired to finish the submarine, but the U-85 boat sank before it could be discharged, settling stern-first into the Atlantic. Because German subs hunted in wolfpacks of two or three, Howe ordered his ship to circle cautiously and drop depth charges. He had heard of skippers torpedoed by a second sub while attempting to rescue submarine crewmen and he wanted to protect against it.

With the Germans still writhing and shouting in the water, the Roper dropped a barrage of 11 depth charges. The powerful underwater concussions killed those Germans not already dead. Some of the Germans were dressed in civilian clothes and were preparing to embark in a rubber raft when the submarine was attacked. When recovered, their wallets were found to contain American currency and identification cards.

The Roper had averted a night landing of German espionage operatives along the lonely Carolina coast, not far away.

For the rest of the night the Roper scoured the area for other subs. Her radioed reports to the Navy at Norfolk—kept brief to avert enemy detection and pursuit—brought a Navy PBY patrol plane at daybreak to look for oil slicks and debris. Two more planes joined and began dropping smoke floats to lead the destroyer to German bodies kept afloat by life jackets. Before the two-hour operation had ended, seven planes, a Navy dirigible and a British trawler were helping.

Clothing and dog tags gave the names of the 29 dead Germans hauled aboard the Roper.

Daily Press

Graves of 29 German naval officers and crewmen were secretly dug at the National Cemetery in Phoebus in 1942.

218 *German Sailors in Hampton*

Daily Press

An Army trumpeter plays taps over graves of servicemen at Phoebus National Cemetery. Among them are 29 German submariners whose u-boat was destroyed in the Atlantic in 1942.

Two were officers, one the U-85's skipper. From empty life jackets floating in the water, it could be seen that others had sunk beneath the waves.

From Norfolk, the Navy sent word to the Roper to mark the sunken sub with a buoy and then return to port. After the destroyer reached the Virginia capes, she transferred the bodies to the Norfolk Naval Air Station for intelligence evaluation.

They were buried in Hampton a night or so later. Protestant and Roman Catholic chaplains read the burial service by lamplight and a squad of Navy seamen fired the volleys in salute. Passers-by were mystified by the nocturnal rites. One of them called a newspaper reporter in Newport News. That's how I first learned of the story.

But the Navy had not finished with the U-85. Divers were sent down to examine the sub as a means of learning the latest German technology. The Navy's sub tender USS Thrasher was summoned from New England to stand over the site while her experts went below to learn all they could from the hulk. Continued U-boat contacts in the area forced the Thrasher and her protecting destroyers finally to break off the inquiry.

The U-boat proved to be one of Hitler's fast new 500-ton submarines, built to carry out Doenitz' undersea war begun in 1940. It had been completed in June 1941 and was on its second cruise in American waters when sunk that April night in 1942. In its 14-month career, it had sunk two allied ships and escaped four plane and two destroyer attacks.

Later, the Navy learned that it was one of the 781 submarines the Germans lost while sinking 3,000 merchant ships and warships—mostly British and American—in the war. The cost to Germany in manpower was astounding. Four out of five Nazi submariners had died in the war.

Today—39 years later—motorists whizzing over Interstate 64 at the Old Point shoreline catch a glimpse of the white headstones of the U-85's crew in the military cemetery nearby.

If they want to read their story, they'll find it in a paragraph of the multi-volume *History of the United States Naval Operations in World War II,* published for the Navy in the 1940s and '50s.

"The old destroyer Roper (Lieutenant Commander H.W. Howe) was the first United States naval vessel to make a kill in the German submarine offensive of 1942," it reads. Then Navy historian Samuel Eliot Morison went on to summarize the story.

Steaming south from Norfolk at 18 knots on the night of 13-14 April, 'Roper' had just passed Wimble Shoal light when her radar screen showed a 'blip' at a range of 2,700 yards. Howe turned up a speed of 20 knots and overhauled the target, which constantly changed its bearing.

A torpedo passed close aboard at a range of 700 yards, but it was not until the range had further closed to a mere 300 yards, and a searchlight had been turned on, that the target was positively identified as a submarine.

'Roper' then opened fire with her main (3-inch) and machine-gun batteries, prevented the Germans from manning their guns, obtained a direct hit near the waterline as the boat began to submerge and then depth-charged on sound contact. Next morning 29 bodies were recovered . . .

And so it is that the U-85 rests today in 14 fathoms off the Outer Banks, while her young victims lie beneath the magnolias of Hampton.

51. *When Newport News Was Fifty*

IF you want to know what America looked like in the 1940s, just find a copy of *Newport News' 325 Years,* published in 1946. There, in the faces of my hometown's morticians, oculists, dentists, and sheet metalsmiths, you'll see the generation that gave birth to ours. Now that generation has largely disappeared.

Lord, what a plain, hard-working city we were! But what good, honest, God-fearing people were its 45,000 citizens! I can remember nearly every face I see in the book, and that was 40 years ago.

World War II was just over in 1946, and Newport News was about to celebrate the 50th anniversary of its chartering, which occurred in 1896. Our nation had never been more powerful. We'd beaten Hitler and Hirohito. We were going to create the United Nations and live in peace, happily ever after.

Newport News shared this euphoria and set up a Golden Anniversary Committee headed by Raymond Bottom. Kemper Kellogg was vice president, L.U. Noland, treasurer, and Bob Smith—all now dead—was secretary. They planned six days of celebration, running from October 13 to 18. It included parades, essay contests, Indian dances, and a pageant at the high school athletic field. To cap the occasion, they hired Alec Brown, just back from the Navy, to edit the city's first history.

I'd just returned from the war and was working for the *Times-Dispatch* in Richmond. One day I got a call from Major Bottom, saying "they" wanted me to write a chapter for the civic history. It was "a great honor," and I would be making "a civic contribution," which meant there would be no pay. Poor as I was, I agreed. Writers are easily flattered.

The hero of this story is Alec Brown. Major Bottom gave him a desk in the Daily Press, then housed in spartan quarters on 25th St., and he went to work. Bob Smith's advertising salesmen solicited and wrote the ads, which were blurbs for local businesses, illustrated with photos of them or their staffs or owners.

I've seen a lot of vanity publications in my time, and they're usually duds, but Messrs. Bottom, Smith, and Brown in 1946 produced a winner. *Newport News' 325 Years* contains 351 double-column pages bulging with the faces, names, and vital statistics of contracting firms, delicatessens, florist shops, and what-have-you. Who can't forgive the owners for being proud of those bakeries and cafeterias? They were entitled to their glow of pride.

The ads in the book are as good as the text. One describes the amenities of Caffee's Fu-

J. Brockenbrough Woodward, chairman of the merger campaign, presides at 1958 ribbon-cutting merging Newport News and Warwick County. Mrs. Philip Hiden and Mrs. Homer Ferguson wield scissors.

neral Home and shows three generations of Caffee morticians, all now gone to their reward. Thanks to Bob Smith and his staff, these commercials give you a good idea of our working-class town, from the arrival of the C&O on the Peninsula in 1880 to the two World Wars that made Newport News big and overgrown.

Ray Bottom conned other unsuspecting souls besides me into writing chapters. Here is Miss Cerinda Evans, telling us how the city got its name. Here are Fairmount "Monk" White and E.O. Smith describing the growth of the shipyard from 1886. And here's skinny little Warner Twyford, later amusement editor of the Virginian-Pilot, glorifying our "Spiritual Life."

Lamar Stanley writes about city schools, and Fred Naff of the Daily Press (Ding Price called him "Nifty Naff") tells the story of Peninsula newspapers. (There were many in the early years.) Other contributors are William M. Harrison, editor of the Times-Herald; attorneys Samuel Buxton Sr. and William T. Stauffer; Elizabeth Buxton Styron (daughter of founder Joseph Buxton of the hospital which became Mary Immaculate and stepmother of novelist William Styron); retired journalist J. Luther Kibler; and George B. Johnson, Andrew Hopkins, Harold Sniffen, Bob Cutler, Arthur Beauchamp, and Matt Fulgham.

One of the best bits is Hairston Seawell's piece on "Entertainment and the Arts," which hymns the Newport News Academy of Music. That was our citadel of culture from 1900 to 1929.

The book concludes with predictions of what Newport News will be in 1996, on its charter's 100th birthday. I especially enjoy those, for they show how perverse and unpredictable the future is. For example, City Manager Joe Biggins foresaw "a successful consolidation of portions of Warwick and Elizabeth City Counties with Newport News." There he woefully underestimated the civic pride of Hampton, which reached out and gobbled up Elizabeth City for its own.

In equally hopeful vein, William E. Blewett of the shipyard thought "All railroad grade crossings will be eliminated"—still not done—and "The Lower Peninsula will be one community, under one government." Ha!

Attorney Charles E. Ford thought he saw "another railroad, coming through Yorktown from the Northern Neck." Delegate Charles K. Hutchens believed Newport News would be "the largest port on the East Coast," while L.U. "Casey" Noland anticipated "more heavy industry" and transoceanic ship companies offering regular Newport News service. We're still looking.

Other predictions have been better fulfilled: the building of a Hampton Roads Bridge-Tunnel and of a Yorktown bridge, the elimination of bridge tolls, the spread of public education, and better opportunities for blacks in education and jobs. The favorite prediction, of course, was the consolidation of the Lower Peninsula into the city of Hampton Roads. I still hope that will come by 1996.

A pathetic note is struck in the book by an extract from an 1885 newspaper which described the unveiling by the Women's Christian Temperance Union of a drinking fountain in Washington Square, then at 28th St. and Washington. Presenting the fountain, temperance advocate Ellen Johnson read a sad little ten-stanza poem, beginning:

"Here, in the heart of the city,
In your midst I take my stand,
To offer water free to all,
The Work of the White Ribbon Band."

Alas for the WCTU, its fountain was moved to the courthouse at 25th and Huntington several decades later, when Washington Square was built on. It has now disappeared.

Menchville on Warwick River became part of Newport News in the 1957 merger of city and county. Fish and oyster boats cluster in the river and in Deep Creek, now a center for pleasure boating.
Newport News Historical Committee

52. *Homer Ferguson: Local Hero*

IF you had worked in the Newport News Shipyard between 1915 and 1946, you'd have seen him. He was a jut-jawed man with a strong nose and a shock of unruly hair. He would watch a laborer do his job, then tell the laborer he'd done a good job or suggest how he could do it better.

He didn't have to introduce himself. Everybody knew Homer Ferguson.

Seldom has a figure dominated his company as Ferguson did the yard. Before he died at 80 in 1953, he made it the biggest private shipyard in the world. It had the biggest payroll of any plant in Virginia.

Today Ferguson is remembered by a dwindling number of older Peninsulans. Many of those have forgotten that he created the Apprentice School and persuaded Archer Huntington to build The Mariners' Museum.

But as the city of Newport News approaches its 100th anniversary in 1996, Ferguson is its nearest thing to a patron saint. His ability to lead a huge work force to build ships won him the appreciation of stockholders and U.S. presidents, especially in the two world wars. During his nearly 40 years' service, the yard built over 430 ships, including America's largest liners and aircraft carriers. The yard's World War II subsidiary yard in Wilmington, N.C., built another 243.

What appealed to me most about Mr. Ferguson was his simplicity. He knew the practical side of shipbuilding from the keel up. He kept up with employees and took pride in their work. He made it his job to walk through the yard every day he was in Newport News and to know his men and their jobs.

"It must be personal," he said, "mixing with men. When you talk to a man about his work, it dignifies the job. Every man needs this."

In his career the yard never had a union strike.

Humor was a Ferguson specialty. He loved to tell of the black shipyard laborer who warned Ferguson against chomping on a cigar—unlighted—as the president walked through the yard. "Mistuh," the man warned, "ef Mistuh Ferguson catch you with that cigar, he gonna run you out."

Once, when Ferguson told the story to laughter at a Christmas party for retired workers, one retiree rose and confessed, "You wanna know who de one told you? I'se the one. I didn't know who you was." It was Ferguson's favorite story.

Ferguson's humor also appealed to Henry E. Huntington, who inherited control of the yard in 1900 on the death of his uncle, Collis Huntington, who had founded it in 1886.

Newport News Shipyard

Homer Ferguson came to work at Newport News Shipyard in 1905. He moved up through the ranks to become president and chairman of the world's largest private shipbuilding firm.

Henry E. Huntington often invited Ferguson to San Marino, California, where the two men talked business. Huntington laughed at Ferguson's stories of his North Carolina boyhood.

After Henry E. Huntington died in 1927, Collis's son, Archer Huntington, was the yard's chairman and principal owner. Tenneco bought control of the company in 1968 and now holds it.

In 1929, when the aging and childless Archer Huntington and his wife, Anna Hyatt, began to give away their estate of art treasures, real estate, and railway and shipyard stock, Ferguson persuaded them to create a nautical museum at Newport News. In 1930 The Mariners' Museum was formed and acreage along the James River and Waters Creek in Warwick County was bought up as its site. The creek is today's Lake Maury. The museum is one of the outstanding maritime museums of the world.

Homer Ferguson was born of Scotch-Irish stock in the mountain town of Waynesville, North Carolina, in 1873. He twice failed the mathematics exam for the U.S. Naval Academy. But he was top man in his class in his graduation in 1892 and won a $1,000 scholarship to study four years at Glasgow University.

After returning to America, he and his wife had two daughters and three sons, whom they reared in the Ferguson family home at 57th Street and Huntington Avenue.

Only their daughter Isobel, now Mrs. Lyman Ayres of Indianapolis, is living. Their daughter Elise, later Mrs. Storer Ware, and their three sons, Homer Jr., Charles, and William McLeod Ferguson, are dead.

Ferguson first came to the Newport News yard in 1905. He moved up through the ranks to be vice president and general manager in 1914. A year later, when yard president Albert Hopkins was lost in 1915 in the sinking of the Lusitania, Ferguson was promoted to president. He remained so until 1946, when he became chairman until his death.

Homer Ferguson (right) greeted workmen on his strolls through the shipyard.

Newport News Historical Committee

Homer Ferguson: Local Hero 225

Newport News Shipyard

Homer Ferguson was America's best-known shipbuilder when he left shipyard presidency in 1946. He and Archer Huntington started Mariners' Museum, and he headed it until he died.

Many stories of Ferguson's regard for "the little guy" still circulate. One is that he once told shipyard owner, Henry E. Huntington, "I think you should share some of the profits with the men who helped you to earn them. A quarter of a million dollars would be about right." Huntington agreed, and Ferguson distributed the money.

The yard president also controlled a $10,000 annual relief fund for needy employees and retirees. He relied on Personnel Director Cargill Johnson to help him use the funds where needed. "You can't imagine the number of people he helped," Johnson said.

Once Ferguson offered to resign as president. When the yard lost $1,250,000 after World War I in converting the German liner Vaterland to the USS Leviathan, the yard president went to New York and told Henry E. Huntington he was ready to take the rap.

Huntington asked if the yard had done a good job.

"The tests were perfect," Ferguson told him.

That was all Huntington wanted to know. Ferguson kept the job.

Looking back over the years of Newport News's growth, it is clear that no one played a major role for so many years as he. The Huntingtons made the yard possible. But Homer Ferguson made it successful. He was a necessary man.

53. *The Muses Smile*

ONE of the changes in Peninsula life in the 20th century has been the spread of the arts and literature. We've grown through generations of hard-working farmers, fishermen, and mechanics into a society that enjoys creativity as an essential to good living.

I suppose it began with the new emphasis on music, arts, and literature in our 20th century public schools. Since then Hampton and Newport News have turned out many talented professional creators as well as thousands of enthusiastic amateurs.

Our Peninsula orchestras, museums, theatres, art galleries, and publications are evidence of that. Cary McMurran, who formed the first Peninsula Symphony in 1947 and who now enjoys a varied professional life in Williamsburg, is a good example.

It was a lot harder to earn a living in the arts in the 1930s and 40s than today. People had less leisure then and fewer organized entertainments. There were no federal grants for performers or scholars. Aspiring musicians lived by working at a 9-to-5 job and "moonlighting" by teaching music, playing in bands, or singing in a choir.

Peninsula history then was written by self-taught researchers—newspapermen, lawyers, or sometimes teachers like Martha Hiden or Annie Jester. The humanist ideal of the gifted "amateur"—exemplified by Jefferson and Teddy Roosevelt—survived then more than today, alas. Many hobbyists then wrote or made music or painted without making it a career. A civilized society needs gifted "amateurs."

I've written before of Professor Aage V. Schmidt, one of Newport News's best known musicians in the 1930s. He led the Newport News Academy of Music orchestra. Further down Washington Avenue, at the Imperial movie house, Professor Albert Michael led another orchestra. Such musicians eked out a thin existence.

In those self-entertainment days, Newport News had many music teachers (whose names could be obtained from clerks at Ferguson's or Gemmell's music stores). E. Gordon Weyburn taught wind instruments and tuned pianos. Ada G. Haughton taught piano and wrote program notes for recitals. Other piano teachers were Ethel Cottrell Epes (Cary McMurran's aunt and first teacher), Professor Blakemore, Mrs. Willis Shell, Eleanor James and Mrs. Richard Marshall.

McMurran taught piano when he returned to his hometown from the conservatory, molding such students as William T. Tim Read, international harpsichordist; Robert Carroll

Smith, pianist at Indiana State College; and William Hudson, conductor of the Fairfax County Symphony.

Other teachers were the well-loved Hampton couple, Harold and Elizabeth Chapman. Harold had studied with Walter Piston at Harvard and wrote much music now in the McMurran Library at Chistropher Newport. (Louise Walker and Marion Huber are continuing the Chapman's Youth Ensemble, and pianist Allan Sternfield of Israel is a notable Chapman product.) .... Another teacher was Eleanor Sherman, now Mrs. Paul Hennig, who directed the Newport News High School orchestra and started its band. Her disciples are legion.

I remember also good-humored Ella Hayes, who supervised Newport News public school music and sang in many groups. A later music supervisor was Margaret Davis, who was a contemporary of the city's most celebrated pop music products, Ella Fitzgerald and Pearl Bailey. The Peninsula has trained many fine jazz performers.

Other products of the '30s and '40s were Fenno Heath, now director of the Yale Glee Club; Howard Boatwright of Syracuse University; and J.S. "Jock" Darling III, Bruton's famous musician. Two others were violist Ronald Marshall and his sister, violinist Dora Marshall Mullins. Both have led groups and starred as soloists. Mrs. Mullins has played New York recitals and performs as a member of the Feldman Chamber Music Society of Norfolk. She taught at Juilliard and is on the summer staff of Alfred University in New York.

Music interested more Peninsulans than any

Instrumentalists of the first Newport News school orchestra line up at John Daniel School about 1920. Irving Nielson and Ella Hayes, at rear, were its leaders.

other art. We have produced few painters or sculptors. The first Peninsula artist to make a name in my day was J.J. Lankes, whose woodcuts of rustic Virginia were widely published in the 1930s. The first professional art teacher I recall was Maribland Bryant, I was one of her students.

In those days the Newport News Woman's Club's annual art show brought out a swarm of housewives and Sunday painters. The first professional artists I remember after Miss Bryant were Jack Clifton and Allan D. Jones Jr., now established painters and teachers, along with the well-known Barclay Sheaks. Allan married Jean Craig, a fellow Pennsylvania Academy graduate and an active painter. Jacqueline Bickford, who studied with Denis Gelin in Paris and became his wife, was well known. They live near Fontainebleau.

Another early local artist was John Needre, now retired from an art career at Fort Eustis. Like the Joneses and Jack Clifton, he graduated from Pennsylvania Academy. His portrait of Cary McMurran hangs in the Christopher Newport library.

Newport News in the 1930s had a good Little Theatre. Those were the times of Dorothy Crane, a dynamo who taught at Newport News High, and of Beatrice Glass Stratford, a dedicated director. Newport News in those days produced such talents as Howard Scammon, later William and Mary's theater director, and actor Tilden Davis, who has retired to Williamsburg.

The first professional Peninsula dancers were Charles Henkel and his wife, Douglas, who taught at the Green Domino Studio, I remember seeing tiny Georgia Hiden, later premiere danseuse of the Vienna State Opera, emerge as a newly-fledged butterfly from a four-foot "cocoon" on a Newport News stage in the 1930s, then begin to dance. Ballet was an unheard-of-career then. Now Georgia is a teacher in New York.

Newport News Historical Committee

Archer Huntington owned the shipyard and founded the Mariners Museum.

In the realm of writing I think of many Peninsulans. Most of them wrote as a hobby, but that doesn't minimize their work. A Newport News lawyer named William T. Stauffer researched early Peninsula land grants, encouraged by such historians as Earl Swem. Mrs. Hiden and Mrs. Jester, mentioned earlier, researched the settlers of Jamestown and the beginnings of Newport News. So did Cerinda Evans, first librarian of the Mariners' Museum. And so did J. Luther Kibler, Fred J. Naff, Alexander Crosby Brown, and Robert Burgess—the latter two former mainstays of the Mariners' Museum.

A Hampton historian was Harry Houston, who published Hampton's Monitor newspaper and was speaker of the House of Delegates.

Others who wrote of Hampton were Marion Starkey, of Hampton Institute; Sclater Montague, attorney and state senator; and Chester Bradley, a scholarly physician who founded the Casemate Museum and wrote Civil War history.

But of all Peninsula writers, the most famous is William Styron, born in Newport News in 1918. His first novel, "Lie Down in Darkness," offers an interesting fictionalized view of his early years. Even so, I think the Peninsula has benefited most from creative people like Cary McMurran, who have stayed and worked here on the Peninsula. They have enriched our life, sometimes without acclaim. Thanks to them, our area is a more stimulating place.

Heroic statue of explorer Leif Ericsson faces entrance of Mariners Museum, founded in 1930. Its exhibits of art and maritime history, built on Lake Maury, are among the world's finest.

City of Newport News

A model shows plan for downtown Newport Centre, facing James River between 26th and 31st Streets. A new interstate highway and new bridge-tunnel in 1990 are expected to revive the area.

230

54. Facing a New Century

AFTER 40 years of decline, downtown Newport News at last seems headed for a revival.

Like Hampton, Newport News in 1990 will benefit from a new interstate highway and a new bridge-tunnel across Hampton Roads.

I have it on the word of Robert Williams, city manager, who is spearheading the $275 million redevelopment plan called Newport Centre. Bob Williams is a persuasive man.

"Completion in 1990 of Interstate 664 and the bridge-tunnel from Newport News to Suffolk will being back the commerce that left us after World War II," Williams says. "Route 664 will create a new downtown city along its way."

A big bluff man whose 12th floor City Hall office on 24th Street and Washington Avenue looks out over a half-deserted downtown, Williams says Newport Centre is needed to control civic growth already coming from new industries and the expanding shipyard.

"The city's need for interstate access to Hampton Roads and west will be met at last," he says. "The 1990 bridge-tunnel will be the last link in a circle between the Peninsula and Suffolk, Portsmouth, Chesapeake, and Norfolk. We've got to be ready for the changes it will bring."

As Williams sees it, Newport News has suffered from inaccessibility ever since Interstate 64 was built from Hampton to Ocean View. "But all that will change" he says "when trucks and motorists can turn off Interstate 64 near Hampton Coliseum and drive over I-664 through the city's new Seafood Park at the Boat Harbor and on to downtown Newport News and the bridge-tunnel."

Williams disagrees with critics who say the city will have trouble luring residents back downtown to its planned Newport Centre housing.

"More than $36 million in private money has been devoted to the plan this fiscal year," he reveals. "Downtown is getting its first new investment in 10 years. The interstate and Newport Centre will give us an expanded tax base plus more than 5,000 new jobs."

The federally-financed bridge-tunnel is on schedule despite congressional delays, Williams says. Route 664 is completed thus far from Hampton Coliseum to Chestnut Avenue. Work is now under way on a new link to 35th Street and Huntington Avenue. And fast-growing traffic over the Hampton bridge-tunnel increases the urgency of the alternative Newport News crossing.

"Newport News is a young city," the executive observes, "but it has been slow to modernize its access. The new interstate will do for this city what I-64 had already done for Norfolk, Hampton, and Richmond. Good access is the key to civic growth."

The Newport Centre concept is the city's effort to control the coming renewal of downtown, the city manager points out. "When I-664 is finished, we must be in control. We don't want haphazard growth."

The heart of the Newport Centre concept is a landscaped sea-walk along the James from 23rd Street and 32nd Street, across the Casino grounds. "It will give back to citizens nearly 1,700 new feet of waterfront," he says. To achieve this, the city has purchased Horne Brothers' shipyard on the James from 23rd to 26th Streets, leasing it for the present to the Newport News Shipyard till the city completes its plans.

"The potential of the downtown waterfront is fantastic," Williams believes, influenced by recent waterside projects in Norfolk and Baltimore. "The future of downtown requires that the city control 15 acres of waterfront and 17 acres of riparian rights." There he envisions city docks for cruise ships as well as a large

Newport News Historical Committee

Coal piers and merchandise docks now overlie onetime Civil War camp site at Newport News point. Completion of the bridge-tunnel route near Boat Harbor at right will ease access to the area.

downtown hotel, a city-owned Cultural Arts Center, and high-rise residential and office buildings with parking garages.

Newport Centre calls for heavy private and public investment in a 22-block area from West Avenue to Huntington and from 23rd Street to 34th. An urban development firm in Madison, Wis., is attempting to interest a hotel chain and condominium builders in putting money in the plan. The city also hopes the shipyard will take part, but thus far it has said no.

"Norfolk is this area's financial center," Williams says. "So Newport News must find another niche. With the city midway between Virginia Beach and Williamsburg, we must create an attraction here to pull people from both. We need something to compete with Waterside and Busch Gardens."

When he became city manager in 1981, Bob Williams found Newport News facing urgent problems. The C&O had thrown its port business to Baltimore, hurting Hampton Roads. The once-independent shipyard had been bought by Tenneco and was controlled from Houston. Peninsula banks had joined chains in Richmond and Norfolk. And the city wasn't getting its share of federal redevelopment money.

"Newport News just watched its neighbors grow while it did nothing," Williams laments.

"The city waited to act till the downtown was desolate. Most businesses moved to Warwick or Mecury Boulevard. People will only go where they can drive their cars," Williams insists. "When the couldn't get to downtown easily, they moved from the inner city. But Interstate 664 will get them back."

Bob Williams refuses to badmouth Norfolk or his predecessors, though he is a competitive man. "We must accept some facts of life and accommodate ourselves to them," he concedes.

"I believe the merger of Newport News and Warwick, expanding the city from four square miles to 68, requires that we diversify and lessen our dependence on the shipyard and C&O. This diversification is towards high-tech corporations such as Oyster Point Industrial Park, Copeland Industrial Park, NASA, and Langley Research Park."

Much as Williams counts on the downtown's rebirth, he knows it can never dominate the Peninsula as it did before Pearl Harbor. The expanded community that came from adding the old city to Warwick in 1958—now 150,000 people—is now a cluster of five or six major commercial areas, he points out. But Williams thinks the downtown is bound to regain strength from new shipping, shopping, banking, and tourism.

In the city's game of catch-up, Williams sees the next five years as crucial. "Timing is the problem. Demand for downtown space is showing up. We're at the point of no return. The economic boom is helping. The shipyard's backlog will keep it booming for years. And local industries like Noland Company, Ferguson Enterprises, Avon Fashions, Mercedes-Benz, the Dominion and A.T. Massey Coal Terminals, and Bendix will help attract other business."

"Our strength as a diversified community is even scaring some Norfolk interests," he says, smiling.

Born in Fauquier County in 1936, Bob Williams worked at the shipyard from 1954 to 1959. He was educated at the University of Virginia. By 1975 he had become Portsmouth's city manager. His success in reviving that city led Newport News to hire him to succeed Frank Smiley as its operating head in 1981.

Bob Williams likes to show his office visitors the scale model of the new downtown as city council envisions it. "When I took office this city had an inferiority complex," he says proudly, looking at the model. "But now we have everything we need to succeed."

After you talk with Bob Williams, you get the feeling that better times are indeed coming to Newport News at last.

Yes, the Peninsula is changing fast.

Daily Press

The Peninsula's biggest asset remains its waterfront. Here York County retirees catch hard crabs with a baited line and crabnet. Rivers, creeks, and marshes are part of the area's appeal.

Index

A

Academy of Music, 75, 91, 118, 120, 126, 129, 115, 161, 162, 199, 221
Accomack County, 4
Acosta, Bert, 95-98
Adams Express Company, 51, 67
Adams Floating Theatre, 148
Aero Club of America, 97
Aircraft carriers, 212-214
Alexander, Fred M., 171-173, 189-191
Allaun, William E., Jr., 74, 96
Almond, Gov. J. Lindsay, Jr., 207
Ambler, Edward, 7
Ambler, Mary (Mrs. Edward), 7
American Academy of Arts and Letters, 47, 48
American Expeditionary Force, 107-110
American Missionary Society, 64
American Theatre, 196
Amos and Andy, 113
Amtrak, 53
Andrews, Gen. Frank, 167
Applewhite, Nancy, 189
Appomattox, 29
Appomattox Manor plantation, 31
Apprentice School, 178, 223
Armistead, Judge Robert, 123
Armistead, William, 70
Armstrong, Rev. Richard, 63
Armstrong, Gen. Samuel C., 55-58, 63-66
Army Air Corps, 95-98, 115-117, 166-170
Army of Northern Va., 20
Army Quartermaster Corps, 93
Army Air Technical Training Command, 170
Arnold, Gen. Hap, 167-170
Ashe, Capt. William, 152
Atlantic Coast Aeronautical Station, 95-98
Atlantic Hotel, 116
A. T. Massey Coal Terminal, 233
Austin Statesman, 44
Avon Fashions, 233
Ayres, Mrs. Lyman (Isobel Ferguson), 224

B

Back River, 166
Bailey, Pearl, 105, 186-188, 227
Baker, James Carr, 186
Baker, Secty. Newton D., 109
Bailey, James T., 53
Baldwin, Capt. Thomas Scott, 95-98
Ballard, William, 56
Ballard Fish & Oyster Co., 159
Baltimore & Ohio Ry., 49
Baltimore Steamship Line, 153
Bancroft, Hubert, 44
Bankhead Magruder School, 184
Barbour, Gov. James, 9, 11
Barclay family, 118
Barclay Jewelry Store, 120
Barham, Mabel, 172, 190
Barham, Judge T. J., 164, 165, 208
Barrett, William E., 188
Barrett Brothers Real Estate, 105
Barthelmess, Richard, 95
Barton, Eleanor Parrish (Mrs. Robert), 145
Barton, James, 122
Bassette, A. W. E., Jr., 206
Battery Park, 143, 146
Battle of Bethel, 18
Bay Shore beach, 195
Beacon newspaper, 189
Beauchamp, Arthur, 221
Beckwith, Sir Sidney, 12
Beecher, Rev. Henry Ward, 44
Behrman, S. N., 39
Belvoir plantation, 7
Ben Greet Players, 127
Benson-Phillips Company, 126
Bentley, Elizabeth Hope (Mrs. George), 160
Bentley, George, 159
Bentley, Bishop John, 206
Berkeley, Capt. Charles C., 123-125, 208
Berkeley plantation, 29, 30
Berlin, Dr. Irving, 190
Berry, Idella, 134
Berryman, John 156-158
Bickford, Robert G., 109
Bide-a-Wee Tea Room, 118, 120, 179, 194
Big Four, 34
Biggins, Joseph, 221
Birley, Sir Oswald, 39
Bivins, A. L., 208
Blackbeard: *see* Edward Teach
Blackbeard's Point, 5, 10
Blackiston, Henry C., 61
Blackstone, Judge J. W. G., 164
Blair, John, 7
Blakemore, Prof. 226
Blewett, William, 118, 222
Bloodfield, 122, 176, 188
Boatwright, Frederic W., 61
Boatwright, Howard, 190, 227
Bob Wallace's College Shop, 155
Booker, Hunter, 61, 167
Booker, George B. A., 128
Bootlegging, 137, 138
Bottom, Cdr. Raymond, 200-202, 220-222
Bowen, Virginia Vaiden (Mrs. William), 145
Bowers, Frederick V., 111
Braddock, Gen. Edward, 7

235

236 Index

Bradley, Dr. Chester, 70, 153, 229
Braxton, Col. Carter, 51
Braxton Court, 104, 108
Breslaw, Dr. William, 86, 87
Briarfield Road, 124, 138, 154
Brick Pond, 138
Broadway Shoe Store, 120
Brown, Alexander Crosby, 87, 180, 220-222, 228
Brown, Arthur, 200
Brown, Judge J. D. G., 93, 164
Brown, Raymond, 158
Bruno, Donald, 82
Brustuen, Melba (Mrs. Sam Hoyle), 190
Bryan, William Jennings, 123
Bryant, Maribland, 228
Buckroe Beach, 57, 97, 98, 153, 160, 195
Burbank, Annye, 171-173
Burgess, Robert, 228
Burma Shave, 152, 153
Burnside, Gen. Ambrose, 31
Buxton, Samuel, 221
Byrd, Gov. Harry, 124, 145
Byrd, Adm. Richard, 96, 134, 191

C

Caffee Funeral Home, 220-221
California gold rush, 34, 49
Calvary Baptist Church, 183
Cameo Theatre, 178
Camp Butler, 32
Camp Eustis. *See* Fort Eustis
Camp Hill, 98, 104-106, 108-110
Camp Hill Hostess House: *see* Hostess House
Camp Morrison, 98, 104-106, 108-110
Camp Stuart, 98, 104-106, 108-110
Campbell, John A., 29
C and O Ry, 13-25, 33, 34-37, 41, 44, 45, 46, 49-53, 59, 67, 71, 161, 232, 233
C and O Depot, 128, 161
C and O piers, 115-117, 232, 233
C and O grain elevator, 91, 93, 161
C and O Historical Soc., 53
Cannon, Bishop James, 124
Cape Henry, 214, 219
Capote, Truman, 117
Caribbean shipping, 3
Carisbrooke plantation, 6
Carleton, Olive, 189
Carlstrom, Carl, 97
Carlstrom, Victor, 96-98
Carmel, Macy, 203-205
Carmel, Percy, 203-205
Carpenter, Bill, 150
Carpenter, Joe, 150
Carroll, Earl, 158
Cartwright crab plant, 159
Cary family, 6-8
Cary, Henry, Jr., 6
Cary, Henry, Sr., 6

Cary, Col. John B., 8
Cary, Mary Wilson Roscow (Mrs. Miles), 7
Cary, Miles, 7
Cary, Sarah Blair (Mrs. Wilson Miles), 7
Cary, Col. Wilson, 7
Cary, Wilson Miles, II, 8
Casemate Club, 124
Casemate Museum, 153, 229
Casino building, 93
Casino grounds, 74-76, 78, 121, 171, 188, 232, 233
Castle, Irene (Mrs. Vernon), 96-98
Castle, Vernon, 96-98
Cedar Hall, 54, 58
Cedar Hall Reading Club, 58
Ceely, Thomas, 7
Ceely's plantation, 6-8, 72
Centennial Special, 53
Central Restaurant, 160
Chamberlin Hotel: *see* Hotel Chamberlin
Chamberlin, John, 71, 73-75
Chapel of the Centurion, 57
Chapman, Elizabeth, 227
Chapman, Harold, 227
Chapman Youth Orchestra, 227
Charles, Dr. Joseph, 74
Charles, Roy, 120
Charles City County, 103, 174
Chase Bag Co., 156
Chautauqua lectures, 75
Chesapeake and Ohio: *see* C and O
Chesapeake City: *see* Phoebus
Chesapeake Dry Dock Co., 33, 35-37, 45: *see* N. N. Shipyard
Chesapeake Hospital, 22
Chesterville plantation, 168
Cheyne, 'Happy', 161
Chickahominy Landing, 18
Chickahominy swamp, 21
China Palace & Gift Shop, 178
Christopher Newport College, 227
Chuckatuck, 155
Church-going, 193-195
Citizens-Marine Bank, 25, 53, 118, 120, 178
Citizens Rapid Transit Co., 160
Civil War, 9, 13-33, 122, 128, 153, 188
Clifton, Jack, 228
Clydebank, 36
Cock, Roland, 203-205
Cockburn, Adm. Sir John, 11
Cofer, Wesley, 146
College of Wm & Mary, 83, 172, 208
College Creek, 175
Collier, Howard, 61
Colonial Inn, 155
Colonial Parkway, 174-176
Colonna, Viola, 133
Commuting, 183-185
Coolidge, Pres. Calvin, 145, 172
Copeland, Mrs. W. Scott, 120

Copeland Industrial Park, 233
Corcoran, Thomas, 213
Cornwallis, General Lord, 52
Coston, Samuel, 162
Cox, Allene, 134
Crab picking, 209-211
Crab town, 154, 159
Crandol, Jeff, 14
Crane, Dorothy, 189
Craney Island, 9-12
Crenshaw, Mayor J. G., 182
Crutchfield, Major Stapleton, 10-12
CSX Corp., 49. *See* C and O Ry.
Cultural life, 226-229
Cumming, Frank, 56
Cumming, Grace Darling (Mrs. James), 57
Cumming, James, 57
Curtis, Simon R., 61
Curtiss, Glenn, 95-98
Curtiss Field 94-98, 161: *see* Atlantic Coast Aeronautical Station

D

Daily Press 99, 109, 121, 123, 190, 200-202, 203-205, 209
Daniels, Jonathan, 115
Danville, 24
Darden, Gov. Colgate, 164
Darling, Frank W., 55, 60, 61, 62, 159-162
Darling, James Sands, I, 55-58, 67, 159-162
Darling, James Sands, II, 55
Darling, James Sands, III, 58
Darling, Mollie Gorton (Mrs. Frank), 57
Darling, Sally, 58
Darling boatyard, 58
Dashiell, Harry, 143
Davis, F. H., 102
Davis, Gertrude, 83, 149-151
Davis, Jefferson, 19, 22, 24, 153
Davis, Margaret, 227
Davis, Gov. Westmoreland, 106
Davis, Tilden, 189, 228
Dawn Patrol, 95
Dawson City, 83
Day's Drug Store, 179
Deep Creek, 222
Delk, Capt. Gordon, 142
Demaray, Arthur, 175
Democratic primaries, 206-208
Dewey, Adm. George, 73
Diggs, Mary, 133
Dickinson, Rev. Alfred, 194
Dixie Hospital, 204
Dodds, William H., 91
Dodge, Horace E., Jr., 156-158
Dodge Boat & Plane Corp., 156-158
Dominion Coal Terminal, 233
Downing farm, 168
Duveen, James Henry, 39, 44, 46-48
Duveen, Lord, 39, 46-48

E

Eaker, Gen. Ira., 167
East End, 183
Eastern Shore, 3, 56
Edwards, Mae Marshall, 172, 190
Elizabeth Buxton Hospital, 7
Elizabeth City County, 51, 83, 183-185
Elizabeth City County Courthouse, 165
Elizabeth River, 9, 10
Elks' Lodge, 151
Endless Harbor, 106
Epes, Cary, 97
Epes, Charles C., Jr., 190-197
Epes, Ethel Cottrell (Mrs. Charles C.), 226
Epes, Horace H., 81, 83
Epes, Lucille Moseley (Mrs. Charles C., Jr.), 190
Epes, W. Perry, Jr., 162
Epes family, 118
Epes Stationery Co., 120, 121, 126, 178
Ericsson, Leif, 229
Evans, Cerinda, 40-48
Evans, William, 159

F

Fairfax, Bryan, 7
Fairfax, Elizabeth Cary (Mrs. Bryan), 7
Fairfax, George William, 6-8
Fairfax, Sally (Mrs. George William), 6-8
Fairfax proprietary, 7
Falconer's Drug Store, 178
Feldman Chamber Music Society, 227
Female Seminary, 83
Ferguson, Charles, 224
Ferguson, Homer, 48, 101, 102, 136, 214, 223-225
Ferguson, Homer, Jr., 224
Ferguson, Mrs. Homer, 119
Ferguson, William McLeod, 224
Ferguson Enterprises, 233
Ferguson Music Store, 178, 226
Fields, Al G., 128
First National Bank, 25, 53, 118, 120
Finkel, Rabbi Jesse J., 151
First Baptist Church, 192-195
First Presbyterian Church, 151, 192-195
First Vermont Regiment, 14
Fitzgerald, Ella, 105, 186-188, 227
Flannagan, Margaret, 202
Florida Orange Store, 179
Ford, Charles E., 208, 222
Ford, Henry, 152
Ford, Lee, 208
Fort Calhoun 12: *see also* Fort Wool, Rip-Raps
Fort Eustis, 98, 104-106, 108-110
Fort McHenry, 12
Fort Monroe, 28-33, 54, 86-87, 153, 154, 168
Fort Monroe post office, 87
Fort Wool, 30
Free, Elma, 172, 190
Freedmen's Bureau, 55-58, 63-66
Freeman, Douglas, 61, 204-205
Fulgham, Matt, 221
Future growth, 231-233

G

Gainsborough's *Blue Boy,* 48
Gallop, H. M. Buck, 95-98
Gallop, Maxine Finch (Mrs. H. M.), 95
Gates, Isaac, 45
Gard, Capt., 142
Gauntlett, Fred, 99-102
Gay, Thomas B., 207
Gelin, Jacqueline Bickford (Mrs. Denis), 228
Gemmell Music Store, 178, 226
Gildersleeve, Ethel, 172
Glasgow, Ellen, 59, 165
Glasgow, Judge, 165
Gloucester County, 103
Godwin, Gov. Mills E., Jr., 148
Gold Coast, 136-139
Goodman, Layton, 190
Gordon, Major J. J., 52
Gordon brothers, 178
Gorsuch's Drug Store, 120, 178
Gospel-Spreading Assoc., 174-176
Grace, Bishop, 176
Grandview Beach, 195
Grant, Gen. Ulysses S., 29, 31
Granville-Barker, Harley, 45
Granville-Barker, Helen Huntington (Mrs. Granville), 45
Great Depression, 151, 156-158, 178, 179, 200-202
Great flu epidemic, 106
Great freeze, 103-106
Great White Fleet, 62, 66, 77-80, 84-87
Green, Paul, 115
Green Domino Studio, 228
Greenwood, Oliver, 82
Griffith, Mrs. E. P., 83
Groner, gen. Virginius, 18
Groome, Nelson, 61, 168
Guittar, Louis, 4
Gwaltney, Henrietta Chapman (Mrs. Julius), 145
Gwaltney, P. D., 142

H

Hallett, Horace, 172, 189
Halsey, P. F., 214
Hampton Album, 65
Hampton & Old Point RR Co., 60
Hampton Bar, 144
Hampton Courthouse, 207
Hampton Electric Light & Power Co., 61
Hampton Fire Department, 87, 96
Hampton High School, 171-173
Hampton Institute: *see* Hampton University
Hampton Memorial Baptist Church, 61
Hampton Military Academy, 8
Hampton Monitor, 51, 104, 228
Hampton National Cemetery, 215-219
Hampton, Phoebus, & Fort Monroe Gas Corp., 61
Hampton Roads Boulevard, 105, 154
Hampton Roads Bridge-Tunnel, 146, 149, 161, 185
Hampton Roads Sanitation Comm., 58
Hampton University, 3, 63-66
Hampton Yacht Club, 159
Hancock, Gen. Winfield, 73
Hankins, Helen, 133
Happy Am I, 174-176
Harmon, Eunice, 133, 134
Harney, Capt., 142
Harper's Weekly, 13, 23, 30, 71
Harrell, Carolyn, 133
Harrell, Lena, 133
Harrison, William M., 221
Hartel, Mrs. Frederick, 57
Hatten, Earl, 156-158
Hawkins-Melson-Finch tract, 74
Hayes, Ella, 134, 227
Heath, Fenno, 81
Heath, Fenno, Jr., 227
Heffelfinger, Jacob, 61
Hell's Half-Acre, 73, 122, 161, 187, 188
Hemingway, Ernest, 117
Henkel, Douglas (Mrs. Charles), 228
Henkel, Charles, 228
Hennig, Eleanor Sherman (Mrs. Paul), 172, 189, 196, 227
Henrico County, 18
Heyman, Harry, 217
Heyman, Peter, 3-5
Herbert, Victor, 127
Hiden, Martha (Mrs. Philip W.), 226, 228
Hiden, Philip W., 121, 136, 146
Hiden, Wallace, 134
Hiden Storage & Forwarding Co., 93, 107
Hilton Village, 104-5, 121, 183-185
Hispanic Society of Am., 47
Holmes, Adm. Ephraim, 209
Holt, Harry, 167
Holt, Quincy, 134
Holt, Robert P., 61
Holt, Lt. Gov. Saxon, 136
Hooper, Henry V., 172
Hooper & Hardy, 161
Hoover, Pres. Herbert, 172

Hopewell, 29-31, 103
Hopkins, Albert L., 99-102, 224
Hopkins, Andrew, 221
Horne, William, 157, 158
Horseman, Howard, 159
Hoster, Charles, 134
Hostess House, 107-110, 137, 138
Hotel Chamberlin, 57, 68-71, 85-87
Hotel de Hirsch, 47, 48
Hotel Hygeia, 11, 67-71
Hotel Monticello, 87, 144
Hotel Warwick, 42, 53, 73-76, 83, 91, 93, 118, 128-129, 162, 179
Houston, Harry R., 228
Howe, Albert, 61
Howe, Arthur, 66
Howe, Cdr. Hamilton, 216-219
Hoyle, N. R., 201
Hoyle, Sam, 190, 200
Hudgins, Robert, 61
Hudson, William, 227
Huffman, Col. E. W., 82
Huffman's Military School, 73
Hunter, Robert M. T., 29
Huntington, Anna Hyatt (Mrs. Archer), 45, 46, 224
Huntington, Arabella Yarrington (Mrs. Collis and Mrs. Henry E.), 38-54
Huntington, Archer M., 38-48, 50, 212, 223, 224
Huntington, Clara Prentice, 45, 46
Huntington, Collis Potter, 34-54, 56, 62, 67, 71, 74-76, 93, 122, 136, 162, 171, 193, 223, 224
Huntington, Elizabeth (Mrs. Collis), 44
Huntington, Henry Edwards, 38-48, 101, 136, 223-225
Huntington Heights, 107-110
Huntington High School, 172
Huntington Hotel, 92
Huntington Library and Art Museum, 38-48
Huntington, W.Va., 50
Hurricane of 1933, 105, 154
Hussey, Wendell, 145
Hussey, Woodroof Hiden (Mrs. Wendell), 145
Hutchens, Charles K., 222
Hygeia Hotel. *See* Hotel Hygeia

I

I Wanted Wings, 167
Ickes, Secty Harold, 175, 176
Influenza epidemic, 103-106, 108-110
International Naval Review, 77
Isle of Wight County, 145-148

J

Jackson, Gen. Stonewall, 25
Jacobs, Ben, 207
Jacobs, Eastman, 168
James, E. Ralph, 208
James, Henry, 45
James River Bridge, 80, 139, 144, 145-148, 155
James River Canal, 20
James River Country Club, 136
James River Line, 121
James River shipping, 141-144
Jamestown, 174-176
Jamestown Exposition, 62, 71, 77-80, 85-87, 97, 98
Jamestown ferries, 152
Jarvis, Sgt. James, 12
Jarvis crab plant, 159
Jefferson, Thomas, 12, 226
Jefferson Bank, 178
Jenkins, Willis, 82
Jester, Annie Lash (Mrs. Lewis), 81, 226, 228
Jester, Capt. A. F., 80, 121, 141, 146, 152, 155
Jester, Lewis T., 204
J. H. Miles Oyster Co., 159
John W. Daniel School, 81, 82, 134, 135, 137, 149-151, 171, 183-185
Johnson, Albert Sydney, 146, 147
Johnson, Cargill, 225
Johnson, George B., 221
Johnson' Academy of Music, 126
Johnston, Gen. Joseph E., 20, 24
Jones, Allan D., 208
Jones, Allan D., Jr., 228
Jones, Grace, 133
Jones, Jean Craig (Mrs. Allan, Jr.), 228
Jones, Mary Mason (Mrs. Isaac), 45
Jones, Mary Wynne, 172
J. S. Darling & Son, 56, 159-162

K

Kane, Elisha Kent, III, 203-205, 206
Kane murder trial, 203-205, 206
Kann, Rudolph, 46
Kearney, Judge Frank, 203-205
Kearney, Ross, 203-205
Kecoughtan Road, 10, 154
Kecoughtan Veterans Hospital: *see* Veterans Admin Hosp, Kecoughtan
Kellogg, Kemper, 220
Kelly, Walter, 122-164, 188
Kennedy, Ambassador Joseph, 213
Kennedy, Rose Fitzgerald (Mrs. Joseph), 213
Kennon, Stanley, 202
Kerlin, Jacob Harry, 81
Kerlin, Nellie, 83
Key, Francis Scott, 12
Kibler, J. Luther, 221, 228
Kimberley Bros. Army & Navy Stores, 56
Kimmich, H. G., 91
King, Rev. Martin Luther, 175
King, Sidney, 32
Knox, H. M., 99-102
Knox, Reba, 133, 134
Kreibohm, Catherine Kearney (Mrs. Rudolph), 145
Krogstad, Gen. Arnold, 167

L

Lafayette House, 73
Lambert's Point, 103
Lake Maury, 162, 224, 229
Lamington plantation, 168
Lancers Confectionary, 125
Land, Adm. Emory, 213
Langley Field, 94-98, 115-117, 166-170
Langley Field, the Early Years, 167
Langley Field dirigibles, 117, 169, 170
Langley Hotel, 160
Langley Research Park, 233
Langley Theatre, 160
Lankes, J. J., 228
Laracy, Pat, 92
LaVallette, Cdr. Albert T., 209-212
LaVallette, Capt. Elie, 209-211
Lavender, David, 42
Lay, Col. Beirne, 167
Lay, Ludwell Lee (Mrs. Beirne), 167
League, Mollie Masters (Mrs. J. B.), 145
Lee, Ann Carter (Mrs. Wm Henry), 19
Lee, Gen. Robert E., 19, 22, 25, 29, 30, 41, 153, 154
Lee Hall, 52, 53
Levinson's Market, 118
Levy, Herman, 173
Liberty Launching Day, 88
Lincoln, Abraham, 28-33, 154
Little Scotland plantation, 64, 66
Locke, Judge John B., 165
Longfellow, Henry Wadsworth, 32-33
Longworth, Alice Roosevelt (Mrs. Nicholas), 86
Longworth, Nicholas, 86
Look Homeward, Angel, 115, 168
Lossing, Benson, 9
Louisa Railroad, 49
Lucky Strike Hit Parade, 113
Lyle, Gladys, 129
Lynchburg, 13-25

M

McRae, Charles, 45
Maddox, Mrs. Richard Milton, 41
Madison, James, 9, 12
Magnolia Tree Tea Room, 154
Magruder, Gen. John Bankhead, 17, 18, 20
Maher, James T., 40, 43, 45
Mariners Museum, 38, 40, 141, 152, 209, 223-225, 228, 229

Index 239

Marrow, Mr., 14, 15
Marrow, Mary Emily West (Mrs.), 18
Marshall, John, 7
Marshall, Mrs. Philip T., 133
Marshall, Capt. Richard Coke, 167, 168
Marshall, Mrs. Richard, 226
Marshall, Ronald, 227
Martin, Sen. Thomas S., 80
Mary Immaculate Hospital, 7, 10
Mathes, Martin, 158
Matthews, Capt., 142
Maynard, Maj. John C., 24
Maynard, Lt. Robert, 5
McIntosh, George, 82
McClellan, Gen. George, 20, 22, 30, 32, 49
McMenamin, James, 159, 162
McMenamin, James, Jr., 159
McMenamin, John, 159
McMenamin crab plant, 159-161, 208
McMurran, Agnes Epes (Mrs. Lewis), 81, 97
McMurran, Cary, 226, 229
McMurran, Lewis, Jr., 162, 199
McMurran Music Library, 227
Memories of Hampton, 163
Menchville, 222
Mennonite market, 121
Mercedes-Benz, 233
Merchants & Miners Line, 144
Metropolitan Museum of Art, 46
Miante, Joe, 138
Michael, Prof. Albert, 226
Michaux, Elder Solomon, 91, 174-176, 188
Miley, Pauline, 133
Miller, Joaquin, 33, 35, 37
Miller, John M., 61
Minstrel shows, 126-129
Mirmelstein, Florence, 133
Mitchell, Gen. William, 95-98, 167
Model A Ford, 155
Model T Ford, 152-155
Monfalcone's Newsstand, 118, 120, 121
Monroe Doctrine, 12
Monroe, James, 12
Montague, Gen. Sclater, 163-165, 208, 229
Moonefield Farm, 143
Moore, Daisy, 189
Morehead, Cynthia Coleman (Mrs. Singleton), 145
Morison, Samuel Eliot, 219
Morrison, 183
Moss, Sally, 189
Mount Vernon, 6, 8
Motley family, 118
Movement to suburbs, 183-185
Mrs. Fox's Nut & Candy Shop, 151, 179
Mrs. Smith's Ice Cream Parlor, 152
Mulberry Island, 108

Mullins, Dora Marshall, 227
Museum of Modern Art, 44

N
NACA, 167-170
Nachman, Herbert, 178
Nachman's Department Store, 118, 178, 179
Naff, Fred, 221, 228
Napier, Lt. Col. Charles James, 11, 12
Napoleon, 12
NASA, 170, 233
National Park Service, 31, 174-176
Needre, John, 228
Nelson, R. O., 82
New Kent County, 18
New York City Directory, 43
New York Home Journal, 75
New York Illustrated News, 17, 31
New York, Philadelphia, & Norfolk Line, 153
New York Shipbuilding Co., 99
New York Times, 207
New York Tribune, 44
Newmarket, 124
Newport Centre, 185, 230-233
Newport News Boys' Academy, 25, 83
Newport News Academy of Music, 126-129, 226-228
Newport News Central School, 81, 83
Newport News and Mississippi Valley Holding Co., 45
Newport NewsBlues, 111-114
Newport News Boat Harbor, 49, 83, 94-98, 108, 154, 156-158, 160, 161, 174-176
Newport News brewery, 90-93
Newport News bridge-tunnel, 231-233
Newport News Courthouse, 164
Newport News Creek, 15
Newport News Federal Bldg, 110
Newport News High School, 81-83, 171-173, 189-191, 227, 228
Newport News Light & Water Co., 76
Newport News Little Theatre, 228
Newport News Pioneers, 73
Newport News Point, 13-25, 50, 74
Newport News Postoffice, 106
Newport News Shipyard, 35, 45, 48, 49, 99-102, 118-121
Newport News Shipyard Apts., 109
Newport News theatres, 120
Newport News theatrical troupe, 128
Newport News' 325 Years, 78, 220-222
Newport News Union Chapel, 53
Newport News Victory Arch, 106, 109

Newport News War Memorial Museum, 111
Newport News Woman's Club, 228
Newsome, J. Thomas, 206, 208
Nicholas, Anne Cary (Mrs. Robert Carter), 7
Nicholas, Robert Carter, 7
Nicholson, Lt. Gov. Francis, 4
Noland, Lloyd U., Sr., 136, 220, 222
Noland Company, 233
Norfleet, Elizabeth Copeland (Mrs. Fillmore), 145
Norfolk, 10, 29, 30, 34, 36, 50, 124, 136
Norfolk & Western Ry., 36, 49, 50
Norfolk County, 4
Norfolk ferries, 91, 161, 185
Norfolk Gazette & Public Ledger, 10
Norfolk Herald, 70, 71, 104
Norfolk Naval Air Station, 170, 218
Norfolk Naval Base, 80, 85-87, 98, 115-117, 161
Norfolk Virginian-Pilot, 221
Northampton County, 4
North Carolina Shipbuilding Co., 214
North End, 105, 107-110, 132-135, 136, 139, 141, 162, 183-185, 186, 188

O
Oakwood Cemetery, 21
Ocean View, 155
Ocracoke, 5
O'Hara, Geoffrey, 111
Old, Col. Robert, 167
Old Bay Line, 96, 153, 160
Old Dominion Brewing & Ice Co., 90-93
Old Dominion Land Co., 73-76, 83, 92
Old Dominion Steamship Line, 77-80
Old Point, 32, 67-76, 144, 162
Old Point Government Pier, 96, 87, 153, 160
Old Point lighthouse, 11
Oliver, Sgt. Hal, 111-114
Olympic Theatre, 178
Orcutt, Calvin, 76, 102
Orton, Col. E. P., 111
Oyster Point Industrial Park, 233

P
Pagan River, 141-144
Palace Theatre, 120, 178, 198
Paramount Theatre, 120, 127, 129, 161, 199
Parker, Anne Victoria
Parker, Col. Richard E., 11
Parker, Frances Lee, 133
Parker, Nancy, 133
Parks, Marshall, 70
Peartree Hall plantation, 6
Peery, Gov. George C., 206
Pembroke Church, 3, 5

Peninsula Campaign, 29-33
Penniman munitions plant, 103
Pennybacker's Drug Store, 120, 178
Perkins, Frank, 158
Perkins Court, 104
Pershing, Gen. John J., 105, 167
Petersburg, 29, 31
Phelps, Gen. Wolcott, 14, 17
Phoebus, 51
Phoebus, Harrison, 62, 67-71, 73
Phoebus Sentinel, 56, 57
Piankatank River, 34, 50
Pier A, 121, 141, 142
Pine Beach, 97, 161
Piracy, 3-5
Pleasants, Kate, 98, 188
Plummer, James, 99
Plummer, Samuel, 119, 137
Plymouth, England, 36
Poe, Edgar Allan, 41
Poe, Virginia Clemm (Mrs. Edgar A.), 41
Point Breeze, 141, 161
Point Comfort: see Old Point
Pope, Arthur, 46
Porter Brothers Shipyard, 116, 117
Portsmouth, 36, 125
Portsmouth Navy Yard, 101
Post, Walter, 74, 102
Post residence, 91
Powell, Thomas Temple, 82
Price, G. Lynwood, 202
Primrose-Dockstader Minstrels, 128
Princess Anne County, 4
Prohibition, 122-125, 188
Prostitution, 98, 161

Q
Queenstown, Ireland, 99-102
Quesada, Gen. Elwood, 167

R
Racial integration, 184
Randolph-Macon Woman's College, 113
Rawlings, Adm. William, 118
Read, J. Winston, 203-205, 208
Read, William T. Tim, 226
Reams, Helen, 201
Reinecke, Theodore, 91
Renssalaer Polytechnic Institute, 102
Restoration of Williamsburg, 155
Reyner, Harry, 128
Reyner's ship chandlery, 119
Rialto Theatre, 178
Richardson, Carolyn, 151
Richmond, 13, 19-25, 29, 30, 32, 38-43
Richmond Daily Dispatch, 42
Richmond Enquirer, 11
Richmond News Leader, 204-5
Richmond, Fredericksburg, & Potomac Ry, 49
Richmond Times-Dispatch, 220

Richneck plantation, 6, 8
Rip Raps, 12: see Fort Monroe, Fort Wool
Riverside Hospital, 25, 53
Roberts, Don, 82
Rockefeller, Mr. & Mrs. John D., Jr., 44, 45
Rodef Sholom Synagogue, 151, 184
Roma dirigible, 169, 170
Roosevelt, Eleanor (Mrs. Franklin), 175, 176
Roosevelt, Franklin, 122, 136
Roosevelt, Theodore, 37, 77, 79, 85-87, 122, 226
Rosenbaum's Hardware Store, 178
Ross, Lula, 98
Rouse, Dashiell, 184
Rouse, Randolph, 103, 186
Rouse, William D., 184
Ruffner, Rev. William H., 82
Russo-Japanese War, 85

S
St. John's Church, Hampton, 9, 10, 11, 25, 55, 71, 154, 206
St. John's Church, Richmond, 18
St. Paul's Church, Newport News, 192-195
St. Paul's Church, Richmond, 22
Saloons, 122-125
Salter's Creek, 6, 7
Saunders, Joseph H., 82, 172
Saunders, Lily, 173
Saunders, Robert, 151, 191
Sayre, Margaret, 171
Scammon, Howard, 172, 173
Schermerhorn, Capt., 142
Schmelz Brothers Bank, 60-62, 118
Schmelz family, 56, 57, 59-62, 67
Schmelz, Francis Anton, 59-62
Schmelz, George, 59-62
Schmelz, Henry Lane, 59-62
Schmidt, Prof. Aage, 126-129, 227
Schubert, Franz, 126
Schumann-Heink, Ernestine, 128
Scribner's Monthly, 35, 50
Scruggs, Anne Perkins, 172
Seabrook tobacco warehouse, 21
Seawell, Hairston, 128
Segar, Cornelia, 173
Seven Days Battles, 19-22, 30
Sewell's Point, 155
Seventh N.Y. Regiment, 14
Seward, Secty. William H., 29
Shafer, Mamie, 164
Sheaks, Barclay, 228
Shell, Mrs. Willis, 226
Shell Road, 154
Shelton, Wilhelmina, 190
Sheridan, Gen. Philip, 73
Sherwood plantation, 168
Shifrin, Cpl. Willie, 111-114
Ships
    Cyclops, 103

Dover, 214
Enterprise, 213
Essex, 214
Franklin, 214
Hampton Roads, 141-144
Hornet, 213
Kearsarge, 76, 86
Kentucky, 76, 86
Kronprinz Wilhelm, 101
La Paix, 4
Leviathan, 225
Lusitania, 99-102, 224
Mayflower, 84, 130
Merrimack, 32
Midway, 214
Monitor, 32
Oneita, 121, 141, 144
Pearl, 5
Pennsylvania, 109
Prinz Eitel Friedrich, 101
Puritan, 33, 35, 76
Quaker, 4
River Queen, 29
Shoreham, 3, 4
Virginia (Smoky Joe), 83, 141-144, 201
Yorktown, 213
Shipbuilding, 212-214
Shirley plantation, 19
Shoemaker, Samuel, 67
Siegrist, Helen, 201
Simpson, Col. Delk, 170
Smith, Douglas, 61
Smith, E. O., 221
Smith, Harriet, 191
Smith, Harry, 203-205
Smith, Robert B., 220-222
Smith, Robert Carroll, 226-227
Smithers, William, 56
Smithfield, 103, 105, 141-144, 145-148, 184
Sniffen, Harold, 78, 221
Sousa marches, 149-151
Southern Pacific, Ry., 41, 45
Southside Virginia, 145-148
Spaatz, Gen. Carl, 167
Spangler, Charles, 172
Spangler, Robert, 172
Spanish-American War, 36, 122, 188
Sparhawk, A lice G. T., 109
Spotswood, Lt.-Gov. Alexander, 5
Spratley, Annie Woodward (Mrs. Vernon), 208
Spratley, Justice C. Vernon, 159, 203, 205, 206-208
Stage shows, 126-129
Stanford, Leland, 48
Stanley, Lamar, 172, 173, 221
Stanton, Sec. Edwin M., 30
Starkey, Marion, 229
Stauffer, William T., 221, 228
Stephens, A. E. S., 148
Stephens, Alexander H., 29
Stinson, Eddie, 95-98

Stonewall Jackson School, 132-135, 149, 150, 152, 171, 198
Stratemeyer, Gen. Robert, 167
Stratford, Beatrice Glass (Mrs. W. W.), 228
Styron, Elizabeth Buxton (Mrs. William), 221
Styron, William, Jr., 105, 117, 229
Submarine warfare, 215-219
Suburban growth, 183-185
Sullivan, Ed, 114
Sunday, Rev. Billy, 75, 121
Surry County, 144-148
Swanson, Secty. Claude, 213
Swem, Earl G., 228
Swinerton, John, 73-76
Syracuse University, 38

T

Taft, Pres. William Howard, 87
Taylor, Ethel, 133
Taylor, Gen. Robert Barraud, 9-12
Teacher pay, 172
Test Pilot, 167
Teach, Edward (Blackbeard), 5
Tenneco Corp., 224
Thomas, Lowell, 113
Tidemill Farm, 168
Tidewater Club, 108
Times-Herald, 92, 163, 165, 186, 200-202
Tobacco growing, 3-5
Todd, Lillian, 133
Tormey, Ann Darling (Mrs. James), 58, 159
Travis, G. Edward, 128, 163-165, 188, 202
Travis House, 155
Trinity Lutheran Church, 192-195
Trinity Methodist Church, 192-195
Trolley cars, 121, 136, 137, 213
Tucker, Katherine Aldridge, 135
Turnbull, Andrew, 115
Turner's Drug Store, 183
Tuskegee Institute, 65
Twyford, Warner, 221

U

U-Boat, 83, 215-219
United States Restaurant, 179
United States Naval Academy, 224
United Virginia Bank, 53
University of Richmond, 25
USS Roper, 215-219

V

Valley of Virginia, 93

Van Buren, Capt. William, 200
Van Buren, William R., Jr., 62
Van Wyck's Academy of Music, 129
Vanderbilt, Frederick Gwynne, 99
Vanderbilt, Cornelius, 45
Veterans Admin Hospital, Kecoughtan, 22, 209
Via, Guy, 81
Virginia capes, 104
Virginia Central Ry., 49
Virginia Engineering Co., 157
Virginia Institute of Marine Science, 158
Virginia Judge, 93, 122, 188
Virginia militia, 4
Virginian Railway, 36

W

Ware Mrs. Storer, 224
Wagner, Richard, 126
Walker, Louise, 227
Walker, Marion, 227
Walter Reed School, 82, 184
War of 1812, 9-12
Wark, Robert, 46, 47
Wartime burials, 215-219
Warwick Brewing & Ice Co., 91
Warwick Courthouse, 8, 15, 74, 93, 164, 183-185
Warwick County, 51, 76, 83, 93
Warwick County Mennonites, 120
Warwick County road, 152, 155
Warwick Hotel: *see* Hotel Warwick
Warwick Machine Co., 121, 142, 161
Warwick River, 222
Washington, Booker, 65
Washington, George, 6-8, 35
Washington, Lawrence, 6
Washington, Martha Dandridge (Mrs. George), 6
Washington Disarmament Conference, 48, 134
Washington Square, 121, 179, 222
Waters Creek, 152, 162, 224
Watson Gies auto repair, 151, 184
Watson, Mammy, 17
Watts Creek: *see* Waters Creek
Weaver, Gen. Walter, 167-170
Wellford, Rev. E. T., 188, 193
Wells Theatre, 129
Wertmann, S. A., 91
West, Mary, 17
West, George Benjamin, 13-25, 53, 67, 83, 105, 178, 188
West, Jimmy, 189
West, Parker, 14-25, 72
West, Mrs. Parker, 18, 20
West, William, 16, 18

West Point, 34, 50
Westmoreland Militia, 11
Westwood, Mr. & Mrs. John, 11
Weyburn, Gordon, 113, 179
Wharton, Edith, 36, 45
White, Fairmount, 221
White, Helen Smith (Mrs. Stuart), 133
White House, 12
Whitman, Walt, 35
Whitney, William C., 45
Wickham, Gen. Williams, 75
Williams, Robert, 231-233
Williams, Capt. Roger, 213
Williamsburg, 4, 18, 20, 35, 51, 52, 53, 174-176
Willoughby Spit, 155
Wilson, Marguerite, 122, 133, 137, 149, 150
Wilson, Col. William, 7
Wilton, Jane, 133
Winder, Capt., 142
Withers, Alfred, 127
Withers, Maj. John, 25
Wolfe, Ben, 117
Wolfe, Thomas, 115-117, 168
Women's Christian Temperance Union, 222
Woodrow Wilson School, 184
Woolworth's 5 & 10¢ Store, 118
World War I, 94-98, 99-102, 107-114, 118-121, 161, 162, 166-168, 188, 198
World War II, 96, 167, 170, 197-199, 212-222
Worsham, John Archer, 42, 44, 45
Wrench, Hazel, 133
Wyatt Brothers store, 55
Wythe, George, 168

Y

Yarrington, Elizabeth Page, 41
Yarrington, Emma, 41
Yarrington, John Blair, 41
Yarrington, John Duval, 41
Yarrington, Richard Milton, 41
Yarrington, Richard Milton, Jr., 41
Yarrington, Mrs. James, 41
York County, 234
Yorktown, 18, 34, 35, 50, 52, 53
Yorktown bridge, 146
Yorktown Centennial, 52
Yorktown ferries, 152
Yorktown National Cemetery, 53

Z

Zeppelin, Count, 169, 170